CAREER EXAMINATION SERIES

D1824993

THIS IS YOUR **PASSBOOK®** FOR ...

INSURANCE FUND HEARING REPRESENTATIVE TRAINEE

NATIONAL LEARNING CORPORATION®
passbooks.com

PASSBOOK® SERIES

THE *PASSBOOK® SERIES* has been created to prepare applicants and candidates for the ultimate academic battlefield – the examination room.

At some time in our lives, each and every one of us may be required to take an examination – for validation, matriculation, admission, qualification, registration, certification, or licensure.

Based on the assumption that every applicant or candidate has met the basic formal educational standards, has taken the required number of courses, and read the necessary texts, the *PASSBOOK® SERIES* furnishes the one special preparation which may assure passing with confidence, instead of failing with insecurity. Examination questions – together with answers – are furnished as the basic vehicle for study so that the mysteries of the examination and its compounding difficulties may be eliminated or diminished by a sure method.

This book is meant to help you pass your examination provided that you qualify and are serious in your objective.

The entire field is reviewed through the huge store of content information which is succinctly presented through a provocative and challenging approach – the question-and-answer method.

A climate of success is established by furnishing the correct answers at the end of each test.

You soon learn to recognize types of questions, forms of questions, and patterns of questioning. You may even begin to anticipate expected outcomes.

You perceive that many questions are repeated or adapted so that you can gain acute insights, which may enable you to score many sure points.

You learn how to confront new questions, or types of questions, and to attack them confidently and work out the correct answers.

You note objectives and emphases, and recognize pitfalls and dangers, so that you may make positive educational adjustments.

Moreover, you are kept fully informed in relation to new concepts, methods, practices, and directions in the field.

You discover that you arre actually taking the examination all the time: you are preparing for the examination by "taking" an examination, not by reading extraneous and/or supererogatory textbooks.

In short, this PASSBOOK®, used directedly, should be an important factor in helping you to pass your test.

INSURANCE FUND
HEARING REPRESENTATIVE TRAINEE

DUTIES

As an Insurance Fund Hearing Representative Trainee, you would prepare workers' compensation cases, generally of ordinary difficulty, for hearing before compensation law judges of the workers' compensation board and represent the state insurance fund at such hearings. You would be assigned to hearing functions in the claims-medical department of the state insurance fund; represent the state insurance fund in hearings of an adversary nature before the compensation law judges of the workers' compensation board; present evidence; examine lay and medical witnesses; and argue questions of fact and law. You would recommend, and might initiate, field investigations or consultations by medical specialists and order such other development of claim cases as might be necessary. You would determine the nature of evidence to be produced at hearings and direct its procurement by correspondence, field investigation or through interviews with claimants, employers, physicians, hospitals, and other witnesses or sources of information. You would perform legal and medical research in preparation for hearings, and analyze and seek final disposition of cases at hearings on the basis of temporary disability, schedule loss, disallowance, or other means of closing. You would decide whether appeal is indicated from awards or decisions, and prepare memoranda to the legal department setting forth the basis for such appeals, or take such other action as might be necessary to protect the fund's interests. You might initiate, negotiate, and conclude lump-sum settlements not in excess of authorized levels in appropriate cases. You would also be required to prepare reports of proceedings at hearings and prepare such briefs or memoranda of law as might be necessary in specific cases.

Upon successful completion of a traineeship, a trainee would be advanced to the position of Insurance Fund Hearing Representative without further examination.

SCOPE OF THE EXAMINATION

The written test will cover knowledge, skills and/or abilities in such areas as:
1. Principles, practices and procedures in the field of administrative law including the ability to make findings of fact;
2. Workers' compensation law and related rules and regulations.
3. Understanding and interpreting written material;
4. Preparing written material; and
5. Arithmetic reasoning.

HOW TO TAKE A TEST

I. YOU MUST PASS AN EXAMINATION

A. *WHAT EVERY CANDIDATE SHOULD KNOW*

Examination applicants often ask us for help in preparing for the written test. What can I study in advance? What kinds of questions will be asked? How will the test be given? How will the papers be graded?

As an applicant for a civil service examination, you may be wondering about some of these things. Our purpose here is to suggest effective methods of advance study and to describe civil service examinations.

Your chances for success on this examination can be increased if you know how to prepare. Those "pre-examination jitters" can be reduced if you know what to expect. You can even experience an adventure in good citizenship if you know why civil service exams are given.

B. *WHY ARE CIVIL SERVICE EXAMINATIONS GIVEN?*

Civil service examinations are important to you in two ways. As a citizen, you want public jobs filled by employees who know how to do their work. As a job seeker, you want a fair chance to compete for that job on an equal footing with other candidates. The best-known means of accomplishing this two-fold goal is the competitive examination.

Exams are widely publicized throughout the nation. They may be administered for jobs in federal, state, city, municipal, town or village governments or agencies.

Any citizen may apply, with some limitations, such as the age or residence of applicants. Your experience and education may be reviewed to see whether you meet the requirements for the particular examination. When these requirements exist, they are reasonable and applied consistently to all applicants. Thus, a competitive examination may cause you some uneasiness now, but it is your privilege and safeguard.

C. *HOW ARE CIVIL SERVICE EXAMS DEVELOPED?*

Examinations are carefully written by trained technicians who are specialists in the field known as "psychological measurement," in consultation with recognized authorities in the field of work that the test will cover. These experts recommend the subject matter areas or skills to be tested; only those knowledges or skills important to your success on the job are included. The most reliable books and source materials available are used as references. Together, the experts and technicians judge the difficulty level of the questions.

Test technicians know how to phrase questions so that the problem is clearly stated. Their ethics do not permit "trick" or "catch" questions. Questions may have been tried out on sample groups, or subjected to statistical analysis, to determine their usefulness.

Written tests are often used in combination with performance tests, ratings of training and experience, and oral interviews. All of these measures combine to form the best-known means of finding the right person for the right job.

II. HOW TO PASS THE WRITTEN TEST

A. NATURE OF THE EXAMINATION

To prepare intelligently for civil service examinations, you should know how they differ from school examinations you have taken. In school you were assigned certain definite pages to read or subjects to cover. The examination questions were quite detailed and usually emphasized memory. Civil service exams, on the other hand, try to discover your present ability to perform the duties of a position, plus your potentiality to learn these duties. In other words, a civil service exam attempts to predict how successful you will be. Questions cover such a broad area that they cannot be as minute and detailed as school exam questions.

In the public service similar kinds of work, or positions, are grouped together in one "class." This process is known as *position-classification*. All the positions in a class are paid according to the salary range for that class. One class title covers all of these positions, and they are all tested by the same examination.

B. FOUR BASIC STEPS

1) Study the announcement

How, then, can you know what subjects to study? Our best answer is: "Learn as much as possible about the class of positions for which you've applied." The exam will test the knowledge, skills and abilities needed to do the work.

Your most valuable source of information about the position you want is the official exam announcement. This announcement lists the training and experience qualifications. Check these standards and apply only if you come reasonably close to meeting them.

The brief description of the position in the examination announcement offers some clues to the subjects which will be tested. Think about the job itself. Review the duties in your mind. Can you perform them, or are there some in which you are rusty? Fill in the blank spots in your preparation.

Many jurisdictions preview the written test in the exam announcement by including a section called "Knowledge and Abilities Required," "Scope of the Examination," or some similar heading. Here you will find out specifically what fields will be tested.

2) Review your own background

Once you learn in general what the position is all about, and what you need to know to do the work, ask yourself which subjects you already know fairly well and which need improvement. You may wonder whether to concentrate on improving your strong areas or on building some background in your fields of weakness. When the announcement has specified "some knowledge" or "considerable knowledge," or has used adjectives like "beginning principles of…" or "advanced … methods," you can get a clue as to the number and difficulty of questions to be asked in any given field. More questions, and hence broader coverage, would be included for those subjects which are more important in the work. Now weigh your strengths and weaknesses against the job requirements and prepare accordingly.

3) Determine the level of the position

Another way to tell how intensively you should prepare is to understand the level of the job for which you are applying. Is it the entering level? In other words, is this the position in which beginners in a field of work are hired? Or is it an intermediate or advanced level? Sometimes this is indicated by such words as "Junior" or "Senior" in the class title. Other jurisdictions use Roman numerals to designate the level – Clerk I, Clerk II, for example. The word "Supervisor" sometimes appears in the title. If the level is not indicated by the title, check the description of duties. Will you be working under very close supervision, or will you have responsibility for independent decisions in this work?

4) Choose appropriate study materials

Now that you know the subjects to be examined and the relative amount of each subject to be covered, you can choose suitable study materials. For beginning level jobs, or even advanced ones, if you have a pronounced weakness in some aspect of your training, read a modern, standard textbook in that field. Be sure it is up to date and has general coverage. Such books are normally available at your library, and the librarian will be glad to help you locate one. For entry-level positions, questions of appropriate difficulty are chosen – neither highly advanced questions, nor those too simple. Such questions require careful thought but not advanced training.

If the position for which you are applying is technical or advanced, you will read more advanced, specialized material. If you are already familiar with the basic principles of your field, elementary textbooks would waste your time. Concentrate on advanced textbooks and technical periodicals. Think through the concepts and review difficult problems in your field.

These are all general sources. You can get more ideas on your own initiative, following these leads. For example, training manuals and publications of the government agency which employs workers in your field can be useful, particularly for technical and professional positions. A letter or visit to the government department involved may result in more specific study suggestions, and certainly will provide you with a more definite idea of the exact nature of the position you are seeking.

III. KINDS OF TESTS

Tests are used for purposes other than measuring knowledge and ability to perform specified duties. For some positions, it is equally important to test ability to make adjustments to new situations or to profit from training. In others, basic mental abilities not dependent on information are essential. Questions which test these things may not appear as pertinent to the duties of the position as those which test for knowledge and information. Yet they are often highly important parts of a fair examination. For very general questions, it is almost impossible to help you direct your study efforts. What we can do is to point out some of the more common of these general abilities needed in public service positions and describe some typical questions.

1) General information

Broad, general information has been found useful for predicting job success in some kinds of work. This is tested in a variety of ways, from vocabulary lists to questions about current events. Basic background in some field of work, such as sociology or economics, may be sampled in a group of questions. Often these are principles which have become familiar to most persons through exposure rather than through formal training. It is difficult to advise you how to study for these questions; being alert to the world around you is our best suggestion.

2) Verbal ability

An example of an ability needed in many positions is verbal or language ability. Verbal ability is, in brief, the ability to use and understand words. Vocabulary and grammar tests are typical measures of this ability. Reading comprehension or paragraph interpretation questions are common in many kinds of civil service tests. You are given a paragraph of written material and asked to find its central meaning.

3) Numerical ability

Number skills can be tested by the familiar arithmetic problem, by checking paired lists of numbers to see which are alike and which are different, or by interpreting charts and graphs. In the latter test, a graph may be printed in the test booklet which you are asked to use as the basis for answering questions.

4) Observation

A popular test for law-enforcement positions is the observation test. A picture is shown to you for several minutes, then taken away. Questions about the picture test your ability to observe both details and larger elements.

5) Following directions

In many positions in the public service, the employee must be able to carry out written instructions dependably and accurately. You may be given a chart with several columns, each column listing a variety of information. The questions require you to carry out directions involving the information given in the chart.

6) Skills and aptitudes

Performance tests effectively measure some manual skills and aptitudes. When the skill is one in which you are trained, such as typing or shorthand, you can practice. These tests are often very much like those given in business school or high school courses. For many of the other skills and aptitudes, however, no short-time preparation can be made. Skills and abilities natural to you or that you have developed throughout your lifetime are being tested.

Many of the general questions just described provide all the data needed to answer the questions and ask you to use your reasoning ability to find the answers. Your best preparation for these tests, as well as for tests of facts and ideas, is to be at your physical and mental best. You, no doubt, have your own methods of getting into an exam-taking mood and keeping "in shape." The next section lists some ideas on this subject.

IV. KINDS OF QUESTIONS

Only rarely is the "essay" question, which you answer in narrative form, used in civil service tests. Civil service tests are usually of the short-answer type. Full instructions for answering these questions will be given to you at the examination. But in case this is your first experience with short-answer questions and separate answer sheets, here is what you need to know:

1) Multiple-choice Questions

Most popular of the short-answer questions is the "multiple choice" or "best answer" question. It can be used, for example, to test for factual knowledge, ability to solve problems or judgment in meeting situations found at work.

A multiple-choice question is normally one of three types—

- It can begin with an incomplete statement followed by several possible endings. You are to find the one ending which *best* completes the statement, although some of the others may not be entirely wrong.
- It can also be a complete statement in the form of a question which is answered by choosing one of the statements listed.
- It can be in the form of a problem – again you select the best answer.

Here is an example of a multiple-choice question with a discussion which should give you some clues as to the method for choosing the right answer:

When an employee has a complaint about his assignment, the action which will *best* help him overcome his difficulty is to
  A. discuss his difficulty with his coworkers
  B. take the problem to the head of the organization
  C. take the problem to the person who gave him the assignment
  D. say nothing to anyone about his complaint

In answering this question, you should study each of the choices to find which is best. Consider choice "A" – Certainly an employee may discuss his complaint with fellow employees, but no change or improvement can result, and the complaint remains unresolved. Choice "B" is a poor choice since the head of the organization probably does not know what assignment you have been given, and taking your problem to him is known as "going over the head" of the supervisor. The supervisor, or person who made the assignment, is the person who can clarify it or correct any injustice. Choice "C" is, therefore, correct. To say nothing, as in choice "D," is unwise. Supervisors have and interest in knowing the problems employees are facing, and the employee is seeking a solution to his problem.

2) True/False Questions

The "true/false" or "right/wrong" form of question is sometimes used. Here a complete statement is given. Your job is to decide whether the statement is right or wrong.

SAMPLE: A roaming cell-phone call to a nearby city costs less than a non-roaming call to a distant city.

This statement is wrong, or false, since roaming calls are more expensive.
This is not a complete list of all possible question forms, although most of the others are variations of these common types. You will always get complete directions for

answering questions. Be sure you understand *how* to mark your answers – ask questions until you do.

V. RECORDING YOUR ANSWERS

Computer terminals are used more and more today for many different kinds of exams.

For an examination with very few applicants, you may be told to record your answers in the test booklet itself. Separate answer sheets are much more common. If this separate answer sheet is to be scored by machine – and this is often the case – it is highly important that you mark your answers correctly in order to get credit.

An electronic scoring machine is often used in civil service offices because of the speed with which papers can be scored. Machine-scored answer sheets must be marked with a pencil, which will be given to you. This pencil has a high graphite content which responds to the electronic scoring machine. As a matter of fact, stray dots may register as answers, so do not let your pencil rest on the answer sheet while you are pondering the correct answer. Also, if your pencil lead breaks or is otherwise defective, ask for another.

Since the answer sheet will be dropped in a slot in the scoring machine, be careful not to bend the corners or get the paper crumpled.

The answer sheet normally has five vertical columns of numbers, with 30 numbers to a column. These numbers correspond to the question numbers in your test booklet. After each number, going across the page are four or five pairs of dotted lines. These short dotted lines have small letters or numbers above them. The first two pairs may also have a "T" or "F" above the letters. This indicates that the first two pairs only are to be used if the questions are of the true-false type. If the questions are multiple choice, disregard the "T" and "F" and pay attention only to the small letters or numbers.

Answer your questions in the manner of the sample that follows:

32. The largest city in the United States is
    A. Washington, D.C.
    B. New York City
    C. Chicago
    D. Detroit
    E. San Francisco

1) Choose the answer you think is best. (New York City is the largest, so "B" is correct.)
2) Find the row of dotted lines numbered the same as the question you are answering. (Find row number 32)
3) Find the pair of dotted lines corresponding to the answer. (Find the pair of lines under the mark "B.")
4) Make a solid black mark between the dotted lines.

VI. BEFORE THE TEST

Common sense will help you find procedures to follow to get ready for an examination. Too many of us, however, overlook these sensible measures. Indeed, nervousness and fatigue have been found to be the most serious reasons why applicants fail to do their best on civil service tests. Here is a list of reminders:

- Begin your preparation early – Don't wait until the last minute to go scurrying around for books and materials or to find out what the position is all about.
- Prepare continuously – An hour a night for a week is better than an all-night cram session. This has been definitely established. What is more, a night a week for a month will return better dividends than crowding your study into a shorter period of time.
- Locate the place of the exam – You have been sent a notice telling you when and where to report for the examination. If the location is in a different town or otherwise unfamiliar to you, it would be well to inquire the best route and learn something about the building.
- Relax the night before the test – Allow your mind to rest. Do not study at all that night. Plan some mild recreation or diversion; then go to bed early and get a good night's sleep.
- Get up early enough to make a leisurely trip to the place for the test – This way unforeseen events, traffic snarls, unfamiliar buildings, etc. will not upset you.
- Dress comfortably – A written test is not a fashion show. You will be known by number and not by name, so wear something comfortable.
- Leave excess paraphernalia at home – Shopping bags and odd bundles will get in your way. You need bring only the items mentioned in the official notice you received; usually everything you need is provided. Do not bring reference books to the exam. They will only confuse those last minutes and be taken away from you when in the test room.
- Arrive somewhat ahead of time – If because of transportation schedules you must get there very early, bring a newspaper or magazine to take your mind off yourself while waiting.
- Locate the examination room – When you have found the proper room, you will be directed to the seat or part of the room where you will sit. Sometimes you are given a sheet of instructions to read while you are waiting. Do not fill out any forms until you are told to do so; just read them and be prepared.
- Relax and prepare to listen to the instructions
- If you have any physical problem that may keep you from doing your best, be sure to tell the test administrator. If you are sick or in poor health, you really cannot do your best on the exam. You can come back and take the test some other time.

VII. AT THE TEST

The day of the test is here and you have the test booklet in your hand. The temptation to get going is very strong. Caution! There is more to success than knowing the right answers. You must know how to identify your papers and understand variations in the type of short-answer question used in this particular examination. Follow these suggestions for maximum results from your efforts:

1) Cooperate with the monitor

The test administrator has a duty to create a situation in which you can be as much at ease as possible. He will give instructions, tell you when to begin, check to see that you are marking your answer sheet correctly, and so on. He is not there to guard you, although he will see that your competitors do not take unfair advantage. He wants to help you do your best.

2) Listen to all instructions

Don't jump the gun! Wait until you understand all directions. In most civil service tests you get more time than you need to answer the questions. So don't be in a hurry. Read each word of instructions until you clearly understand the meaning. Study the examples, listen to all announcements and follow directions. Ask questions if you do not understand what to do.

3) Identify your papers

Civil service exams are usually identified by number only. You will be assigned a number; you must not put your name on your test papers. Be sure to copy your number correctly. Since more than one exam may be given, copy your exact examination title.

4) Plan your time

Unless you are told that a test is a "speed" or "rate of work" test, speed itself is usually not important. Time enough to answer all the questions will be provided, but this does not mean that you have all day. An overall time limit has been set. Divide the total time (in minutes) by the number of questions to determine the approximate time you have for each question.

5) Do not linger over difficult questions

If you come across a difficult question, mark it with a paper clip (useful to have along) and come back to it when you have been through the booklet. One caution if you do this – be sure to skip a number on your answer sheet as well. Check often to be sure that you have not lost your place and that you are marking in the row numbered the same as the question you are answering.

6) Read the questions

Be sure you know what the question asks! Many capable people are unsuccessful because they failed to *read* the questions correctly.

7) Answer all questions

Unless you have been instructed that a penalty will be deducted for incorrect answers, it is better to guess than to omit a question.

8) Speed tests

It is often better NOT to guess on speed tests. It has been found that on timed tests people are tempted to spend the last few seconds before time is called in marking answers at random – without even reading them – in the hope of picking up a few extra points. To discourage this practice, the instructions may warn you that your score will be "corrected" for guessing. That is, a penalty will be applied. The incorrect answers will be deducted from the correct ones, or some other penalty formula will be used.

9) Review your answers

If you finish before time is called, go back to the questions you guessed or omitted to give them further thought. Review other answers if you have time.

10) Return your test materials

If you are ready to leave before others have finished or time is called, take ALL your materials to the monitor and leave quietly. Never take any test material with you. The monitor can discover whose papers are not complete, and taking a test booklet may be grounds for disqualification.

VIII. EXAMINATION TECHNIQUES

1) Read the general instructions carefully. These are usually printed on the first page of the exam booklet. As a rule, these instructions refer to the timing of the examination; the fact that you should not start work until the signal and must stop work at a signal, etc. If there are any *special* instructions, such as a choice of questions to be answered, make sure that you note this instruction carefully.

2) When you are ready to start work on the examination, that is as soon as the signal has been given, read the instructions to each question booklet, underline any key words or phrases, such as *least, best, outline, describe* and the like. In this way you will tend to answer as requested rather than discover on reviewing your paper that you *listed without describing*, that you selected the *worst* choice rather than the *best* choice, etc.

3) If the examination is of the objective or multiple-choice type – that is, each question will also give a series of possible answers: A, B, C or D, and you are called upon to select the best answer and write the letter next to that answer on your answer paper – it is advisable to start answering each question in turn. There may be anywhere from 50 to 100 such questions in the three or four hours allotted and you can see how much time would be taken if you read through all the questions before beginning to answer any. Furthermore, if you come across a question or group of questions which you know would be difficult to answer, it would undoubtedly affect your handling of all the other questions.

4) If the examination is of the essay type and contains but a few questions, it is a moot point as to whether you should read all the questions before starting to answer any one. Of course, if you are given a choice – say five out of seven and the like – then it is essential to read all the questions so you can eliminate the two that are most difficult. If, however, you are asked to answer all the questions, there may be danger in trying to answer the easiest one first because you may find that you will spend too much time on it. The best technique is to answer the first question, then proceed to the second, etc.

5) Time your answers. Before the exam begins, write down the time it started, then add the time allowed for the examination and write down the time it must be completed, then divide the time available somewhat as follows:

- If 3-1/2 hours are allowed, that would be 210 minutes. If you have 80 objective-type questions, that would be an average of 2-1/2 minutes per question. Allow yourself no more than 2 minutes per question, or a total of 160 minutes, which will permit about 50 minutes to review.
- If for the time allotment of 210 minutes there are 7 essay questions to answer, that would average about 30 minutes a question. Give yourself only 25 minutes per question so that you have about 35 minutes to review.

6) The most important instruction is to *read each question* and make sure you know what is wanted. The second most important instruction is to *time yourself properly* so that you answer every question. The third most important instruction is to *answer every question*. Guess if you have to but include something for each question. Remember that you will receive no credit for a blank and will probably receive some credit if you write something in answer to an essay question. If you guess a letter – say "B" for a multiple-choice question – you may have guessed right. If you leave a blank as an answer to a multiple-choice question, the examiners may respect your feelings but it will not add a point to your score. Some exams may penalize you for wrong answers, so in such cases *only*, you may not want to guess unless you have some basis for your answer.

7) Suggestions
   a. Objective-type questions
      1. Examine the question booklet for proper sequence of pages and questions
      2. Read all instructions carefully
      3. Skip any question which seems too difficult; return to it after all other questions have been answered
      4. Apportion your time properly; do not spend too much time on any single question or group of questions
      5. Note and underline key words – *all, most, fewest, least, best, worst, same, opposite*, etc.
      6. Pay particular attention to negatives
      7. Note unusual option, e.g., unduly long, short, complex, different or similar in content to the body of the question
      8. Observe the use of "hedging" words – *probably, may, most likely*, etc.
      9. Make sure that your answer is put next to the same number as the question
      10. Do not second-guess unless you have good reason to believe the second answer is definitely more correct
      11. Cross out original answer if you decide another answer is more accurate; do not erase until you are ready to hand your paper in
      12. Answer all questions; guess unless instructed otherwise
      13. Leave time for review

   b. Essay questions
      1. Read each question carefully
      2. Determine exactly what is wanted. Underline key words or phrases.
      3. Decide on outline or paragraph answer

4. Include many different points and elements unless asked to develop any one or two points or elements
5. Show impartiality by giving pros and cons unless directed to select one side only
6. Make and write down any assumptions you find necessary to answer the questions
7. Watch your English, grammar, punctuation and choice of words
8. Time your answers; don't crowd material

8) Answering the essay question

Most essay questions can be answered by framing the specific response around several key words or ideas. Here are a few such key words or ideas:

M's: manpower, materials, methods, money, management
P's: purpose, program, policy, plan, procedure, practice, problems, pitfalls, personnel, public relations
  a. Six basic steps in handling problems:
    1. Preliminary plan and background development
    2. Collect information, data and facts
    3. Analyze and interpret information, data and facts
    4. Analyze and develop solutions as well as make recommendations
    5. Prepare report and sell recommendations
    6. Install recommendations and follow up effectiveness

  b. Pitfalls to avoid
    1. *Taking things for granted* – A statement of the situation does not necessarily imply that each of the elements is necessarily true; for example, a complaint may be invalid and biased so that all that can be taken for granted is that a complaint has been registered
    2. *Considering only one side of a situation* – Wherever possible, indicate several alternatives and then point out the reasons you selected the best one
    3. *Failing to indicate follow up* – Whenever your answer indicates action on your part, make certain that you will take proper follow-up action to see how successful your recommendations, procedures or actions turn out to be
    4. *Taking too long in answering any single question* – Remember to time your answers properly

IX. AFTER THE TEST

Scoring procedures differ in detail among civil service jurisdictions although the general principles are the same. Whether the papers are hand-scored or graded by machine we have described, they are nearly always graded by number. That is, the person who marks the paper knows only the number – never the name – of the applicant. Not until all the papers have been graded will they be matched with names. If other tests, such as training and experience or oral interview ratings have been given, scores will be combined. Different parts of the examination usually have different weights. For example, the written test might count 60 percent of the final grade, and a rating of training and experience 40 percent. In many jurisdictions, veterans will have a certain number of points added to their grades.

After the final grade has been determined, the names are placed in grade order and an eligible list is established. There are various methods for resolving ties between those who get the same final grade – probably the most common is to place first the name of the person whose application was received first. Job offers are made from the eligible list in the order the names appear on it. You will be notified of your grade and your rank as soon as all these computations have been made. This will be done as rapidly as possible.

People who are found to meet the requirements in the announcement are called "eligibles." Their names are put on a list of eligible candidates. An eligible's chances of getting a job depend on how high he stands on this list and how fast agencies are filling jobs from the list.

When a job is to be filled from a list of eligibles, the agency asks for the names of people on the list of eligibles for that job. When the civil service commission receives this request, it sends to the agency the names of the three people highest on this list. Or, if the job to be filled has specialized requirements, the office sends the agency the names of the top three persons who meet these requirements from the general list.

The appointing officer makes a choice from among the three people whose names were sent to him. If the selected person accepts the appointment, the names of the others are put back on the list to be considered for future openings.

That is the rule in hiring from all kinds of eligible lists, whether they are for typist, carpenter, chemist, or something else. For every vacancy, the appointing officer has his choice of any one of the top three eligibles on the list. This explains why the person whose name is on top of the list sometimes does not get an appointment when some of the persons lower on the list do. If the appointing officer chooses the second or third eligible, the No. 1 eligible does not get a job at once, but stays on the list until he is appointed or the list is terminated.

X. HOW TO PASS THE INTERVIEW TEST

The examination for which you applied requires an oral interview test. You have already taken the written test and you are now being called for the interview test – the final part of the formal examination.

You may think that it is not possible to prepare for an interview test and that there are no procedures to follow during an interview. Our purpose is to point out some things you can do in advance that will help you and some good rules to follow and pitfalls to avoid while you are being interviewed.

What is an interview supposed to test?
The written examination is designed to test the technical knowledge and competence of the candidate; the oral is designed to evaluate intangible qualities, not readily measured otherwise, and to establish a list showing the relative fitness of each candidate – as measured against his competitors – for the position sought. Scoring is not on the basis of "right" and "wrong," but on a sliding scale of values ranging from "not passable" to "outstanding." As a matter of fact, it is possible to achieve a relatively low score without a single "incorrect" answer because of evident weakness in the qualities being measured.

Occasionally, an examination may consist entirely of an oral test – either an individual or a group oral. In such cases, information is sought concerning the technical knowledges and abilities of the candidate, since there has been no written examination for this purpose. More commonly, however, an oral test is used to supplement a written examination.

Who conducts interviews?

The composition of oral boards varies among different jurisdictions. In nearly all, a representative of the personnel department serves as chairman. One of the members of the board may be a representative of the department in which the candidate would work. In some cases, "outside experts" are used, and, frequently, a businessman or some other representative of the general public is asked to serve. Labor and management or other special groups may be represented. The aim is to secure the services of experts in the appropriate field.

However the board is composed, it is a good idea (and not at all improper or unethical) to ascertain in advance of the interview who the members are and what groups they represent. When you are introduced to them, you will have some idea of their backgrounds and interests, and at least you will not stutter and stammer over their names.

What should be done before the interview?

While knowledge about the board members is useful and takes some of the surprise element out of the interview, there is other preparation which is more substantive. It *is* possible to prepare for an oral interview – in several ways:

1) Keep a copy of your application and review it carefully before the interview

This may be the only document before the oral board, and the starting point of the interview. Know what education and experience you have listed there, and the sequence and dates of all of it. Sometimes the board will ask you to review the highlights of your experience for them; you should not have to hem and haw doing it.

2) Study the class specification and the examination announcement

Usually, the oral board has one or both of these to guide them. The qualities, characteristics or knowledges required by the position sought are stated in these documents. They offer valuable clues as to the nature of the oral interview. For example, if the job involves supervisory responsibilities, the announcement will usually indicate that knowledge of modern supervisory methods and the qualifications of the candidate as a supervisor will be tested. If so, you can expect such questions, frequently in the form of a hypothetical situation which you are expected to solve. NEVER go into an oral without knowledge of the duties and responsibilities of the job you seek.

3) Think through each qualification required

Try to visualize the kind of questions you would ask if you were a board member. How well could you answer them? Try especially to appraise your own knowledge and background in each area, *measured against the job sought*, and identify any areas in which you are weak. Be critical and realistic – do not flatter yourself.

4) Do some general reading in areas in which you feel you may be weak

For example, if the job involves supervision and your past experience has NOT, some general reading in supervisory methods and practices, particularly in the field of human relations, might be useful. Do NOT study agency procedures or detailed manuals. The oral board will be testing your understanding and capacity, not your memory.

5) Get a good night's sleep and watch your general health and mental attitude

You will want a clear head at the interview. Take care of a cold or any other minor ailment, and of course, no hangovers.

What should be done on the day of the interview?

Now comes the day of the interview itself. Give yourself plenty of time to get there. Plan to arrive somewhat ahead of the scheduled time, particularly if your appointment is in the fore part of the day. If a previous candidate fails to appear, the board might be ready for you a bit early. By early afternoon an oral board is almost invariably behind schedule if there are many candidates, and you may have to wait. Take along a book or magazine to read, or your application to review, but leave any extraneous material in the waiting room when you go in for your interview. In any event, relax and compose yourself.

The matter of dress is important. The board is forming impressions about you – from your experience, your manners, your attitude, and your appearance. Give your personal appearance careful attention. Dress your best, but not your flashiest. Choose conservative, appropriate clothing, and be sure it is immaculate. This is a business interview, and your appearance should indicate that you regard it as such. Besides, being well groomed and properly dressed will help boost your confidence.

Sooner or later, someone will call your name and escort you into the interview room. *This is it.* From here on you are on your own. It is too late for any more preparation. But remember, you asked for this opportunity to prove your fitness, and you are here because your request was granted.

What happens when you go in?

The usual sequence of events will be as follows: The clerk (who is often the board stenographer) will introduce you to the chairman of the oral board, who will introduce you to the other members of the board. Acknowledge the introductions before you sit down. Do not be surprised if you find a microphone facing you or a stenotypist sitting by. Oral interviews are usually recorded in the event of an appeal or other review.

Usually the chairman of the board will open the interview by reviewing the highlights of your education and work experience from your application – primarily for the benefit of the other members of the board, as well as to get the material into the record. Do not interrupt or comment unless there is an error or significant misinterpretation; if that is the case, do not hesitate. But do not quibble about insignificant matters. Also, he will usually ask you some question about your education, experience or your present job – partly to get you to start talking and to establish the interviewing "rapport." He may start the actual questioning, or turn it over to one of the other members. Frequently, each member undertakes the questioning on a particular area, one in which he is perhaps most competent, so you can expect each member to participate in the examination. Because time is limited, you may also expect some rather abrupt switches in the direction the questioning takes, so do not be upset by it. Normally, a board member will not pursue a single line of questioning unless he discovers a particular strength or weakness.

After each member has participated, the chairman will usually ask whether any member has any further questions, then will ask you if you have anything you wish to add. Unless you are expecting this question, it may floor you. Worse, it may start you off on an extended, extemporaneous speech. The board is not usually seeking more information. The question is principally to offer you a last opportunity to present further qualifications or to indicate that you have nothing to add. So, if you feel that a significant qualification or characteristic has been overlooked, it is proper to point it out in a sentence or so. Do not compliment the board on the thoroughness of their examination – they have been sketchy, and you know it. If you wish, merely say, "No thank you, I have nothing further to add." This is a point where you can "talk yourself out" of a good impression or fail to present an important bit of information. Remember, *you close the interview yourself.*

The chairman will then say, "That is all, Mr. _____, thank you." Do not be startled; the interview is over, and quicker than you think. Thank him, gather your belongings and take your leave. Save your sigh of relief for the other side of the door.

How to put your best foot forward
Throughout this entire process, you may feel that the board individually and collectively is trying to pierce your defenses, seek out your hidden weaknesses and embarrass and confuse you. Actually, this is not true. They are obliged to make an appraisal of your qualifications for the job you are seeking, and they want to see you in your best light. Remember, they must interview all candidates and a non-cooperative candidate may become a failure in spite of their best efforts to bring out his qualifications. Here are 15 suggestions that will help you:

1) Be natural – Keep your attitude confident, not cocky
If you are not confident that you can do the job, do not expect the board to be. Do not apologize for your weaknesses, try to bring out your strong points. The board is interested in a positive, not negative, presentation. Cockiness will antagonize any board member and make him wonder if you are covering up a weakness by a false show of strength.

2) Get comfortable, but don't lounge or sprawl
Sit erectly but not stiffly. A careless posture may lead the board to conclude that you are careless in other things, or at least that you are not impressed by the importance of the occasion. Either conclusion is natural, even if incorrect. Do not fuss with your clothing, a pencil or an ashtray. Your hands may occasionally be useful to emphasize a point; do not let them become a point of distraction.

3) Do not wisecrack or make small talk
This is a serious situation, and your attitude should show that you consider it as such. Further, the time of the board is limited – they do not want to waste it, and neither should you.

4) Do not exaggerate your experience or abilities
In the first place, from information in the application or other interviews and sources, the board may know more about you than you think. Secondly, you probably will not get away with it. An experienced board is rather adept at spotting such a situation, so do not take the chance.

5) If you know a board member, do not make a point of it, yet do not hide it

Certainly you are not fooling him, and probably not the other members of the board. Do not try to take advantage of your acquaintanceship – it will probably do you little good.

6) Do not dominate the interview

Let the board do that. They will give you the clues – do not assume that you have to do all the talking. Realize that the board has a number of questions to ask you, and do not try to take up all the interview time by showing off your extensive knowledge of the answer to the first one.

7) Be attentive

You only have 20 minutes or so, and you should keep your attention at its sharpest throughout. When a member is addressing a problem or question to you, give him your undivided attention. Address your reply principally to him, but do not exclude the other board members.

8) Do not interrupt

A board member may be stating a problem for you to analyze. He will ask you a question when the time comes. Let him state the problem, and wait for the question.

9) Make sure you understand the question

Do not try to answer until you are sure what the question is. If it is not clear, restate it in your own words or ask the board member to clarify it for you. However, do not haggle about minor elements.

10) Reply promptly but not hastily

A common entry on oral board rating sheets is "candidate responded readily," or "candidate hesitated in replies." Respond as promptly and quickly as you can, but do not jump to a hasty, ill-considered answer.

11) Do not be peremptory in your answers

A brief answer is proper – but do not fire your answer back. That is a losing game from your point of view. The board member can probably ask questions much faster than you can answer them.

12) Do not try to create the answer you think the board member wants

He is interested in what kind of mind you have and how it works – not in playing games. Furthermore, he can usually spot this practice and will actually grade you down on it.

13) Do not switch sides in your reply merely to agree with a board member

Frequently, a member will take a contrary position merely to draw you out and to see if you are willing and able to defend your point of view. Do not start a debate, yet do not surrender a good position. If a position is worth taking, it is worth defending.

14) Do not be afraid to admit an error in judgment if you are shown to be wrong

The board knows that you are forced to reply without any opportunity for careful consideration. Your answer may be demonstrably wrong. If so, admit it and get on with the interview.

15) Do not dwell at length on your present job

The opening question may relate to your present assignment. Answer the question but do not go into an extended discussion. You are being examined for a *new* job, not your present one. As a matter of fact, try to phrase ALL your answers in terms of the job for which you are being examined.

Basis of Rating

Probably you will forget most of these "do's" and "don'ts" when you walk into the oral interview room. Even remembering them all will not ensure you a passing grade. Perhaps you did not have the qualifications in the first place. But remembering them will help you to put your best foot forward, without treading on the toes of the board members.

Rumor and popular opinion to the contrary notwithstanding, an oral board wants you to make the best appearance possible. They know you are under pressure – but they also want to see how you respond to it as a guide to what your reaction would be under the pressures of the job you seek. They will be influenced by the degree of poise you display, the personal traits you show and the manner in which you respond.

ABOUT THIS BOOK

This book contains tests divided into Examination Sections. Go through each test, answering every question in the margin. At the end of each test look at the answer key and check your answers. On the ones you got wrong, look at the right answer choice and learn. Do not fill in the answers first. Do not memorize the questions and answers, but understand the answer and principles involved. On your test, the questions will likely be different from the samples. Questions are changed and new ones added. If you understand these past questions you should have success with any changes that arise. Tests may consist of several types of questions. We have additional books on each subject should more study be advisable or necessary for you. Finally, the more you study, the better prepared you will be. This book is intended to be the last thing you study before you walk into the examination room. Prior study of relevant texts is also recommended. NLC publishes some of these in our Fundamental Series. Knowledge and good sense are important factors in passing your exam. Good luck also helps. So now study this Passbook, absorb the material contained within and take that knowledge into the examination. Then do your best to pass that exam.

EXAMINATION SECTION

EXAMINATION SECTION
TEST 1

DIRECTIONS: Each question or incomplete statement is followed by several suggested answers or completions. Select the one that BEST answers the question or completes the statement. *PRINT THE LETTER OF THE CORRECT ANSWER IN THE SPACE AT THE RIGHT.*

1. The reliability of information obtained increases with the number of persons interviewed. The more the interviewees differ in their statements, the more persons it is necessary to interview to ascertain the true facts.
   According to this statement, the dependability of the information about an occurrence obtained from interviews is related to

   A. how many people are interviewed
   B. how soon after the occurrence an interview can be arranged
   C. the individual technique of the interviewer
   D. the interviewer's ability to detect differences in the statements of interviewees

1.____

2. A sufficient quantity of the material supplied as evidence enables the laboratory expert to determine the true nature of the substance, whereas an extremely limited specimen may be an abnormal sample containing foreign matter not indicative of the true nature of the material.
   On the basis of this statement alone, it may be concluded that a reason for giving an adequate sample of material for evidence to a laboratory expert is that

   A. a limited specimen spoils more quickly than a larger sample
   B. a small sample may not truly represent the evidence
   C. he cannot analyze a small sample correctly
   D. he must have enough material to keep a part of it untouched to show in court

2.____

Questions 3-4.

DIRECTIONS: Questions 3 and 4 are based ONLY on the information given in the following paragraph.

Credibility of a witness is usually governed by his character and is evidenced by his reputation for truthfulness. Personal or financial reasons or a criminal record may cause a witness to give false information to avoid being implicated. Age, sex, physical and mental abnormalities, loyalty, revenge, social and economic status, indulgence in alcohol, and the influence of other persons are some of the many factors which may affect the accuracy, willingness, or ability with which witnesses observe, interpret, and describe occurrences.

3. According to the above paragraph, a witness may, for personal reasons, give wrong information about an occurrence because he

   A. wants to protect his reputation for truthfulness
   B. wants to embarrass the investigator
   C. doesn't want to become involved
   D. doesn't really remember what happened

3.____

4. According to the above paragraph, factors which influence the witness of an occurrence may affect   4.____

    A. not only what he tells about it, but what he was able and wanted to see of it
    B. only what he describes and interprets later but not what he actually sees at the time of the event
    C. what he sees but not what he describes
    D. what he is willing to see but not what he is able to see

5. There are few individuals or organizations on whom some records are not kept. This sentence means MOST NEARLY that   5.____

    A. a few organizations keep most of the records on individuals
    B. some of the records on a few individuals are destroyed and not kept
    C. there are few records kept on individuals
    D. there is some kind of record kept on almost every individual

Questions 6-10.

DIRECTIONS: Questions 6 through 10 are based SOLELY on the following paragraph.

Those statutes of limitations which are of interest to a claim examiner are the ones affecting third party actions brought against an insured covered by a liability policy of insurance. Such statutes of limitations are legislative enactments limiting the time within which such actions at law may be brought. Research shows that such periods differ from state to state and vary within the states with the type of action brought. The laws of the jurisdiction in which the action is brought govern and determine the period within which the action may be instituted, regardless of the place of the cause of action or the residence of the parties at the time of cause of action. The period of time set by a statute of limitations for a tort action starts from the moment the alleged tort is committed. The period usually extends continuously until its expiration, upon which legal action may no longer be brought. However, there is a suspension of the running of the period when a defendant has concealed himself in order to avoid service of legal process. The suspension continues until the defendant discontinues his concealment and then the period starts running again. A defendant may, by his agreement or conduct, be legally barred from asserting the statute of limitations as a defense to an action. The insurance carrier for the defendant may, by the misrepresentation of the claims man, cause such a bar against use of the statute of limitations by the defendant. If the claim examiner of the insurance carrier has by his conduct or assertion lulled the plaintiff into a false sense of security by false representations, the defendant may be barred from setting up the statute of limitations as a defense.

6. Of the following, the MOST suitable title for the above paragraph is   6.____

    A. Fraudulent Use of the Statute of Limitations
    B. Parties at Interest in a Lawsuit
    C. The Claim Examiner and the Law
    D. The Statute of Limitations in Claims Work

2

7. The period of time during which a third party action may be brought against an insured   7.____
   covered by a liability policy depends on

   A. the laws of the jurisdiction in which the action is brought
   B. where the cause of action which is the subject of the suit took place
   C. where the claimant lived at the time of the cause of action
   D. where the insured lived at the time of the cause of action

8. Time limits in third party actions which are set by the statutes of limitations described   8.____
   above are

   A. determined by claimant's place of residence at start of action
   B. different in a state for different actions
   C. the same from state to state for the same type of action
   D. the same within a state regardless of type of action

9. According to the above paragraph, grounds which may be legally used to prevent a   9.____
   defendant from using the statute of limitations as a defense in the action described are

   A. defendant's agreement or concealment; a charge of liability for death and injury
   B. defendant's agreement or conduct; misrepresentation by the claims man
   C. fraudulent concealment by claim examiner; a charge of liability for death or injury;
      defendant's agreement
   D. misrepresentation by claim examiner of carrier; defendant's agreement; plaintiff's
      concealment

10. Suppose an alleged tort was committed on January 1, 2013 and that the period in which   10.____
    action may be taken is set at three years by the statute of limitations. Suppose further
    that the defendant, in order to avoid service of legal process, had concealed himself from
    July 1, 2015 through December 31, 2015.
    In this case, the defendant may NOT use the statute of limitations as a defense unless
    action is brought by the plaintiff after

    A. January 1, 2016   B. February 28, 2016
    C. June 30, 2016   D. August 1, 2016

Questions 11-15.

DIRECTIONS: Questions 11 through 15 are based SOLELY on the information given in the
               following paragraph.

*The nature of the interview varies with the aim or the use to which it is put. While these
uses vary widely, interviews are basically of three types: fact-finding, informing, and motivat-
ing. One of these purposes usually predominates in an interview, but not the exclusion of the
other two. If the main purpose is fact-finding, for example, the interviewer must often motivate
the interviewee to cooperate in revealing the facts. A major factor in the interview is the inter-
action of the personalities of the interviewer and the interviewee. The interviewee may not
wish to reveal the facts sought, or even though willing enough to impart them, he may not be
able to do so because of a lack of clear understanding as to what is wanted or because of
lack of ability to put into words the information he has to give. On the other hand, the interviewer may not be able to grasp and report accurately the facts which the one being interviewed is trying to convey. Also, the interviewer's prejudice may make him not want to get at
the real facts or make him unable to recognize the truth.*

3

11. According to the above paragraph, the purpose of an interview   11._____

    A. determines the nature of the interview
    B. is usually the same for the three basic types of interviews
    C. is predominantly motivation of the interviewee
    D. is usually to check on the accuracy of facts previously obtained

12. In discussing the use or purpose of an interview, the above paragraph points out that   12._____

    A. a good interview should have only one purpose
    B. an interview usually has several uses that are equally important
    C. fact-finding should be the main purpose of an interview
    D. the interview usually has one main purpose

13. According to the above paragraph, an obstacle to the successful interview sometimes attributable to the interviewee is   13._____

    A. a lack of understanding of how to conduct an interview
    B. an inability to express himself
    C. prejudice toward the interviewer
    D. too great a desire to please

14. According to the above paragraph, one way in which the interviewer may help the interviewee to reveal the facts sought is to   14._____

    A. make him willing to impart the facts by stating clearly the consequences of false information
    B. make sure he understands what information is wanted
    C. motivate him by telling him how important he is in the investigation
    D. tell him what words to use to convey the information wanted

15. According to the above paragraph, bias on the part of the interviewer could   15._____

    A. be due to inability to understand the facts being imparted
    B. lead him to report the facts accurately
    C. make the interviewee unwilling to impart the truth
    D. prevent him from determining the facts

Questions 16-20.

DIRECTIONS: Questions 16 through 20 are to be based SOLELY on the information given in the following paragraph.

PROCEDURE TO OBTAIN REIMBURSEMENT FROM DEPARTMENT OF HEALTH
FOR CARE OF PHYSICALLY HANDICAPPED CHILDREN

Application for reimbursement must be received by the Department of Health within 30 days of the date of hospital admission in order that the Department of Hospitals may be reimbursed from the date of admission. Upon determination that the patient is physically handicapped, as defined under Chapter 780 of the State Laws, the ward clerk shall prepare seven copies of Department of Health Form A-1 or A-2 "Application and Authorization," and shall submit six copies to the institutional Collections Unit. The ward clerk shall also initiate two copies of Department of Health Form B-1 or B-2 "Financial and Social Report," and shall for-

ward them to the institutional Collections Unit for completion of page 1 and routing to the Social Service Division for completion of the Social Summary on page 2. Social Service Division shall return Form B-1 or B-2 to the institutional Collections Unit, which shall forward one copy of Form B-1 or B-2 and six copies of Form A-1 or A-2 to Central Office Division of Collections for transmission to Bureau of Handicapped Children, Department of Health.

16. According to the above paragraph, the Department of Health will pay for hospital care for   16._____

    A. children who are physically handicapped
    B. any children who are ward patients
    C. physically handicapped adults and children
    D. thirty days for eligible children

17. According to the procedure described in the above paragraph, the definition of what constitutes a physical handicap is made by the   17._____

    A. attending physician   B. laws of the state
    C. Social Service Division   D. ward clerk

18. According to the above paragraph, Form B-1 or B-2 is   18._____

    A. a three page form containing detachable pages
    B. an authorization form issued by the Department of Hospitals
    C. completed by the ward clerk after the Social Summary has been entered
    D. sent to the institutional Collections Unit by the Social Service Division

19. According to the above paragraph, after their return by the Social Service Division, the institutional Collections Unit keeps   19._____

    A. one copy of Form A-1 or A-2
    B. one copy of Form A-1 or A-2 and one copy of Form B-1 or B-2
    C. one copy of Form B-1 or B-2
    D. no copies of Forms A-1 or A-2 or B-1 or B-2

20. According to the above paragraph, forwarding the "Application and Authorization" to the Department of Health is the responsibility of the   20._____

    A. Bureau for Handicapped Children
    B. Central Office Division of Collections
    C. Institutional Collections Unit
    D. Social Service Division

21. An investigator interviews members of the public at his desk.
The attitude of the public toward this department will probably be LEAST affected by this investigator's   21._____

    A. courtesy   B. efficiency   C. height   D. neatness

22. While you are conducting an interview, the telephone on your desk rings.
Of the following, it would be BEST for you to   22._____

    A. ask the interviewer at the next desk to answer your telephone and take the message for you
    B. excuse yourself, pick up the telephone, and tell the person on the other end you are busy and will call him back later

C. ignore the ringing telephone and continue with the interview
D. use another telephone to inform the operator not to put calls through to you while you are conducting an interview

23. An interviewee is at your desk, which is quite near to desks where other people work. He beckons you a little closer and starts to talk in a low voice as though he does not want anyone else to hear him.
Under these circumstances, the BEST thing for you to do is to

    23._____

A. ask him to speak a little louder so that he can be heard
B. cut the interview short and not get involved in his problems
C. explain that people at other desks are not eavesdroppers
D. listen carefully to what he says and give it consideration

24. In the course of your work, you have developed a good relationship with the clerk in charge of the information section of a certain government agency from which you must frequently obtain information. This agency's procedures require that a number of long complicated forms be prepared by you before the information can be released.
For you to ask the clerk in charge to release information to you without your presenting the forms would be

    24._____

A. *unwise* mainly because the information so obtained is no longer considered official
B. *wise* mainly because a great deal of time will be saved by you and by the clerk
C. *unwise* mainly because it may impair the good relations you have established
D. *wise* mainly because more information can usually be obtained through friendly contacts

25. Sometimes city employees are offered gifts by members of the public in an effort to show appreciation for acts performed purely as a matter of duty. An investigator to whom such a gift was offered refused to accept it.
The action of the investigator was

    25._____

A. *bad;* the gift should have been accepted to avoid being rude to the person making the offer
B. *bad;* salaries paid city employees are not high enough to justify such refusals
C. *good;* he should accept such a gift only when he has done a special favor for someone
D. *good;* the acceptance of such gifts may raise doubts as to the honesty of the employee

26. From the point of view of current correct English usage and grammar, the MOST accept-able of the following sentences is:

    26._____

A. Each claimant was allowed the full amount of their medical expenses,
B. Either of the three witnesses is available
C. Every one of the witnesses was asked to tell his story
D. Neither of the witnesses are right

27. From the point of view of current correct English usage and grammar, the MOST accept-able of the following sentences is:

    27._____

A. Beside the statement to the police, the witness spoke to no one
B. He made no statement other than to the police and I

C. He made no statement to any one else, aside from the police
D. The witness spoke to no one but me

28. From the point of view of current correct English usage and grammar, the MOST accept-   28.____
able of the following sentences is:

A. The claimant has no one to blame but himself
B. The boss sent us, he and I, to deliver the packages
C. The lights come from mine and not his car
D. There was room on the stairs for him and myself

29. Of the following excerpts selected from letters, the one which is considered by modern   29.____
letter writing experts to be the BEST is:

A. Attached please find the application form to be filled out by you. Return the form to
this office at the above address.
B. Forward to this office your check accompanied by the application form enclosed
with this letter
C. If you wish to apply, please complete and return the enclosed form with your check
D. In reply to your letter of December _____, enclosed herewith please find the
application form you requested

30. Which of the following sentences would be MOST acceptable, from the point of view of   30.____
current correct English usage and grammar, in a letter answering a request for information about eligibility for clinic care?

A. Admission to this clinic is limited to patients' inability to pay for medical care.
B. Patients who can pay little or nothing for medical care are treated in this clinic.
C. The patient's ability to pay for medical care is the determining factor in his admissi-
bility to this clinic.
D. This clinic is for the patient's that cannot afford to pay or that can pay a little for
medical care.

31. A city employee who writes a letter requesting information from a business man should   31.____
realize that, of the following, it is MOST important to

A. end the letter with a polite closing
B. make the letter short enough to fit on one page
C. use a form, such as a questionnaire, to save the businessman's time
D. use a courteous tone that will get the desired cooperation

Questions 32-35.

DIRECTIONS: Each of Questions 32 through 35 consists of a sentence which may be classi-
fied appropriately under one of the following four categories:
A. incorrect because of faulty grammar or sentence structure
B. incorrect because of faulty punctuation
C. incorrect because of faulty capitalization
D. correct
Examine each sentence carefully. Then, in the space at the right, print the letter
preceding the category which is the BEST of the four suggested above. Each
incorrect sentence contains only one type of error. Consider a sentence correct
if it contains none of the types of errors mentioned, although there may be
other correct ways of expressing the same thought.

32. Despite the efforts of the Supervising mechanic, the elevator could not be started. 32.____

33. The U.S. Weather Bureau, weather record for the accident date was checked. 33.____

34. John Jones accidentally pushed the wrong button and then all the lights went out. 34.____

35. The investigator ought to of had the witness sign the statement. 35.____

Questions 36-45.

DIRECTIONS: Each of Questions 36 to 45 consists of a capitalized word followed by four suggested meanings of the word. For each question, choose the word or phrase which means MOST NEARLY the same as the word in capital letters.

36. ABUT 36.____

    A.   abandon   B.   assist   C.   border on   D.   renounce

37. ABSCOND 37.____

    A.   draw in   B.   give up
    C.   refrain from   D.   steal off

38. BEQUEATH 38.____

    A.   deaden   B.   hand down   C.   make sad   D.   scold

39. BOGUS 39.____

    A.   sad   B.   false   C.   shocking   D.   stolen

40. CALAMITY 40.____

    A.   disaster   B.   female   C.   insanity   D.   patriot

41. COMPULSORY 41.____

    A.   binding   B.   ordinary   C.   protected   D.   ruling

42. CONSIGN 42.____

    A.   agree with   B.   benefit   C.   commit   D.   drive down

43. DEBILITY 43.____

    A.   failure   B.   legality   C.   quality   D.   weakness

44. DEFRAUD 44.____

    A.   cheat   B.   deny   C.   reveal   D.   tie

45. DEPOSITION 45.____

    A.   absence   B.   publication   C.   removal   D.   testimony

KEY (CORRECT ANSWERS)

1.	A	11.	A	21.	C	31.	D	41.	A
2.	B	12.	D	22.	B	32.	C	42.	C
3.	C	13.	B	23.	D	33.	B	43.	D
4.	A	14.	B	24.	C	34.	D	44.	A
5.	D	15.	D	25.	D	35.	A	45.	D
6.	D	16.	A	26.	C	36.	C		
7.	A	17.	B	27.	D	37.	D		
8.	B	18.	D	28.	A	38.	B		
9.	B	19.	C	29.	C	39.	B		
10.	C	20.	B	30.	B	40.	A		

TEST 2

DIRECTIONS: Each of Questions 1 to 10 consists of a capitalized word followed by four suggested meanings of the word. For each question, choose the word or phrase
which means MOST NEARLY the same as the word in capital letters.

1. DOMICILE   1.____
   A. anger   B. dwelling   C. tame   D. willing

2. HEARSAY   2.____
   A. selfish   B. serious   C. rumor   D. unlikely

3. HOMOGENEOUS   3.____
   A. human   B. racial   C. similar   D. unwise

4. ILLICIT   4.____
   A. understood   B. uneven   C. unkind   D. unlawful

5. LEDGER   5.____
   A. book of accounts   B. editor
   C. periodical   D. shelf

6. NARRATIVE   6.____
   A. gossip   B. natural   C. negative   D. story

7. PLAUSIBLE   7.____
   A. reasonable   B. respectful
   C. responsible   D. rightful

8. RECIPIENT   8.____
   A. absentee   B. receiver   C. speaker   D. substitute

9. SUBSTANTIATE   9.____
   A. appear for   B. arrange   C. confirm   D. combine

10. SURMISE   10.____
   A. aim   B. break   C. guess   D. order

Questions 11-14.

DIRECTIONS: In Questions 11 to 14, one of the four words is misspelled. For each question,
choose the word which is misspelled.

11.   A. absence   B. accummulate   11.____
      C. acknowledgment   D. audible

12. A. benificiary   B. disbursement   12.____
     C. exorbitant   D. incidentally

13. A. inoculate   B. liaison   C. acquire   D. noticable   13.____

14. A. peddler   B. permissible   C. persuade   D. pertenant   14.____

15. A. reconciliation   B. responsable   15.____
     C. sizable   D. substantial

16. Suppose a badly cracked sidewalk, 160 feet long and 14 feet wide, is to be torn up and   16.____
     replaced in four equal sections.
     Each section will measure _____ square feet.

     A. 40   B. 220   C. 560   D. 680

17. A businessman pays R dollars a month in rent, has a weekly payroll of P dollars, and a   17.____
     utility bill of U dollars for each two months.
     His annual expenses can be expressed by

     A. $12(R+P+U)$ B. $52(R+P+U)$
     C. $12(R+52P+6U)$ D. $12(R+4P+2U)$

18. An interviewer can interview P number of people in H number of hours, including the time   18.____
     needed to prepare a report on each interview.
     The number of people he can interview in a work week of W hours is represented by

     A. $\dfrac{HW}{P}$ B. $\dfrac{PW}{H}$ C. $\dfrac{PH}{W}$ D. $\dfrac{35H}{P}$

19. Claims investigated by a certain unit total $8,430,000 for the year.   19.____
     If the cost of investigating these claims is 17.3 cents per $100, the yearly cost of inves-
     tigating these claims is MOST NEARLY

     A. $1,450   B. $14,500   C. $145,000   D. $1,450,000

20. Suppose that a business you are investigating presents the following figures: 20.____

Year	Net Income	Tax Rate on Net Income
1994	$55,000	20%
1995	55,000	30%
1996	65,000	20%
1997	52,000	25%
1998	62,000	30%
1999	68,000	25%

According to these figures, it is MOST accurate to say that   20.____

     A. less tax was due in 1998 than in 1999
     B. more tax was due in 1994 than in 1997
     C. the same amount of tax was due in 1994 and 1995
     D. the same amount of tax was due in 1996 and 1997

21. In 1996, the number of investigations completed in a certain unit had increased 230 over   21.____
the number completed in 1995, an increase of 10%. In 1997, the number completed
decreased 10% from the number completed in 1996.
Therefore, the number of investigations completed in 1997 was _____ the number
completed in 1995.

    A. 23 less than   B. 123 less than
    C. 230 more than   D. the same as

22. Assume that during a certain period Unit A investigated 400 cases and Unit B investi-   22.____
gated 300 cases.
If each unit doubled its number of investigations, the proportion of Unit A's investigations to Unit B's investigations would then be _____ it was.

    A. twice what   B. one-half as large as
    C. one-third larger than   D. the same as

23. In a certain family, the teenage daughter's annual earnings are 5/8 the earnings of her   23.____
brother and 1/5 the earnings of her father.
If her brother earns $19,200 a year, then her father's annual earnings are

    A. $60,000   B. $75,000   C. $80,000   D. $96,000

24. Assume that of the 1,700 verifications made by a certain investigating unit in a one week   24.____
period, 40% were birth records, 30% were military records, 10% were citizenship
records, and the remainder were miscellaneous records. Then the MOST accurate of the
following statements about the relative number of different records is that

    A. citizenship records verifications equaled 20% of military record verifications
    B. fewer than 700 verifications were birth records
    C. miscellaneous records verifications were 20% more than citizenship records verifi-
        cations
    D. more than 550 verifications were military records

25. Two units, A and B, answer, respectively, 1,000 and 1,500 inquiries a month.   25.____
Assuming that the number of inquiries answered by Unit A increase at the rate of 20
each month, while those answered by Unit B decrease at the rate of 5 each month, the
two units will answer the same number of inquiries at the end of _____ months.

    A. 10   B. 15   C. 20   D. 25

26. For the claim examiner to obtain a signed statement the very first time he interviews a   26.____
witness to an accident is USUALLY

    A. *bad;* the witness should be given more time in which to recall the details of the
        accident
    B. *good;* delay might result in the witness forgetting details
    C. *good;* no further appointments with the witness would then be needed
    D. *good;* the story given by this witness would then be the first description of the acci-
        dent

Questions 27-30.

DIRECTIONS: Questions 27 to 30 are based on the following description by a physician of the injuries sustained by the victim of an accident.

Compound fracture of the right humerus. Contusions and ecchymoses of the right chest. Four-inch long laceration on the dorsal surface of the right hand.

27.   According to this description, the victim has a broken   27._____

   A.   ankle   B.   arm   C.   knee   D.   thigh

28.   The broken bone is   28._____

   A.   broken in more than one place
   B.   crushed
   C.   protruding through the skin
   D.   splintered

29.   Contusions are   29._____

   A.   bruises   B.   skin scrapes or cuts
   C.   swellings   D.   torn muscles

30.   The laceration of the right hand is on the   30._____

   A.   back of the hand   B.   little finger side
   C.   palm   D.   thumb side

31.   Suppose a claim examiner desires to obtain a signed statement during an appointment   31._____
in a witness's home. He finds that the witness is cooperative, but has a large family
whose members stay with him in the living room, talking and looking at television.
After considering the problem of getting the signed statement, the claim examiner
should

   A.   leave after making another appointment since his visit is an intrusion at this time
   B.   suggest that he and the witness use another room where they can give the state-
        ment their full attention
   C.   take advantage of the friendly atmosphere in the living room by having the state-
        ment drawn up and signed there
   D.   tell the witness to get his family to stop talking and to turn off the television set so
        that he and the witness can concentrate

32.   Claim examiners occasionally expose fake automobile injury claims in which bruises and   32._____
lacerations from falls, barroom brawls, or other mishaps are attributed to an insured commercial vehicle.
Since the claimant usually tries to pick a situation in which the driver is likely to be
unaware of the accident and so can not contradict the claim, which of the following is
MOST likely to be the claimant's story?

   A.   The front end of a truck with defective brake struck him and the truck kept going.
   B.   The front end of a truck sideswiped him as the driver backed into a parking space.
   C.   A truck knocked him over while backing into a loading space.
   D.   The rear end of a truck making a sharp turn struck him.

33. Suppose there is a rule in your office that signed statements of claimants should be witnessed by a person who has no direct interest in the claim.
In accordance with this rule, when a claimant is willing to sign a statement in his home, it would be BEST for you to have the claimant's signature witnessed by

 A. a neighbor   B. his attorney
 C. his wife   D. yourself

33.____

34. The attitude presented by the claim examiner to the claimant should ALWAYS leave the claimant with the feeling that

 A. he will be treated fairly
 B. he will receive damages
 C. his claim has no basis
 D. the claim examiner is his friend

34.____

35. If a claimant states that his vision has been impaired by an accident, it would be BEST to have him examined by a physician who is a specialist in

 A. dermatology   B. opthalmology
 C. otology   D. urology

35.____

36. Suppose that witness W tells you, the claim examiner, that Mr. X also witnessed the accident you are investigating. Mr. X denies that he has any knowledge of the accident. For you to have Mr. X sign a statement that he has no knowledge of the accident is wise MAINLY because such a statement

 A. casts doubt on Mr. X's reliability if he should be a surprise witness for the opposition
 B. makes it unnecessary for you to further investigate Mr. X
 C. proves that Mr. X is telling the truth
 D. proves that the statements made by witness W are unreliable and should be investigated further

36.____

37. A claim examiner admitted that the settlement negotiations were not progressing because of a clash of personalities and suggested that another claim examiner continue the negotiations.
Such an action by the claim examiner is

 A. *sensible;* it reduces his responsibility if the settlement negotiations fail
 B. *foolish;* it is an admission that he has an irritating personality and can not get along with people
 C. *sensible;* it shows he recognizes the problem and a possible method of completing the settlement
 D. *foolish;* it gives the claimant an advantage in the negotiations

37.____

38. In evaluating a doctor's fitness to serve as an expert witness in a negligence case, the claim examiner should give FIRST consideration to the doctor's

 A. field of specialization
 B. previous total experience as a witness in negligence cases
 C. standing in the community and in his profession
 D. total formal schooling

38.____

39. A claim examiner, showing his identification, introduced himself to a housewife by saying, *I am Mr. Nichols from the Department of... We are trying to get information about an accident which occurred in front of your house.*
The claim examiner's approach was

    A. *good;* by identifying himself and stating his purpose, he is apt to get better cooperation
    B. *good;* by giving his name, he puts the interview on a non-personal basis
    C. *poor;* by revealing his purpose immediately, he may lose the woman's cooperation because of fear
    D. *poor;* he should stress the importance of cooperating with city departments

40. Witness A describes an individual as being *of medium height.* Witness B describes the same individual as being *tall and thin.*
To clear up this difference in description of the individual's height, it would be BEST for you to

    A. ask another witness to describe the individual
    B. ask both witnesses to compare the individual's height with that of a person of known height
    C. average the difference and describe the individual as being *medium tall*
    D. check both witnesses' judgment on other factors to decide which witness is more reliable

41. A claimant against the city is in the hospital as the result of an automobile accident. An interview with this claimant might eliminate confusion caused by contradictory statements of witnesses to the accident.
Under these circumstances, the BEST action for the claim examiner assigned to the case to take FIRST is to

    A. determine whether the claimant is in a condition that would permit an interview
    B. postpone interviewing the claimant until he leaves the hospital
    C. try to resolve the problem by re-examining the witnesses whose statements are in conflict
    D. try to get an immediate short interview in case the person should die

42. The claimant is an occupant of a building, ownership of which was taken over by the city one day before his accident. He has bruises and contusions which he attributes to tripping on a loose board on a stairway. Several tenants state that they had complained many times to the previous owner of the building about the same loose board.
Which of the following would tend MOST to suggest fraudulent intent on the part of the claimant?

    A. The claimant is represented by an insurance company with which he holds a policy covering this type of accident.
    B. The claimant is the previous owner of the building, and there are no witnesses to the accident.
    C. It is established by reliable witnesses that the claimant tripped over the loose board while intoxicated.
    D. Witnesses state that the claimant tripped over the loose board while chasing a stray dog down the stairway.

43. At the request of the investigator, witness A added a signed paragraph to a statement   43.____
already signed by witness B while witness B was present. This paragraph stated that witness A's version of the accident was exactly the same as that of witness B.
Authorities in the field of claim examining would GENERALLY consider the addition of
such a paragraph as

    A. *good;* it makes the statement of witness B more believable
    B. *bad;* witness A should have been asked to add his statement after witness B had
       left
    C. *good;* the effect is to make both witnesses more cooperative
    D. *bad;* since witnesses rarely give identical versions of an accident, the validity of this
       additional statement would be questioned

44. The train operator's statement was that he had applied brakes immediately on seeing   44.____
the man collapse and fall onto the tracks, but he could not stop soon enough and ran
over him.
If proving absence of negligence in this case depends entirely on showing that the
accident was beyond the train operator's control, which, of the following circumstances
would, by itself, show that there was no negligence?

    A. Five witnesses agreed independently that the man had apparently collapsed from
       a heart attack.
    B. Five witnesses agreed independently that the train was traveling at a speed which
       was far under the normal approach speed.
    C. The train operator's record showed that he had been involved in no previous accident
       although employed thirty years as a train operator.
    D. At the moment the man fell, the distance between him and the train was less than
       the minimum distance at which the train could stop at normal approach speed.

45. No proper evaluation of a claim can be made without a working knowledge of the law of   45.____
the jurisdiction in which an accident occurred.
Of the following, the CHIEF implication of this statement is that

    A. claims are based on where the accident occurred
    B. evaluation of the law is a proper function of the claim examiner
    C. local laws affect the claim examiner's decisions
    D. the best claim examiners are attorneys

———————

KEY (CORRECT ANSWERS)

1.	B	11.	B	21.	A	31.	B	41.	A
2.	C	12.	A	22.	D	32.	D	42.	B
3.	C	13.	D	23.	A	33.	A	43.	D
4.	D	14.	D	24.	B	34.	A	44.	D
5.	A	15.	B	25.	C	35.	B	45.	C
6.	D	16.	C	26.	B	36.	A		
7.	A	17.	C	27.	B	37.	C		
8.	B	18.	B	28.	C	38.	A		
9.	C	19.	B	29.	A	39.	A		
10.	C	20.	D	30.	A	40.	B		

EXAMINATION SECTION
TEST 1

DIRECTIONS: Each question or incomplete statement is followed by several suggested answers or completions. Select the one that BEST answers the question or completes the statement. *PRINT THE LETTER OF THE CORRECT ANSWER IN THE SPACE AT THE RIGHT.*

1. It is desirable for an examiner to keep a regular periodic check on witnesses for the city in a negligence suit MAINLY because, in this way, he can   1._____

    A.   coach the witnesses thoroughly on the testimony they are to give
    B.   develop new leads to previously unknown sources of information
    C.   lessen the chance of losing track of witnesses before the suit goes to trial
    D.   show these witnesses how important they are to the city's case

2. A certain examiner follows the practice of having the claimant or his attorney place a settlement value on their claim before he makes any settlement offer himself. Such a practice is GENERALLY   2._____

    A.   *desirable* because the claimant will realize that his interests are being given consideration by the examiner
    B.   *undesirable* because it leads to delays in settlements by encouraging differences between claims and offers
    C.   *desirable* because the demand made by the claimant or his attorney may show the examiner that he has overvalued the claim
    D.   *undesirable* because the claimant and attorney will always set a high settlement figure

3. The preliminary investigation of a fatal subway accident reveals that the wife of the victim took out a large insurance policy on his life shortly before the accident. In evaluating this information, the examiner should realize that it   3._____

    A.   is important enough to warrant further investigation
    B.   is important evidence of the criminal involvement of the wife
    C.   is purely coincidental and no special significance should be attached to it
    D.   points strongly to the probability of suicide

4. In a vehicle collision case involving a city vehicle and a privately-owned vehicle legally parked at the curb, the driver of the city vehicle admitted to the examiner for the city that the accident was entirely his fault.
The action of the city driver in admitting blame for the accident should   4._____

    A.   *be* criticized; it will encourage the claimant in his suit against the city
    B.   *not be* criticized; it will influence the claimant to make a more reasonable settlement demand against the city
    C.   *be* criticized; the question of liability must be decided by a competent court of law
    D.   *not be* criticized; liability is clear-cut in view of the conditions that existed at the time of the accident

5. Of the following, the CHIEF objective of the examiner who investigates an automobile accident claim should be to 5.____

    A. complete his investigation in the shortest possible time while the memory of the event is still fresh
    B. get the facts for use as evidence in court or as a basis for settlement
    C. steer the claimant toward accepting a settlement of the claim
    D. try to lay a basis for disproving the liability of the city

6. In law, the rule of negligence provides that to hold a person liable for another's injury, there must have been a duty owed by the former to the latter. 6.____
The duty MOST probably referred to in the preceding statement is the duty to

    A. advise regarding the possible consequences of the action contemplated
    B. exercise reasonable care to prevent the injury
    C. provide speedy medical assistance when needed
    D. refuse entry into the vehicle or the premises

7. Claimants and witnesses become suspicious when the examiner makes a *callback* to get additional information which he should have obtained in the initial contact. 7.____
Of the following, the CHIEF implication of this statement for the examiner in his work is that he should

    A. carefully plan the *callback* interview in such a way as to avoid arousing suspicions of claimants and witnesses
    B. frankly state the reason for the *callback* to the claimant or witness so that suspicions will be allayed
    C. not make any *callbacks* in order not to arouse the suspicions of claimants and witnesses
    D. thoroughly plan his initial interview so as to obtain complete and correct information and avoid the need for *callback*

8. It is desirable for an examiner to be familiar with medical terminology relating to bodily injuries MAINLY because this familiarity will 8.____

    A. assist him in determining whether a claimant is being given proper care
    B. enable him to determine whether a claimant's injuries have been fully and properly described on the hospital records
    C. give him a sympathetic approach to discussing a claim with the injured person
    D. help him understand medical reports that he may refer to in the course of the investigation of a claim

9. Assume that a city vehicle is forced to stop short by another vehicle in front of it. As a result, a third vehicle runs into the rear of the city vehicle. The driver of the third vehicle files a claim against the city alleging that the city vehicle's short stop caused the accident. 9.____
The examiner assigned to this case should recommend

    A. denial of the claim since the rear vehicle in such a situation should be at a sufficient distance to stop in time
    B. settling the claim since the city vehicle is the direct cause of the actual collision
    C. denial of this claim since the real cause of the accident is the first vehicle's improper stop

D. settling the claim but bringing in the driver of the first vehicle as the defendant liable for all the damage

10. The investigating staff of the Department of Hospitals often processes liability claims for accident victims who are hospitalized in municipal hospitals.
Of the following, the MOST probable reason why the investigating staff processes such claims is that   10._____

    A. reimbursement of the hospital for the victim's care may be facilitated by such action
    B. such action is required by and consistent with the effort to reduce the number of accidents in the city
    C. the processing of such liability claims requires little effort and results in better public relations
    D. the welfare of the patient is usually considered above everything else

11. Suppose that, as a matter of policy, insurance company representatives are not permitted to inspect the hospital records of patients without the latter's written consent. Such a policy is   11._____

    A. *justified* because information about a patient's ailment or disease is confidential and private
    B. *unjustified* because nobody should be required to give information about his medical condition
    C. *justified* because these records may be meaningful to a medical person but not to a layman
    D. *unjustified* because such matters should be left to the hospital administrator

12. Continuous taking of notes during an interview is GENERALLY   12._____

    A. *desirable* because no important facts will be forgotten
    B. *undesirable* because it gives the person being interviewed a clue to the importance of the information being obtained from him
    C. *desirable* because the interviewer cannot write as fast as the person being interviewed can speak
    D. *undesirable* because it may put the person being interviewed ill at ease

13. In deciding whether to make use of a source of information in connection with an investigation, the examiner should be influenced MAINLY by the   13._____

    A. expense entailed in the use of the source
    B. relative availability of the source
    C. relative proximity of the source
    D. reliability of the information offered by the source

14. An examiner's report always includes his personal judgment of the credibility of witnesses mentioned in his report.
This practice is   14._____

    A. *desirable*, mainly because it can be used to support the position that the examiner wants to take with respect to the case
    B. *undesirable*, mainly because it is of no value to the reader of the report
    C. *desirable*, mainly because it is part of the claim examining function to evaluate the credibility of witnesses

D. *undesirable*, mainly because judgments should be formed on the basis of facts, not opinions

15. When a statement which may be submitted as evidence in court has been secured from a person after questioning, it is often typed up with intentional errors and given to the person to read.
Such action is USUALLY based on a   15._____

   A. desire to be able to counteract any later denial by the person that he was aware of the contents; if the person corrects and initials the errors and then signs the statement, it is evidence that he was aware of the contents
   B. desire to distinguish the truthful from the untruthful person; an error which makes for inconsistency within the statement will be noticed much more readily by the truthful person
   C. need for careful proofreading; when the person discovers several mistakes, he will be alerted to watch for other possible mistakes
   D. need for testing the mental functioning of the person at the time of making the statement; if he does not detect the errors, he is functioning abnormally

16. Suppose you are checking an alphabetical card reference file to locate information about a *George Dyerly*. After checking all the *D*'s, you can find a card only for a *George Dypely*. Of the following, the BEST action for you to take is to   16._____

   A. check the balance of the file to see if the card you are interested in has been misfiled
   B. check the data on the card to see if it relates to the same person in whom you are interested
   C. correct the spelling of the name on your records and reports to conform to the spelling on the card
   D. reject this reference file as a source of information regarding this person

17. Mary Hartley, age 40, wife of William Hartley, had stated in an application that she was a graduate of a certain high school and had completed 2 years of college in another city. A written inquiry to these two schools brought the reply that they had no record of Mary Hartley ever having attended their respective schools.
Of the following, it is MOST probable that the   17._____

   A. records in question, being rather old, had been destroyed
   B. records in question had been lost or misplaced
   C. woman exaggerated her education in her application
   D. woman was listed on the school records under another name

18. Of the following, the MOST important reason why an examiner should maintain a good working relationship with law enforcement officers in the community is that   18._____

   A. all government employees, whether city, state, or federal, should keep in close touch with each other in view of their common interests
   B. community law enforcement officers may sometimes need the assistance of the examiner in a police matter
   C. law enforcement is most effective when all elements in the community cooperate
   D. these officers often know a great many facts regarding the citizens of a community which are not matters of public record

19. In fidelity bond investigations, the employer applying for the bond is investigated in addition to the employee to be bonded.
The MOST likely reason for this is that

    A. employers can be depended upon to be reliable but fraud by an employer involves greater sums of money
    B. the employer's auditing methods and his methods of handling valuables affect his risk status
    C. there are as many dishonest employers as there are dishonest employees
    D. there is such a great number of cases where the employer and the employee conspire to defraud the insurance company

19.____

20. An examiner who wanted to interview the head of a business firm introduced himself by saying, *I am James Smith of the State Legal Department, and I would like to check with you certain information given us by Herbert Brown, a former employee of yours.*
The approach used by the examiner was

    A. *good* because by giving so little information, he has lost nothing if the employer should refuse to cooperate
    B. *poor* because he should first try to establish a friendly relationship with the employer before stating the purpose of his visit
    C. *good* because he came directly to the point by stating who he was and what he wanted
    D. *poor* because he should have stressed with the employer the importance of cooperating with government agencies in all investigative matters

20.____

21. The examiner should never rely entirely on the data given him by a witness.
Of the following, the CHIEF justification for this statement is the fact that

    A. human perceptions are often incomplete and frequently affected by distortions
    B. recall and recognition are apt to be more accurate when the passage of time has caused momentary passions and prejudices to cool
    C. a witness to an occurrence cannot always be found
    D. witnesses usually contradict each other

21.____

22. The first 3 numerals in a social security number indicate the state where the employee resided when the number was assigned.
According to the preceding statement, if your investigation indicates that the first 3 numerals of a New York resident's Social Security number do not correspond to the numbers for the state, it is MOST reasonable to conclude that

    A. the numbers assigned to New York have been revised
    B. there is an error in the Social Security number
    C. this person at one time did not live in New York
    D. this person is not a bona fide New York resident

22.____

23. The examiner's general plans for the investigation should be determined before he starts on a case.
Of the following, the BEST argument in favor of this procedure is that

    A. a plan once adopted should not be modified unless there are very good reasons for doing so

23.____

B.   steps in the investigation which duplicate each other or are of little value will be minimized
C.   the plan for each investigation will be different
D.   until an investigation is actually begun, it is difficult to know the problems that will be encountered

24.   An examiner is only as good as the technique he employs. Of the following, the MOST logical conclusion from this statement is that   24.____

A.   examiners employing the same technique will achieve the same results
B.   poor results in examining work are traced inevitably to poor technique
C.   potentially good examiners may do poor work through the use of improper technique
D.   successful examiners employ the same technique

25.   The examiner must always bear in mind that he has no power to force the interviewee to give him information. Of the following, the CHIEF implication of this statement for the examiner in his work is that   25.____

A.   he may nevertheless utilize forceful persuasion as a tool since the interviewee is not aware of his lack of power to apply pressure
B.   he should develop techniques for leading the interviewee into making certain admissions without the latter being aware of it
C.   he should place considerable emphasis on developing the voluntary cooperation of the interviewee
D.   information that he obtains by force is of doubtful validity

26.   Carefully planned interviews tend to impose restrictions which leave little room for spontaneity.
A flaw in this criticism of the planned interview is that it does NOT take into account that   26.____

A.   a planned interview obviates the need for spontaneity
B.   even the planned interview may be flexible
C.   not all planned interviews impose restrictions
D.   restrictions that result from planning are undesirable

27.   In New York State, compulsory automobile liability insurance   27.____

A.   is optional with each municipality
B.   must be carried in minimum amounts of $5,000, $10,000, and $5,000
C.   was defeated at the last session of the legislature
D.   is required

28.   The State Vehicle and Traffic Law requires that when a vehicular accident has occurred, an accident report be filed with the Commissioner of Motor Vehicles   28.____

A.   if anyone has been injured or there has been property damage of more than a certain amount
B.   if someone has been injured or there has been property damage in any amount
C.   only if someone has been injured seriously
D.   regardless of whether there has been any property damage or personal injury

29. A form relating to possible insurance coverage of accident victims has a space headed 29.____
Name of Carrier.
The word *carrier* in this case MOST probably refers to the

    A. accident victim   B. insurance company
    C. policy beneficiary   D. policy holder

30. In the business world, title companies are GENERALLY concerned with matters relating 30.____
to the

    A. investment in securities
    B. laws of copyright
    C. ownership of real property
    D. registration of patents

31. A person who has *derivative* United States citizenship is one who has citizenship through 31.____

    A. birth in the United States
    B. his own naturalization proceedings
    C. marriage with a naturalized citizen
    D. the naturalization of a parent

32. As most commonly employed, the term *vital statistics* refers to records of 32.____

    A. automobile accidents
    B. births and deaths
    C. crimes known to the police
    D. stock market transactions

Questions 33-35.

DIRECTIONS: Questions 33 through 35 are to be answered SOLELY on the basis of the information given in the following statement.

    When a voluntary hospital admits a Blue Cross subscriber who has been referred from a city hospital, a concurrent submission of the case shall be made by it to both Blue Cross and the city investigator who routinely visits the voluntary hospital. This procedure will be advantageous to both the voluntary hospital and the city since the hospital would be notified immediately of the ability of the city to reimburse should Blue Cross coverage be inapplicable or insufficient; furthermore, the city will be able to assure itself of potential state aid for those cases for whom it may have to assume some responsibility. Necessary time limits to process applications for state aid can also be made if this referral is concurrent, such as for state charges and relief clients, who are frequently Blue Cross members. This investigation can best be conducted by the city staff assigned to the voluntary hospital, rather than by the staff in the referring municipal hospital.

33. According to the above statement, one responsibility of a voluntary hospital with respect   33.____
to an admission who is a Blue Cross subscriber is to

    A.   get the city to reimburse its fair share if Blue Cross coverage is inapplicable or
insufficient
    B.   refer the case to the city hospital for possible collection of state aid
    C.   submit the case concurrently to both Blue Cross and the city investigator
    D.   submit the case to the city investigator if the patient has been referred by a city
hospital

34. According to the above statement, it is NOT an advantage of the procedure described   34.____
that the

    A.   city can make sure of getting possible state aid for those cases for whom it may be
partly responsible
    B.   cost of caring for the cases referred to will be shared by Blue Cross, the voluntary
hospital, the city, and the state
    C.   needed time limits to handle state aid applications can be made
    D.   voluntary hospitals will know immediately if the city will pay for its referrals who do
not have enough Blue Cross coverage

35. According to the above statement, the investigation referred to can be carried out MOST   35.____
advantageously by the

    A.   city investigator who routinely visits the voluntary hospital
    B.   city staff assigned to the hospital that admitted the patient
    C.   staff of the hospital that referred the patient
    D.   staff of the voluntary hospital that accepted the referral

36. To have analytical habits and a scientific approach is a necessary qualification for the   36.____
development of a first-rate examiner. But it is also true that the main source of people
with such qualifications, the body of scientists, mathematicians, and logicians who con-
stantly advance the state of human knowledge, does not contain many people who could
be developed into first-rate examiners.
On the basis of this statement, it is MOST reasonable to assume that

    A.   in order to develop into a very good examiner, a person needs something more
than analytical habits and a scientific approach
    B.   examiners should receive intensive training in science, mathematics, and logic
    C.   most successful examiners are drawn from the fields of science, mathematics, and
logic
    D.   the eccentricities usually found in the behavior of scientists, mathematicians, and
logicians are not conducive to the development of first-rate examiners

37. A greater variety of accounts of the circumstances of an accident is likely to result when   37.____
the witnesses are interviewed separately than when they are interviewed as a group.
Of the following, the MOST valid inference from this statement is that

    A.   a truer picture of the circumstances of an accident can be obtained through inter-
viewing the witnesses as a group than through interviewing them separately
    B.   interviewing of accident witnesses individually offers a greater chance that individ-
ual versions of the accident will be obtained than interviewing the same witnesses
as a group

C. people who witness an accident as part of a group are more likely to agree on the circumstances of the accident than those witnesses who are separated at the time of the accident and see the accident from different angles

D. witnesses are not as likely to tell the truth when they are interviewed privately as when they are interviewed as a group

Questions 38-39.

DIRECTIONS: Questions 38 and 39 are to be answered SOLELY on the basis of the information given in the following paragraph.

It is argued by some that the locale of the trial should be given little or no consideration. Facts are facts, they say; and if presented properly to a jury panel, they will be productive of the same results regardless of where the trial is held. However, experience shows great differences in the methods of handling claims by juries. In some counties, large demands in personal injury suits are viewed with suspicion by the jury. In others, the jurors are liberal in dealing with someone else's funds.

38. According to the above paragraph, it would be advisable for an examiner on a personal injury case to   38.____

    A. get information as to the kind of verdicts that are usually awarded by juries in the county of trial
    B. give little or no consideration to the locale of the trial
    C. look for incomplete and improper presentation of facts to the jury if the verdict was not justified by the facts
    D. offer a high but realistic initial settlement figure so that no temptation is left to the claimant to gamble on the jury's verdict

39. According to the above statement, the argument that the location of a trial in a personal injury suit CANNOT counteract the weight of the evidence is   39.____

    A. basically sound
    B. disproven by the differences in awards for similar claims
    C. substantiated in those cases where the facts are properly and carefully presented to the injury
    D. supported by experience which shows great differences in the methods of handling claims by juries

Questions 40-42.

DIRECTIONS: Questions 40 through 42 are to be answered SOLELY on the basis of the information given in the following paragraph.

A loan receipt is an instrument devised to permit the insurance company to bring an action against the wrongdoer in the name of the insured despite the fact that the insured no longer has any financial interest in the outcome. It provides, in effect, that the amount of the loss is advanced to the insured as a loan which is repayable only up to the extent of any recovery made from the wrongdoer. The insured further agrees to enter and prosecute suit against the wrongdoer in his own name. Such a receipt substitutes a loan for a payment for the purpose of permitting the insurance company to press its action against the wrongdoer in the name of the insured.

40. According to the above paragraph, the purpose behind the use of a loan receipt is to   40._____

    A. guarantee that the insurance company gets repayment from the person insured
    B. insure repayment of all expenditures to the named insured
    C. make it possible for the insurance company to sue in the name of the policy owner
    D. prevent the wrongdoer from escaping the natural consequences of his act

41. According to the above paragraph, the amount of the loan which must be paid back to   41._____
the insurance company equals but does NOT exceed the amount

    A. of the loss
    B. on the face of the policy
    C. paid to the insured
    D. recovered from the wrongdoer

42. According to the above paragraph, by giving a loan receipt, the person insured agrees to   42._____

    A. a suit against the wrongdoer in his own name
    B. forego any financial gain from the outcome of the suit
    C. institute an action on behalf of the insurance company
    D. repay the insurance company for the loan received

Questions 43-44.

DIRECTIONS: Questions 43 and 44 are to be answered SOLELY on the basis of the information given in the following paragraph.

Hospitals maintained wholly by public taxation may treat only those compensation cases which are emergencies and may not treat such emergency cases longer than the emergency exists; provided, however, that these restrictions shall not be applicable where there is not available a hospital other than a hospital maintained wholly by taxation.

43. According to the above paragraph, compensation cases   43._____

    A. are regarded as emergency cases by hospitals maintained wholly by public taxation
    B. are seldom treated by hospitals maintained wholly by public taxation
    C. are treated mainly by privately endowed hospitals
    D. may be treated by hospitals maintained wholly by public taxation if they are emergencies

44. According to the above paragraph, it is MOST reasonable to conclude that where a privately endowed hospital is available   44._____

    A. a hospital supported wholly by public taxation may treat emergency compensation cases only so long as the emergency exists
    B. a hospital supported wholly by public taxation may treat any compensation cases
    C. a hospital supported wholly by public taxation must refer emergency compensation cases to such a hospital
    D. the restrictions regarding the treatment of compensation cases by a tax-supported hospital are not wholly applicable

Questions 45-46.

DIRECTIONS: Questions 45 and 46 are to be answered SOLELY on the basis of the information given in the following paragraph.

*An assumption commonly made in regard to the reliability of testimony is that when a
number of persons report upon the same matter, those details upon which there is an agreement may, in general, be considered as substantiated. Experiments have shown, however,
that there is a tendency for the same errors to appear in the testimony of different individuals,
and that, quite apart from any collusion, agreement of testimony is no proof of dependability.*

45. According to the above paragraph, it is commonly assumed that details of an event are   45._____
     substantiated when

     A.   a number of persons report upon them
     B.   a reliable person testifies to them
     C.   no errors are apparent in the testimony of different individuals
     D.   several witnesses are in agreement about them

46. According to the above paragraph, agreement in the testimony of different witnesses to   46._____
     the same event is

     A.   evaluated more reliably when considered apart from collusion
     B.   not the result of chance
     C.   not a guarantee of the accuracy of the facts
     D.   the result of a mass reaction of the witnesses

Questions 47-48.

DIRECTIONS: Questions 47 and 48 are to be answered SOLELY on the basis of the information given in the following paragraph.

*The accuracy of the information about past occurrence obtainable in an interview is so
low that one must take the stand that the best use to be made of the interview in this connection is a means of finding clues and avenues of access to more reliable sources of information. On the other hand, feelings and attitudes have been found to be clearly and correctly
revealed in a properly conducted personal interview.*

47. According to the above paragraph, information obtained in a personal interview   47._____

     A.   can be corroborated by other clues and more reliable sources of information
          revealed at the interview
     B.   can be used to develop leads to other sources of information about past events
     C.   is not reliable
     D.   is reliable if it relates to recent occurrences

48. According to the above paragraph, the personal interview is suitable for obtaining   48._____

     A.   emotional reactions to a given situation
     B.   fresh information on factors which may be forgotten
     C.   revived recollection of previous events for later use as testimony
     D.   specific information on material already reduced to writing

49. Even if no one else is interested in the case you are investigating, it is still recommended   49.____
that you keep a record of the progress of the case by means of regular reports for the file.
Of the following, the one which is NOT a good reason for this recommendation is that

    A.   it is difficult for the memory to retain all the information gathered on every case during the course of daily investigations
    B.   it may become necessary to review the case while the person assigned to it is temporarily away from the office because of illness or other reason
    C.   the final report on the investigation will be briefer if it includes only the important material from the daily reports
    D.   the person investigating the case may resign or transfer to another job

50. The most thorough investigation is of no value if the report written by the investigator   50.____
does not enable the reader to readily decide the correct action to be taken. Of the following, the LEAST direct implication of the preceding paragraph is that the

    A.   investigation conducted must be very thorough to be of value
    B.   investigation report is generally written by the person who made the investigation
    C.   purpose of the investigation report is to give superiors a basis for action
    D.   worth of the investigation is affected by the report submitted

_____

KEY (CORRECT ANSWERS)

1. C	11. A	21. A	31. D	41. D
2. C	12. D	22. C	32. B	42. A
3. A	13. D	23. B	33. D	43. D
4. D	14. C	24. C	34. B	44. A
5. B	15. A	25. C	35. B	45. D
6. B	16. B	26. B	36. A	46. C
7. D	17. D	27. D	37. B	47. B
8. D	18. D	28. A	38. A	48. A
9. A	19. B	29. B	39. B	49. C
10. A	20. C	30. C	40. C	50. A

_____

TEST 2

DIRECTIONS: Each question or incomplete statement is followed by several suggested answers or completions. Select the one that BEST answers the question or completes the statement. *PRINT THE LETTER OF THE CORRECT ANSWER IN THE SPACE AT THE RIGHT.*

1. Before you submit the written report of an investigation which you conducted, you become aware of some previously unknown information relating to the case.
Your decision as to whether to rewrite your report to include this additional information should be influenced MAINLY by the

    A. amount of time remaining in which to submit the report
    B. bearing this additional information will have on the findings and recommendations of the report
    C. extent of the revision that will be required in the original report in order to include this additional information
    D. feasibility of submitting a supplementary report at a later date

1.____

2. When dictating a report to a stenographer, it is LEAST important to

    A. be brief and say only what is essential
    B. be emphatic and speak with expression
    C. spell out all involved words
    D. work from an outline previously prepared

2.____

3. When signed statements of witnesses are forwarded with the report of an investigation, it is generally BEST to

    A. merely highlight the main points of the statements in the report, commenting on any contradictions
    B. repeat the statements verbatim in the body of the report and call attention to the original statements attached
    C. retype in the report those parts of the statements that are not significant and of doubtful validity, thus calling the reader's attention to them and avoiding misinterpretation
    D. save space by not taking up the statements in the report since they are attached and available to the reader of the report

3.____

Questions 4-18.

DIRECTIONS: In each of Questions 4 through 18, select the lettered word or phrase which means MOST NEARLY the same as the italicized word.

4. *abet*

    A. crush   B. encourage
    C. gamble   D. reduce

4.____

5. *abeyance*

    A. assistance   B. conclusion
    C. obedience   D. suspension

5.____

6. *allege*   6.____

    A. affirm   B. increase
    C. legalize   D. prove

7. *allusion*   7.____

    A. deposit   B. image
    C. impression   D. reference

8. *brevity*   8.____

    A. fearless   B. pointless
    C. shortness   D. truthfulness

9. *cognizance*   9.____

    A. awareness   B. convincing
    C. soundness   D. timeliness

10. *collusion*   10.____

    A. accident   B. deceit
    C. deduction   D. imagination

11. *conjecture*   11.____

    A. agreement   B. conjunction
    C. failure   D. guess

12. *defalcation*   12.____

    A. absence   B. dying
    C. embezzlement   D. rejection

13. *derogatory*   13.____

    A. concealed   B. deserving
    C. detracting   D. questioning

14. *interlocutory*   14.____

    A. intermediate   B. prompt
    C. soothing   D. wordy

15. *suborn*   15.____

    A. decorate   B. distribute
    C. incite   D. subtract

16. *subrogate*   16.____

    A. legislate   B. remove
    C. substitute   D. support

17. *surety*   17.____

    A. gain   B. guarantee
    C. increase   D. spoilage

18. *tort*   18.____

    A. active interest   B. concise
    C. involved interpretation   D. wrongful act

Questions 18-23.

DIRECTIONS: Each of Questions 18 through 23 consists of four words. Three of the words are spelled correctly; one is spelled incorrectly. For each question, select the word that is spelled INCORRECTLY.

19. A. collateral   B. possesion   19.____
    C. relevant   D. superficial

20. A. fluorescent   B. maintenance   20.____
    C. occurrence   D. tecnical

21. A. hindrance   B. interval   21.____
    C. liquidate   D. preceeding

22. A. questionnaire   B. superintendant   22.____
    C. temporarily   D. vaccination

23. A. resipient   B. significant   23.____
    C. unanimous   D. variable

24. From the point of view of current correct English usage and grammar, the MOST acceptable of the following sentences is: 24.____

    A. An agreement was reached between the defendant, the plaintiff, the plaintiff's attorney and the insurance company as to the amount of the settlement.
    B. Everybody was asked to give their versions of the accident.
    C. The consensus of opinion was that the evidence was inconclusive.
    D. The witness stated that if he was rich, he wouldn't have had to loan the money.

25. From the point of view of current correct English usage and grammar, the MOST acceptable of the following sentences is: 25.____

    A. Before beginning the investigation, all the materials relating to the case were carefully assembled.
    B. The reason for his inability to keep the appointment is because of his injury in the accident.
    C. This here evidence tends to support the claim of the defendant.
    D. We interviewed all the witnesses who, according to the driver, were still in town.

KEY (CORRECT ANSWERS)

1.	B		11.	D
2.	B		12.	C
3.	A		13.	C
4.	B		14.	A
5.	D		15.	C
6.	A		16.	C
7.	D		17.	B
8.	C		18.	D
9.	A		19.	B
10.	B		20.	D

21.	D
22.	B
23.	A
24.	C
25.	D

READING COMPREHENSION
UNDERSTANDING AND INTERPRETING WRITTEN MATERIAL
EXAMINATION SECTION
TEST 1

DIRECTIONS: Each question or incomplete statement is followed by several suggested answers or completions. Select the one that BEST answers the question or completes the statement. *PRINT THE LETTER OF THE CORRECT ANSWER IN THE SPACE AT THE RIGHT.*

Questions 1-4.

DIRECTIONS: Questions 1 through 4 are to be answered SOLELY on the basis of the following paragraph.

An annual leave allowance, which combines leaves previously given for vacation, personal business, family illness, and other reasons shall be granted members. Calculation of credits for such leave shall be on an annual basis beginning January 1st of each year. Annual leave credits shall be based on time served by members during preceding calendar year. However, when credits have been accrued and member retires during current year, additional annual leave credits shall, in this instance, be granted at accrual rate of three days for each completed month of service, excluding terminal leave. If accruals granted for completed months of service extend into following month, member shall be granted an additional three days accrual for completed month. This shall be the only condition where accruals in a current year are granted for vacation period in such year.

1. According to the above paragraph, if a fireman's wife were to become seriously ill so that he would take time off from work to be with her, such time off would be deducted from his _____ allowance.

    A. annual leave   B. vacation leave
    C. personal business leave   D. family illness leave

1.____

2. Terminal leave means leave taken

    A. at the end of the calendar year
    B. at the end of the vacation year
    C. immediately before retirement
    D. before actually earned, because of an emergency

2.____

3. A fireman appointed on July 1, 2007 will be able to take his first full or normal annual leave during the period

    A. July 1, 2007 to June 30, 2008
    B. Jan. 1, 2008 to Dec. 31, 2008
    C. July 1, 2008 to June 30, 2009
    D. Jan. 1, 2009 to Dec. 31, 2009

3.____

4. According to the above paragraph, a member who retires on July 15 of this year will be entitled to receive leave allowance based on this year of _____ days.   4._____

   A. 15   B. 18   C. 22   D. 24

5. Fire alarm boxes are electromechanical devices for transmitting a coded signal. In each box, there is a trainwork of wheels. When the box is operated, a spring-activated code wheel within begins to revolve. The code number of the box is notched on the circumference of the code wheel, and the latter is associated with the circuit in such a way that when it revolves it causes the circuit to open and close in a predetermined manner, thereby transmitting its particular signal to the central station. A fire alarm box is nothing more than a device for interrupting the flow of current in a circuit in such a way as to produce a coded signal that may be decoded by the dispatchers in the central office.   5._____
   Based on the above, select the FALSE statement:

   A. Each standard fire alarm box has its own code wheel
   B. The code wheel operates when the box is pulled
   C. The code wheel is operated electrically
   D. Only the break in the circuit by the notched wheel causes the alarm signal to be transmitted to the central office

Questions 6-9.

DIRECTIONS: Questions 6 through 9 are to be answered SOLELY on the basis of the following paragraph.

   Ventilation, as used in fire fighting operations, means opening up a building or structure in which a fire is burning to release the accumulated heat, smoke, and gases. Lack of knowledge of the principles of ventilation on the part of firemen may result in unnecessary punishment due to ventilation being neglected or improperly handled. While ventilation itself extinguishes no fires, when used in an intelligent manner, it allows firemen to get at the fire more quickly, easily, and with less danger and hardship.

6. According to the above paragraph, the MOST important result of failure to apply the principles of ventilation at a fire may be   6._____

   A. loss of public confidence
   B. waste of water
   C. excessive use of equipment
   D. injury to firemen

7. It may be inferred from the above paragraph that the CHIEF advantage of ventilation is that it   7._____

   A. eliminates the need for gas masks
   B. reduces smoke damage
   C. permits firemen to work closer to the fire
   D. cools the fire

8. Knowledge of the principles of ventilation, as defined in the above paragraph, would be LEAST important in a fire in a   8.____

    A. tenement house   B. grocery store
    C. ship's hold   D. lumberyard

9. We may conclude from the above paragraph that for the well-trained and equipped fire-man, ventilation is   9.____

    A. a simple matter   B. rarely necessary
    C. relatively unimportant   D. a basic tool

Questions 10-13.

DIRECTIONS: Questions 10 through 13 are to be answered SOLELY on the basis of the following passage.

Fire exit drills should be established and held periodically to effectively train personnel to leave their working area promptly upon proper signal and to evacuate the building, speedily but without confusion. All fire exit drills should be carefully planned and carried out in a serious manner under rigid discipline so as to provide positive protection in the event of a real emergency. As a general rule, the local fire department should be furnished advance information regarding the exact date and time the exit drill is scheduled. When it is impossible to hold regular drills, written instructions should be distributed to all employees.

Depending upon individual circumstances, fires in warehouses vary from those of fast development that are almost instantly beyond any possibility of employee control to others of relatively slow development where a small readily attackable flame may be present for periods of time up to 15 minutes or more during which simple attack with fire extinguishers or small building hoses may prevent the fire development. In any case, it is characteristic of many warehouse fires that at a certain point in development they flash up to the top of the stack, increase heat quickly, and spread rapidly. There is a degree of inherent danger in attacking warehouse type fires, and all employees should be thoroughly trained in the use of the types of extinguishers or small hoses in the buildings and well instructed in the necessity of always staying between the fire and a direct pass to an exit.

10. Employees should be instructed that, when fighting a fire, they MUST   10.____

    A. try to control the blaze
    B. extinguish any fire in 15 minutes
    C. remain between the fire and a direct passage to the exit
    D. keep the fire between themselves and the fire exit

11. Whenever conditions are such that regular fire drills cannot be held, then which one of the following actions should be taken?   11.____

    A. The local fire department should be notified.
    B. Rigid discipline should be maintained during work hours.
    C. Personnel should be instructed to leave their working area by whatever means are available.
    D. Employees should receive fire drill procedures in writing.

12. The above passage indicates that the purpose of fire exit drills is to train employees to   12.____

    A. control a fire before it becomes uncontrollable
    B. act as firefighters
    C. leave the working area promptly
    D. be serious

13. According to the above passage, fire exit drills will prove to be of UTMOST effectiveness   13.____
if

    A. employee participation is made voluntary
    B. they take place periodically
    C. the fire department actively participates
    D. they are held without advance planning

Questions 14-16.

DIRECTIONS: Questions 14 through 16 are to be answered SOLELY on the basis of the following paragraph.

    The heat output from unit heaters will depend on how fast and how completely dry hot steam fills the unit core. For complete and fast air removal and rapid drainage of condensate, use a trap actuated by water or vapor (inverted bucket trap) and not a trap operated by temperature only (thermostatic or bellows trap). A temperature-actuated trap will hold back the hot condensate until it cools to a point where the thermal element opens. When this happens, the condensate backs up in the heater and reduces the heat output. With a water-actuated trap, this will not happen as the water or condensate is discharged as fast as it is formed.

14. On the basis of the information given in the above paragraph, it can be concluded that   14.____
the PROPER type of trap to use for a unit heater is a(n) _____ trap.

    A. thermostatic   B. bellows-type
    C. inverted bucket   D. temperature

15. According to the above paragraph, the MAIN reason for using the type of trap specified   15.____
for a unit heater is to

    A. bring the condensate up to steam temperature
    B. prevent reduction in the heat output of the unit heater
    C. permit cycling of the heater
    D. maintain constant temperature of condensate in the trap

16. As used in the above paragraph, the word *actuated* means MOST NEARLY   16.____

    A. clogged   B. operated   C. cleaned   D. vented

Question 17 -25.

DIRECTIONS: Questions 17 through 25 are to be answered SOLELY on the basis of the following passage. Each question consists of a statement. You are to indicate
whether the statement is TRUE (T) or FALSE (F).

MOVING AN OFFICE

An office with all its equipment is sometimes moved during working hours. This is a difficult task and must be done in an orderly manner to avoid confusion. The operation should be planned in such a way as not to interrupt the progress of work usually done in the office and to make possible the accurate placement of the furniture and records in the new location. If the office moves to a place inside the same building, the desks and files are moved with all their contents. If the movement is to another building, the contents of each desk and file are placed in boxes. Each box is marked with a letter showing the particular section in the new quarters to which it is to be moved. Also marked on each box is the number of the desk or file on which the box is to be placed. Each piece of equipment must have a numbered tag. The number of each piece of equipment is put in soft chalk on the floor in the new office to show the proper location, and several floor plans are made to show where each piece of equipment goes. When the moving is done, someone is stationed at each of the several exits of the old office to see that each box or piece of equipment has its destination clearly marked on it. At the new office, someone stands at each of the several entrances with a copy of the floor plan and directs the placing of the furniture and equipment according to the floor plan. No one should interfere at this point with the arrangements shown on the plan. Improvements in arrangement can be considered and made at a later date.

17. It is a hard job to move an office from one place to another during working hours.   17.____

18. Confusion cannot be avoided if an office is moved during working hours.   18.____

19. The work usually done in an office must be stopped for the day when the office is moved during working hours.   19.____

20. If an office is moved from one floor to another in the same building, the contents of a desk are taken out and put into boxes for moving.   20.____

21. If boxes are used to hold material from desks when moving an office, the box is numbered the same as the desk on which it is to be put.   21.____

22. Letters are marked in soft chalk on the floor at the new quarters to show where the desks should go when moved.   22.____

23. When the moving begins, a person is put at each exit of the old office to check that each box and piece of equipment has clearly marked on it where it to go.   23.____

24. A person stationed at each entrance of the new quarters to direct the placing of the furniture and equipment has a copy of the floor plan of the new quarters.   24.____

25. If, while the furniture is being moved into the new office, a person helping at a doorway gets an idea of a better way to arrange the furniture, he should change the planned arrangement and make a record of the change.   25.____

KEY (CORRECT ANSWERS)

1.	A	11.	D
2.	C	12.	C
3.	D	13.	B
4.	B	14.	C
5.	C	15.	B
6.	D	16.	B
7.	C	17.	T
8.	D	18.	F
9.	D	19.	F
10.	C	20.	F

21.	T
22.	F
23.	T
24.	T
25.	F

TEST 2

DIRECTIONS: Questions 1 through 4 are to be answered SOLELY on the basis of the following paragraph.

In all cases of homicide, members of the Police Department who investigate will make every effort to obtain statements from dying persons. Such statements are of the greatest importance to the District Attorney. In many cases, there may be a failure to solve the crime if they are not taken. The principal element to be considered in taking the declaration of a dying person is his mental attitude. In order to be admissible in evidence, the person must have no hope of recovery. The patient will be fully interrogated on that point before a statement is taken.

1. In cases of homicide, according to the above paragraph, members of the police force will   1._____

    A. try to change the mental attitude of the dying person
    B. attempt to obtain a statement from the dying person
    C. not give the information they obtain directly to the District Attorney
    D. be careful not to injure the dying person unnecessarily

2. The mental attitude of the person making the dying statement is of GREAT importance because it can determine, according to the above paragraph, whether the   2._____

    A. victim should be interrogated in the presence of witnesses
    B. victim will be willing to make a statement of any kind
    C. statement will tell the District Attorney who committed the crime
    D. the statement can be used as evidence

3. District Attorneys find that statements of a dying person are important, according to the above paragraph, because   3._____

    A. it may be that the victim will recover and then refuse to testify
    B. they are important elements in determining the mental attitude of the victim
    C. they present a point of view
    D. it may be impossible to punish the criminal without such a statement

4. A well-known gangster is found dying from a bullet wound. The patrolman first on the scene, in the presence of witnesses, tells the man that he is going to die and asks, *Who shot you?* The gangster says, *Jones shot me, but he hasn't killed me. I'll live to get him.* He then falls back dead. According to the above paragraph, this statement is   4._____

    A. *admissible* in evidence; the man was obviously speaking the truth
    B. *not admissible* in evidence; the man obviously did not believe that he was dying
    C. *admissible* in evidence; there were witnesses to the statement
    D. *not admissible* in evidence; the victim did not sign any statement and the evidence is merely hearsay

Questions 5-7.

DIRECTIONS: Questions 5 through 7 are to be answered SOLELY on the basis of the following paragraph.

The factors contributing to crime and delinquency are varied and complex. The home and its immediate environment have been found to be crucial in determining the behavior patterns of the individual, and criminality can frequently be traced to faulty family relationships and a bad neighborhood. But in the search for a clearer understanding of the underlying causes of delinquent and criminal behavior, the total environment must be taken into consideration.

5. According to the above paragraph, family relationships   5._____

    A.   tend to become faulty in bad neighborhoods
    B.   are important in determining the actions of honest people as well as criminals
    C.   are the only important element in the understanding of causes of delinquency
    D.   are determined by the total environment

6. According to the above paragraph, the causes of crime and delinquency are   6._____

    A.   not simple   B.   not meaningless
    C.   meaningless   D.   simple

7. According to the above paragraph, faulty family relationships FREQUENTLY are   7._____

    A.   responsible for varied and complex results
    B.   caused when one or both parents have a criminal behavior pattern
    C.   independent of the total environment
    D.   the cause of criminal acts

Questions 8-10.

DIRECTIONS: Questions 8 through 10 are to be answered SOLELY on the basis of the following paragraph.

A change in the specific problems which confront the police and in the methods for dealing with them has taken place in the last few decades. The automobile is a two-way symbol of this change in policing. It menaces every city with a complicated traffic problem and has speeded up the process of committing a crime and making a getaway, but at the same time has increased the effectiveness of police operations. However, the major concern of police departments continues to be the antisocial or criminal actions and behavior of human beings.

8. On the basis of the above paragraph, it can be stated that, for the most part, in the past   8._____
   few decades the specific problems of a police force

    A.   have changed but the general problems have not
    B.   as well as the general problems have changed
    C.   have remained the same but the general problems have changed
    D.   as well as the general problems have remained the same

9. According to the above paragraph, advances in science and industry have, in general,   9._____
   made the police

    A.   operations less effective from the overall point of view
    B.   operations more effective from the overall point of view
    C.   abandon older methods of solving police problems
    D.   concern themselves more with the antisocial acts of human beings

10. The automobile is a *two-way symbol,* according to the above paragraph, because its use   10.____

    A. has speeded up getting to and away from the scene of a crime
    B. both helps and hurts police operations
    C. introduces a new antisocial act – traffic violation – and does away with criminals like horse thieves
    D. both increases and decreases speed by introducing traffic problems

Questions 11-14.

DIRECTIONS: Questions 11 through 14 are to be answered SOLELY on the basis of the following passage on INSTRUCTIONS TO COIN AND TOKEN CASHIERS.

INSTRUCTIONS TO COIN AND TOKEN CASHIERS

Cashiers should reset the machine registers to an even starting number before commencing the day's work. Money bags received directly from collecting agents shall be counted and receipted for on the collecting agent's form. Each cashier shall be responsible for all coin or token bags accepted by him. He must examine all bags to be used for bank deposits for cuts and holes before placing them in use. Care must be exercised so that bags are not cut in opening them. Each bag must be opened separately and verified before another bag is opened. The machine register must be cleared before starting the count of another bag. The amount shown on the machine register must be compared with the amount on the bag tag. The empty bag must be kept on the table for re-examination should there be a difference between the amount on the bag tag and the amount on the machine register.

11. A cashier should BEGIN his day's assignment by   11.____

    A. counting and accepting all money bags
    B. resetting the counting machine register
    C. examining all bags for cuts and holes
    D. verifying the contents of all money bags

12. In verifying the amount of money in the bags received from the collecting agent, it is BEST to   12.____

    A. check the amount in one bag at a time
    B. base the total on the amount on the collecting agent's form
    C. repeat the total shown on the bag tag
    D. refer to the bank deposit receipt

13. A cashier is instructed to keep each empty coin bag on. his table while verifying its contents CHIEFLY because, long as the bag is on the table,   13.____

    A. it cannot be misplaced
    B. the supervisor can see how quickly the cashier works
    C. cuts and holes are easily noticed
    D. a recheck is possible in case the machine count disagrees with the bag tag total

14. The INSTRUCTIONS indicate that it is NOT proper procedure for a cashier to　　　14._____

    A. assume that coin bags are free of cuts and holes
    B. compare the machine register total with the total shown on the bag tag
    C. sign a form when he receives coin bags
    D. reset the machine register before starting the day's counting

Questions 15-17.

DIRECTIONS: Questions 15 through 17 are to be answered SOLELY on the basis of the following passage.

The mass media are an integral part of the daily life of virtually every American. Among these media the youngest, television, is the most pervasive. Ninety-five percent of American homes have at least one T.V. set, and on the average that set is in use for about 40 hours each week. The central place of television in American life makes this medium the focal point of a growing national concern over the effects of media portrayals of violence on the values, attitudes, and behavior of an ever increasing audience.

In our concern about violence and its causes, it is easy to make television a scapegoat. But we emphasize the fact that there is no simple answer to the problem of violence—no single explanation of its causes, and no single prescription for its control. It should be remembered that America also experienced high levels of crime and violence in periods before the advent of television.

The problem of balance, taste, and artistic merit in entertaining programs on television are complex. We cannot countenance government censorship of television. Nor would we seek to impose arbitrary limitations on programming which might jeopardize television's ability to deal in dramatic presentations with controversial social issues. Nonetheless, we are deeply troubled by television's constant portrayal of violence, not in any genuine attempt to focus artistic expression on the human condition, but rather in pandering to a public preoccupation with violence that television itself has helped to generate.

15. According to the above passage, television uses violence MAINLY　　　15._____

    A. to highlight the reality of everyday existence
    B. to satisfy the audience's hunger for destructive action
    C. to shape the values and attitudes of the public
    D. when it films documentaries concerning human conflict

16. Which one of the following statements is BEST supported by the above passage?　　　16._____

    A. Early American history reveals a crime pattern which is not related to television.
    B. Programs should give presentations of social issues and never portray violent acts.
    C. Television has proven that entertainment programs can easily make the balance between taste and artistic merit a simple matter.
    D. Values and behavior should be regulated by governmental censorship.

17. Of the following, which word has the same meaning as *countenance,* as used in the above passage?　　　17._____

    A. Approve   B. Exhibit   C. Oppose   D. Reject

DIRECTIONS: Questions 18 through 21 are to be answered SOLELY on the basis of the following passage.

Maintenance of leased or licensed areas on public parks or lands has always been a problem. A good rule to follow in the administration and maintenance of such areas is to limit the responsibility of any lessee or licensee to the maintenance of the structures and grounds essential to the efficient operation of the concession, not including areas for the general use of the public, such as picnic areas, public comfort stations, etc.; except where such facilities are leased to another public agency or where special conditions make such inclusion practicable, and where a good standard of maintenance can be assured and enforced. If local conditions and requirements are such that public use areas are included, adequate safeguards to the public should be written into contracts and enforced in their administration, to insure that maintenance by the concessionaire shall be equal to the maintenance standards for other park property.

18. According to the above passage, when an area on a public park is leased to a concessionaire, it is usually BEST to 18.____

    A. confine the responsibility of the concessionaire to operation of the facilities and leave the maintenance function to the park agency
    B. exclude areas of general public use from the maintenance obligation of the concessionaire
    C. make the concessionaire responsible for maintenance of the entire area including areas of general public use
    D. provide additional comfort station facilities for the area

19. According to the above passage, a valid reason for giving a concessionaire responsibility for maintenance of a picnic area within his leased area is that 19.____

    A. local conditions and requirements make it practicable
    B. more than half of the picnic area falls within his leased area
    C. the concessionaire has leased picnic facilities to another public agency
    D. the picnic area falls entirely within his leased area

20. According to the above passage, a precaution that should be taken when a concessionaire is made responsible for maintenance of an area of general public use in a park is 20.____

    A. making sure that another public agency has not previously been made responsible for this area
    B. providing the concessionaire with up-to-date equipment, if practicable
    C. requiring that the concessionaire take out adequate insurance for the protection of the public
    D. writing safeguards to the public into the contract

KEY (CORRECT ANSWERS)

1.	B		11.	B
2.	D		12.	A
3.	D		13.	D
4.	B		14.	A
5.	B		15.	B
6.	A		16.	A
7.	D		17.	A
8.	A		18.	B
9.	B		19.	A
10.	B		20.	D

TEST 3

Questions 1-5.

DIRECTIONS: Questions 1 through 5 are to be answered SOLELY on the basis of the following paragraph.

Physical inspections are an important tool for the examiner because he will have to decide the case in many instances on the basis of the inspection report. Most proceedings in a rent office are commenced by the filing of a written application or complaint by an interested party; that is, either the landlord or the tenant. Such an application or complaint must be filed in duplicate in order that the opposing party may be served with a copy of the application or complaint and thus be given an opportunity to answer and oppose it. Sometimes, a further opportunity is given the applicant to file a written rebuttal or reply to his adversary's answer. Often an examiner can make a determination or decision based on the written application, the answer, and the reply to the answer; and, of course, it would speed up operations if it were always possible to make decisions based on written documents only. Unfortunately, decisions can't always be made that way. There are numerous occasions where <u>disputed</u> issues of fact remain which cannot be <u>resolved</u> on the basis of the written statements of the parties. Typical examples are the following: The tenant claims that the refrigerator or stove or bathroom fixture is not functioning properly and the landlord denies this. It is obvious that in such cases an inspection of the accommodations is almost the only means of resolving such disputed issues.

1. According to the above paragraph,   1.____

    A. physical inspections are made in all cases
    B. physical inspections are seldom made
    C. it is sometimes possible to determine the facts in a case without a physical inspection
    D. physical inspections are made when it is necessary to verify the examiner's determination

2. According to the above paragraph, in MOST cases, proceedings are started by a(n)   2.____

    A. inspector discovering a violation
    B. oral complaint by a tenant or landlord
    C. request from another agency, such as the Building Department
    D. written complaint by a tenant or landlord

3. According to the above paragraph, when a tenant files an application with the rent office,   3.____
the landlord is

    A. not told about the proceeding until after the examiner makes his determination
    B. given the duplicate copy of the application
    C. notified by means of an inspector visiting the premises
    D. not told about the proceeding until after the inspector has visited the Premises

4. As used in the above paragraph, the word *disputed* means MOST NEARLY   4.____

    A. unsettled   B. contested
    C. definite   D. difficult

5. As used in the above paragraph, the word *resolved* means MOST NEARLY   5._____

   A. settled   B. fixed   C. helped   D. amended

Questions 6-10.

DIRECTIONS: Questions 6 through 10 are to be answered SOLELY on the basis of the following paragraph.

   The examiner should order or request an inspection of the housing accommodations. His request for a physical inspection should be in writing, identify the accommodations and the landlord and the tenant, and specify <u>precisely</u> just what the inspector is to look for and report on. Unless this request is specific and lists <u>in detail</u> every item which the examiner wishes to be reported, the examiner will find that the inspection has not served its purpose and that even with the inspector's report, he is still in no position to decide the case due to loose ends which have not been completely tied up. The items that the examiner is interested in should be separately numbered on the inspection request and the same number referred to in the inspector's report. You can see what it would mean if an inspector came back with a report that did not cover everything. It may mean a tremendous waste of time and often require a re-inspection.

6. According to the above paragraph, the inspector makes an inspection on the order of   6._____

   A. the landlord
   B. the tenant
   C. the examiner
   D. both the landlord and the tenant

7. According to the above paragraph, the reason for numbering each item that an inspector reports on is so that   7._____

   A. the report is neat
   B. the report can be easily read and referred to
   C. none of the examiner's requests for information is missed
   D. the report will be specific

8. The one of the following items that is NOT necessarily included in the request for inspection is   8._____

   A. location of dwelling   B. name of landlord
   C. item to be checked   D. type of building

9. As used in the above paragraph, the word precisely means MOST NEARLY   9._____

   A. exactly   B. generally   C. Usually   D. strongly

10. As used in the above paragraph, the words in detail mean MOST NEARLY   10._____

   A. clearly   B. item by item
   C. substantially   D. completely

Questions 11-13.

DIRECTIONS: Questions 11 through 13 are to be answered SOLELY on the basis of the following passage.

The agreement under which a tenant rents property from a landlord is known as a lease. Generally speaking, leases are classified as either short-term or long-term in duration. They are further subdivided according to the method used to determine the amount of periodic rent payments. Of the following types of lease in use, the more commonly used ones are the following:

1. The straight or fixed lease is one in which rent may be paid in equal amounts throughout the duration of the lease. These are usually restricted to short-term leasing, or somewhat longer-term if clauses in the lease provide for periodic escalation of payments as the economy shifts.
2. Percentage leasing, used for short-term commercial leasing, provides the landlord with a stipulated percentage of a tenant's gross sales from goods and services sold on the premises, in addition to a fixed amount of rent.
3. The net lease, generally long-term (ten years or more), requires the tenant to pay all operating costs, including real estate taxes and insurance. In a net-net lease, the tenant further agrees to meet mortgage interest and principal payments.
4. An escalated lease, which is a long-term lease, requires rent to be of a stipulated base amount which periodically is subject to escalation in accordance with cost-of-living index scales, or in direct proportion to taxes, insurance, and operating costs.

11. Based on the information given in the passage, which type of lease is MOST likely to be advantageous to a landlord if there is a high rate of inflation? _____ lease.   11._____

  A. Fixed   B. Percentage   C. Net   D. Escalated

12. On the basis of the above passage, which types of lease would generally be MOST suitable for a well-established textile company which requires permanent facilities for its large operations?   12._____
  _____ lease and _____ lease.

  A. Percentage; escalated   B. Escalated; net
  C. Straight; net   D. Straight; percentage

13. According to the above passage, the ONLY type of lease which assures the same amount of rent throughout a specified interval is the _____ lease.   13._____

  A. straight   B. percentage   C. net-net   D. escalated

Questions 14-15.

DIRECTIONS: Questions 14 and 15 are to be answered SOLELY on the basis of the following passage.

If you like people, if you seek contact with them rather than hide yourself in a corner, if you study your fellow men sympathetically, if you try consistently to contribute something to their success and happiness, if you are reasonably generous with your thought and your time, if you have a partial reserve with everyone but a seeming reserve with no one, you will get along with your superiors, your subordinates, and the human race.

By the scores of thousands, precepts and platitudes have been written for the guidance of personal conduct. The odd part of it is that, despite all of this labor, most of the frictions in modern society arise from the individual's feeling of inferiority, his false pride, his vanity, his unwillingness to yield space to any other man and his consequent urge to throw his own weight around. Goethe said that the quality which best enables a man to renew his own life, in his relation to others, is his capability of renouncing particular things at the right moment in order warmly to embrace something new in the next.

14.　On the basis of the above passage, it may be INFERRED that　　　　　　　　14.____

    A.　a person should be unwilling to renounce privileges
    B.　a person should realize that loss of a desirable job assignment may come at an opportune moment
    C.　it is advisable for a person to maintain a considerable amount of reserve in his relationship with unfamiliar people
    D.　people should be ready to contribute generously to a worthy charity

15.　Of the following, the MOST valid implication made by the above passage is that　　15.____

    A.　a wealthy person who spends a considerable amount of money entertaining his friends is not really getting along with them
    B.　if a person studies his fellow men carefully and impartially, he will tend to have good relationships with them
    C.　individuals who maintain seemingly little reserve in their relationships with people have in some measure overcome their own feelings of inferiority
    D.　most precepts that have been written for the guidance of personal conduct in relationships with other people are invalid

Questions 16-17.

DIRECTIONS:　Questions 16 and 17 are to be answered SOLELY on the basis of the following passage.

When a design for a new bank note of the Federal Government has been prepared by the Bureau of Engraving and Printing and has been approved by the Secretary of the Treasury, the engravers begin the work of cutting the design in steel. No one engraver does all the work. Each man is a specialist. One works only on portraits, another on lettering, another on scroll work, and so on. Each engraver, with a steel tool known as a graver, and aided by a powerful magnifying glass, carefully carves his portion of the design into the steel. He knows that one false cut or a slip of his tool, or one miscalculation of width or depth of line, may destroy the merit of his work. A single mistake means that months or weeks of labor will have been in vain. The Bureau is proud of the fact that no counterfeiter ever has duplicated the excellent work of its expert engravers.

16.　According to the above passage, each engraver in the Bureau of Engraving and Printing　16.____

    A.　must be approved by the Secretary of the Treasury before he can begin work on the design for a new bank note
    B.　is responsible for engraving a complete design of a new bank note by himself
    C.　designs new bank notes and submits them for approval to the Secretary of the Treasury
    D.　performs only a specific part of the work of engraving a design for a new bank note

17. According to the above passage,

    A. an engraver's tools are not available to a counterfeiter
    B. mistakes made in engraving a design can be corrected immediately with little delay in the work of the Bureau
    C. the skilled work of the engravers has not been successfully reproduced by counterfeiter
    D. careful carving and cutting by the engravers is essential to prevent damage to equipment

17.____

Questions 18-21.

DIRECTIONS: Questions 18 through 21 are to be answered SOLELY on the basis of the following passage.

In the late fifties, the average American housewife spent $4.50 per day for a family of four on food and 5.15 hours in food preparation, if all of her food was *home prepared*; she spent $5.80 per day and 3.25 hours if all of her food was purchased *partially prepared*; and $6.70 per day and 1.65 hours if all of her food was purchased *ready to serve*.

Americans spent about 20 billion dollars for food products in 1941. They spent nearly 70 billion dollars in 1958. They spent 25 percent of their cash income on food in 1958. For the same kinds and quantities of food that consumers bought in 1941, they would have spent only 16% of their cash income in 1958. It is obvious that our food does cost more. Many factors contribute to this increase besides the additional cost that might be attributed to processing. Consumption of more expensive food items, higher marketing margins, and more food eaten in restaurants are other factors.

The Census of Manufacturers gives some indication of the total bill for processing. The value added by manufacturing of food and kindred products amounted to 3.5 billion of the 20 billion dollars spent for food in 1941. In the year 1958, the comparable figure had climbed to 14 billion dollars.

18. According to the above passage, the cash income of Americans in 1958 was MOST NEARLY _____ billion dollars.

    A. 11.2   B. 17.5   C. 70   D. 280

18.____

19. According to the above passage, if Americans bought the same kinds and quantities of food in 1958 as they did in 1941, they would have spent MOST NEARLY _____ billion dollars.

    A. 20   B. 45   C. 74   D. 84

19.____

20. According to the above passage, the percent increase in money spent for food in 1958 over 1941, as compared with the percentage increase in money spent for food processing in the same years,

    A. was greater
    B. was less
    C. was the same
    D. cannot be determined from the passage

20.____

21. In 1958, an American housewife who bought all of her food ready-to-serve saved in time, as compared with the housewife who prepared all of her food at home   21._____

    A. 1.6 hours daily
    B. 1.9 hours daily
    C. 3.5 hours daily
    D. an amount of time which cannot be determined from the above passage

Questions 22-25.

DIRECTIONS: Questions 22 through 25 are to be answered SOLELY on the basis of the following passage.

    Any member of the retirement system who is in city service, who files a proper application for service credit and agrees to deductions from his compensation at triple his normal rate of contribution, shall be credited with a period of city service previous to the beginning of his present membership in the retirement system. The period of service credited shall be equal to the period throughout which such triple deductions are made, but may not exceed the total of the city service the member rendered between his first day of eligibility for membership in the retirement system and the day he last became a member. After triple contributions for all of the first three years of service credit claimed, the remaining service credit may be purchased by a single payment of the sum of the remaining payments. If the total time purchasable exceeds ten years, triple contributions may be made for one-half of such time, and the remaining time purchased by a single payment of the sum of the remaining payments. Credit for service acquired in the above manner may be used only in determining the amount of any retirement benefit. Eligibility for such benefit will, in all cases, be based upon service rendered after the employee's membership last began, and will be exclusive of service credit purchased as described below.

22. According to the above passage, in order to obtain credit for city service previous to the beginning of an employee's present membership in the retirement system, the employee must   22._____

    A. apply for the service credit and consent to additional contributions to the retirement system
    B. apply for the service credit before he renews his membership in the retirement system
    C. have previous city service which does not exceed ten years
    D. make contributions to the retirement system for three years

23. According to the information in the above passage, credit for city service previous to the beginning of an employee's present membership in the retirement system, is   23._____

    A. credited up to a maximum of ten years
    B. credited to any member of the retirement system
    C. used in determining the amount of the employee's benefits
    D. used in establishing the employee's eligibility to receive benefits

24. According to the information in the above passage, a member of the retirement system may purchase service credit for   24.____

   A. the period of time between his first day of eligibility for membership in the retirement system and the date he applies for the service credit
   B. one-half of the total of his previous city service if the total time exceeds ten years
   C. the period of time throughout which triple deductions are made
   D. the period of city service between his first day of eligibility for membership in the retirement system and the day he last became a member

25. Suppose that a member of the retirement system has filed an application for service credit for five years of previous city service.   25.____
   Based on the information in the above passage, the employee may purchase credit for this previous city service by making

   A. triple contributions for three years
   B. triple contributions for one-half of the time and a single payment of the sum of the remaining payments
   C. triple contributions for three years and a single payment of the sum of the remaining payments
   D. a single payment of the sum of the payments

KEY (CORRECT ANSWERS)

1.	C	11.	D
2.	D	12.	B
3.	B	13.	A
4.	B	14.	B
5.	A	15.	C
6.	C	16.	D
7.	C	17.	C
8.	D	18.	D
9.	A	19.	B
10.	B	20.	B

21.	C
22.	A
23.	C
24.	D
25.	C

PREPARING WRITTEN MATERIAL

PARAGRAPH REARRANGEMENT
COMMENTARY

The sentences which follow are in scrambled order. You are to rearrange them in proper order and indicate the letter choice containing the correct answer at the space at the right.

Each group of sentences in this section is actually a paragraph presented in scrambled order. Each sentence in the group has a place in that paragraph; no sentence is to be left out. You are to read each group of sentences and decide upon the best order in which to put the sentences so as to form as well-organized paragraph.

The questions in this section measure the ability to solve a problem when all the facts relevant to its solution are not given.

More specifically, certain positions of responsibility and authority require the employee to discover connections between events sometimes, apparently, unrelated. In order to do this, the employee will find it necessary to correctly infer that unspecified events have probably occurred or are likely to occur. This ability becomes especially important when action must be taken on incomplete information.

Accordingly, these questions require competitors to choose among several suggested alternatives, each of which presents a different sequential arrangement of the events. Competitors must choose the MOST logical of the suggested sequences.

In order to do so, they may be required to draw on general knowledge to infer missing concepts or events that are essential to sequencing the given events. Competitors should be careful to infer only what is essential to the sequence. The plausibility of the wrong alternatives will always require the inclusion of unlikely events or of additional chains of events which are NOT essential to sequencing the given events.

It's very important to remember that you are looking for the best of the four possible choices, and that the best choice of all may not even be one of the answers you're given to choose from.

There is no one right way to solve these problems. Many people have found it helpful to first write out the order of the sentences, as they would have arranged them, on their scrap paper before looking at the possible answers. If their optimum answer is there, this can save them some time. If it isn't, this method can still give insight into solving the problem. Others find it most helpful to just go through each of the possible choices, contrasting each as they go along. You should use whatever method feels comfortable, and works, for you.

While most of these types of questions are not that difficult, we've added a higher percentage of the difficult type, just to give you more practice. Usually there are only one or two questions on this section that contain such subtle distinctions that you're unable to answer confidently, and you then may find yourself stuck deciding between two possible choices, neither of which you're sure about.

———

EXAMINATION SECTION
TEST 1

DIRECTIONS: The sentences that follow are in scrambled order. You are to rearrange them in proper order and indicate the letter choice containing the correct answer. *PRINT THE LETTER OF THE CORRECT ANSWER IN THE SPACE AT THE RIGHT.*

1. Below are four statements labeled W., X., Y., and Z.   1.____
   W.   He was a strict and fanatic drillmaster.
   X.   The word is always used in a derogatory sense and generally shows resent-
         ment and anger on the part of the user.
   Y.   It is from the name of this Frenchman that we derive our English word, martinet.
   Z.   Jean Martinet was the Inspector-General of Infantry during the reign of King
         Louis XIV.
   The *PROPER* order in which these sentences should be placed in a paragraph is:

   A. X, Z, W, Y   B. X, Z, Y, W   C. Z, W, Y, X   D. Z, Y, W, X

2. In the following paragraph, the sentences which are numbered, have been jumbled.   2.____
   1.   Since then it has undergone changes.
   2.   It was incorporated in 1955 under the laws of the State of New York.
   3.   Its primary purpose, a cleaner city, has, however, remained the same.
   4.   The Citizens Committee works in cooperation with the Mayor's Inter-departmen-
        tal Committee for a Clean City.
   The order in which these sentences should be arranged to form a well-organized paragraph is:

   A. 2, 4, 1, 3   B. 3, 4, 1, 2   C. 4, 2, 1, 3   D. 4, 3, 2, 1

Questions 3-5.

DIRECTIONS: The sentences listed below are part of a meaningful paragraph but they are not given in their proper order. You are to decide what would be the *best order* in which to put the sentences so as to form a well-organized paragraph. Each sentence has a place in the paragraph; there are no extra sentences. You are then to answer questions 3 to 5 inclusive on the basis of your rearrangements of these scrambled sentences into a properly organized paragraph.

In 1887 some insurance companies organized an Inspection Department to advise their clients on all phases of fire prevention and protection. Probably this has been due to the smaller annual fire losses in Great Britain than in the United States. It tests various fire prevention devices and appliances and determines manufacturing hazards and their safeguards. Fire research began earlier in the United States and is more advanced than in Great Britain. Later they established a laboratory specializing in electrical, mechanical, hydraulic, and chemical fields.

3. When the five sentences are arranged in proper order, the paragraph starts with the sen-   3.____
    tence which begins

    A. "In 1887..."   B. "Probably this ..."   C. "It tests ..."
    D. "Fire research ..." E. "Later they ..."

4. In the last sentence listed above, "they" refers to   4.____

    A. insurance companies
    B. the United States and Great Britain
    C. the Inspection Department
    D. clients
    E. technicians

5. When the above paragraph is properly arranged, it ends with the words   5.____

    A. "... and protection."   B. "... the United States."
    C. "... their safeguards."   D. "... in Great Britain."
    E. "... chemical fields."

———————

KEY (CORRECT ANSWERS)

    1. C
    2. C
    3. D
    4. A
    5. C

———————

TEST 2

1. 1. It is established when one shows that the landlord has prevented the tenant's enjoyment of his interest in the property leased.
   2. Constructive eviction is the result of a breach of the covenant of quiet enjoyment implied in all leases.
   3. In some parts of the United States, it is not complete until the tenant vacates within a reasonable time.
   4. Generally, the acts must be of such serious and permanent character as to deny the tenant the enjoyment of his possessing rights.
   5. In this event, upon abandonment of the premises, the tenant's liability for that ceases.

   The CORRECT answer is:

   A. 2, 1, 4, 3, 5   B. 5, 2, 3, 1, 4   C. 4, 3, 1, 2, 5
   D. 1, 3, 5, 4, 2

   1.____

2. 1. The powerlessness before private and public authorities that is the typical experience of the slum tenant is reminiscent of the situation of blue-collar workers all through the nineteenth century.
   2. Similarly, in recent years, this chapter of history has been reopened by anti-poverty groups which have attempted to organize slum tenants to enable them to bargain collectively with their landlords about the conditions of their tenancies.
   3. It is familiar history that many of the workers remedied their condition by joining together and presenting their demands collectively.
   4. Like the workers, tenants are forced by the conditions of modern life into substantial dependence on these who possess great political arid economic power.
   5. What's more, the very fact of dependence coupled with an absence of education and self-confidence makes them hesitant and unable to stand up for what they need from those in power.

   The CORRECT answer is:

   A. 5, 4, 1, 2, 3   B. 2, 3, 1, 5, 4   C. 3, 1, 5, 4, 2
   D. 1, 4, 5, 3, 2

   2.____

3. 1. A railroad, for example, when not acting as a common carrier may contract away responsibility for its own negligence.
   2. As to a landlord, however, no decision has been found relating to the legal effect of a clause shifting the statutory duty of repair to the tenant.
   3. The courts have not passed on the validity of clauses relieving the landlord of this duty and liability.
   4. They have, however, upheld the validity of exculpatory clauses in other types of contracts.
   5. Housing regulations impose a duty upon the landlord to maintain leased premises in safe condition.

   3.____

6. As another example, a bailee may limit his liability except for gross negligence, willful acts, or fraud.

The CORRECT answer is:

A. 2, 1, 6, 4, 3, 5 B. 1, 3, 4, 5, 6, 2 C. 3, 5, 1, 4, 2, 6
D. 5, 3, 4, 1, 6, 2

4. 1. Since there are only samples in the building, retail or consumer sales are generally eschewed by mart occupants, and in some instances, rigid controls are maintained to limit entrance to the mart only to those persons engaged in retailing.   4.____
    2. Since World War I, in many larger cities, there has developed a new type of property, called the mart building.
    3. It can, therefore, be used by wholesalers and jobbers for the display of sample merchandise.
    4. This type of building is most frequently a multi-storied, finished interior property which is a cross between a retail arcade and a loft building.
    5. This limitation enables the mart occupants to ship the orders from another location after the retailer or dealer makes his selection from the samples.

The CORRECT answer is:

A. 2, 4, 3, 1, 5 B. 4, 3, 5, 1, 2 C. 1, 3, 2, 4, 5
D. 1, 4, 2, 3, 5

5. 1. In general, staff-line friction reduces the distinctive contribution of staff personnel.   5.____
    2. The conflicts, however, introduce an uncontrolled element into the managerial system.
    3. On the other hand, the natural resistance of the line to staff innovations probably usefully restrains over-eager efforts to apply untested procedures on a large scale.
    4. Under such conditions, it is difficult to know when valuable ideas are being sacrificed.
    5. The relatively weak position of staff, requiring accommodation to the line, tends to restrict their ability to engage in free, experimental innovation.

The CORRECT answer is:

A. 4, 2, 3, 1, 3 B. 1, 5, 3, 2, 4 C. 5, 3, 1, 2, 4
D. 2, 1, 4, 5, 3

KEY (CORRECT ANSWERS)

1. A
2. D
3. D
4. A
5. B

TEST 3

DIRECTIONS: Questions 1 through 4 consist of six sentences which can be arranged in a logical sequence. For each question, select the choice which places the numbered sentences in the *most logical* sequence. *PRINT THE LETTER OF THE CORRECT ANSWER IN THE SPACE AT THE RIGHT.*

1. 1. The burden of proof as to each issue is determined before trial and remains upon the same party throughout the trial.
   2. The jury is at liberty to believe one witness' testimony as against a number of contradictory witnesses.
   3. In a civil case, the party bearing the burden of proof is required to prove his contention by a fair preponderance of the evidence.
   4. However, it must be noted that a fair preponderance of evidence does not necessarily mean a greater number of witnesses.
   5. The burden of proof is the burden which rests upon one of the parties to an action to persuade the trier of the facts, generally the jury, that a proposition he asserts is true.
   6. If the evidence is equally balanced, or if it leaves the jury in such doubt as to be unable to decide the controversy either way, judgment must be given against the party upon whom the burden of proof rests.

   The CORRECT answer is:

   A. 3, 2, 5, 4, 1, 6   B. 1, 2, 6, 5, 3, 4   C. 3, 4, 5, 1, 2, 6
   D. 5, 1, 3, 6, 4, 2

   1.____

2. 1. If a parent is without assets and is unemployed, he cannot be convicted of the crime of non-support of a child.
   2. The term "sufficient ability" has been held to mean sufficient financial ability.
   3. It does not matter if his unemployment is by choice or unavoidable circumstances.
   4. If he fails to take any steps at all, he may be liable to prosecution for endangering the welfare of a child.
   5. Under the penal law, a parent is responsible for the support of his minor child only if the parent is "of sufficient ability."
   6. An indigent parent may meet his obligation by borrowing money or by seeking aid under the provisions of the Social Welfare Law.

   The CORRECT answer is:

   A. 6, 1, 5, 3, 2, 4   B. 1, 3, 5, 2, 4, 6   C. 5, 2, 1, 3, 6, 4
   D. 1, 6, 4, 5, 2, 3

   2.____

3.
1. Consider, for example, the case of a rabble rouser who urges a group of twenty people to go out and break the windows of a nearby factory.
2. Therefore, the law fills the indicated gap with the crime of inciting to riot.
3. A person is considered guilty of inciting to riot when he urges ten or more persons to engage in tumultuous and violent conduct of a kind likely to create public alarm.
4. However, if he has not obtained the cooperation of at least four people, he cannot be charged with unlawful assembly.
5. The charge of inciting to riot was added to the law to cover types of conduct which cannot be classified as either the crime of "riot" or the crime of "unlawful assembly."
6. If he acquires the acquiescence of at least four of them, he is guilty of unlawful assembly even if the project does not materialize.

The CORRECT answer is:

A. 3, 5, 1, 6, 4, 2   B. 5, 1, 4, 6, 2, 3   C. 3, 4, 1, 5, 2, 6
D. 5, 1, 4, 6, 3, 2

3.____

4.
1. If, however, the rebuttal evidence presents an issue of credibility, it is for the jury to determine whether the presumption has, in fact, been destroyed.
2. Once sufficient evidence to the contrary is introduced, the presumption disappears from the trial.
3. The effect of a presumption is to place the burden upon the adversary to come forward with evidence to rebut the presumption.
4. When a presumption is overcome and ceases to exist in the case, the fact or facts which gave rise to the presumption still remain.
5. Whether a presumption has been overcome is ordinarily a question for the court.
6. Such information may furnish a basis for a logical inference.

The CORRECT answer is:

A. 4, 6, 2, 5, 1, 3   B. 3, 2, 5, 1, 4, 6   C. 5, 3, 6, 4, 2, 1
D. 5, 4, 1, 2, 6, 3

4.____

_____

KEY (CORRECT ANSWERS)

1. D
2. C
3. A
4. B

_____

PREPARING WRITTEN MATERIAL

EXAMINATION SECTION
TEST 1

DIRECTIONS: Each question consists of a sentence which may or may not be an example of good English usage. Examine each sentence, considering grammar, punctuation, spelling, capitalization, and awkwardness. Then choose the correct statement about it from the four choices below it. If the English usage in the sentence given is better than any of the changes suggested in choices B, C, or D, pick choice A. (Do not pick a choice that will change the meaning of the sentence.)

1. We attended a staff conference on Wednesday the new safety and fire rules were discussed.

    A. This is an example of acceptable writing.
    B. The words "safety," "fire" and "rules" should begin with capital letters.
    C. There should be a comma after the word "Wednesday."
    D. There should be a period after the word "Wednesday" and the word "the" should begin with a capital letter

1.____

2. Neither the dictionary or the telephone directory could be found in the office library.

    A. This is an example of acceptable writing.
    B. The word "or" should be changed to "nor."
    C. The word "library" should be spelled "libery."
    D. The word "neither" should be changed to "either."

2.____

3. The report would have been typed correctly if the typist could read the draft.

    A. This is an example of acceptable writing.
    B. The word "would" should be removed.
    C. The word "have" should be inserted after the word "could."
    D. The word "correctly" should be changed to "correct."

3.____

4. The supervisor brought the reports and forms to an employees desk.

    A. This is an example of acceptable writing.
    B. The word "brought" should be changed to "took."
    C. There should be a comma after the word "reports" and a comma after the word "forms."
    D. The word "employees" should be spelled "employee's."

4.____

5. It's important for all the office personnel to submit their vacation schedules on time.

    A. This is an example of acceptable writing.
    B. The word "It's" should be spelled "Its."
    C. The word "their" should be spelled "they're."
    D. The word "personnel" should be spelled "personal."

5.____

6. The report, along with the accompanying documents, were submitted for review.   6.____

    A.   This is an example of acceptable writing.
    B.   The words "were submitted" should be changed to "was submitted."
    C.   The word "accompanying" should be spelled "accompaning."
    D.   The comma after the word "report" should be taken out.

7. If others must use your files, be certain that they understand how the system works, but   7.____
insist that you do all the filing and refiling.

    A.   This is an example of acceptable writing.
    B.   There should be a period after the word "works," and the word "but" should start a
        new sentence
    C.   The words "filing" and "refiling" should be spelled "fileing" and "refileing."
    D.   There should be a comma after the word "but."

8. The appeal was not considered because of its late arrival.   8.____

    A.   This is an example of acceptable writing.
    B.   The word "its" should be changed to "it's."
    C.   The word "its" should be changed to "the."
    D.   The words "late arrival" should be changed to "arrival late."

9. The letter must be read carefuly to determine under which subject it should be filed.   9.____

    A.   This is an example of acceptable writing.
    B.   The word "under" should be changed to "at."
    C.   The word "determine" should be spelled "determin."
    D.   The word "carefuly" should be spelled "carefully."

10. He showed potential as an office manager, but he lacked skill in delegating work.   10.____

    A.   This is an example of acceptable writing.
    B.   The word "delegating" should be spelled "delagating."
    C.   The word "potential" should be spelled "potencial."
    D.   The words "he lacked" should be changed to "was lacking."

KEY (CORRECT ANSWERS)

1.	D	6.	B
2.	B	7.	A
3.	C	8.	A
4.	D	9.	D
5.	A	10.	A

TEST 2

DIRECTIONS: Each question consists of a sentence which may or may not be an example of good English usage. Examine each sentence, considering grammar, punctuation, spelling, capitalization, and awkwardness. Then choose the correct statement about it from the four choices below it. If the English usage in the sentence given is better than any of the changes suggested in choices B, C, or D, pick choice A. (Do not pick a choice that will change the meaning of the sentence.)

1. The supervisor wants that all staff members report to the office at 9:00 A.M.   1.____

     A. This is an example of acceptable writing.
     B. The word "that" should be removed and the word "to" should be inserted after the word "members."
     C. There should be a comma after the word "wants" and a comma after the word "office."
     D. The word "wants" should be changed to "want" and the word "shall" should be inserted after the word "members."

2. Every morning the clerk opens the office mail and distributes it.   2.____

     A. This is an example of acceptable writing.
     B. The word "opens" should be changed to "open."
     C. The word "mail" should be changed to "letters."
     D. The word "it" should be changed to "them."

3. The secretary typed more fast on a desktop computer than on a laptop computer.   3.____

     A. This is an example of acceptable writing.
     B. The words "more fast" should be changed to "faster."
     C. There should be a comma after the words "desktop computer."
     D. The word "than" should be changed to "then."

4. The new stenographer needed a desk a computer, a chair and a blotter.   4.____

     A. This is an example of acceptable writing.
     B. The word "blotter" should be spelled "blodder."
     C. The word "stenographer" should begin with a capital letter.
     D. There should be a comma after the word "desk."

5. The recruiting officer said, "There are many different goverment jobs available."   5.____

     A. This is an example of acceptable writing.
     B. The word "There" should not be capitalized.
     C. The word "goverment" should be spelled "government".
     D. The comma after the word "said" should be removed.

6. He can recommend a mechanic whose work is reliable.   6.____

     A. This is an example of acceptable writing.
     B. The word "reliable" should be spelled "relyable."
     C. The word "whose" should be spelled "who's."
     D. The word "mechanic" should be spelled "mecanic."

7. She typed quickly; like someone who had not a moment to lose. 7.____

    A. This is an example of acceptable writing.
    B. The word "not" should be removed.
    C. The semicolon should be changed to a comma.
    D. The word "quickly" should be placed before instead of after the word "typed."

8. She insisted that she had to much work to do. 8.____

    A. This is an example of acceptable writing.
    B. The word "insisted" should be spelled "incisted."
    C. The word "to" used in front of "much" should be spelled "too."
    D. The word "do" should be changed to "be done."

9. He excepted praise from his supervisor for a job well done. 9.____

    A. This is an example of acceptable writing.
    B. The word "excepted" should be spelled "accepted."
    C. The order of the words "well done" should be changed to "done well."
    D. There should be a comma after the word "supervisor."

10. What appears to be intentional errors in grammar occur several times in the passage. 10.____

    A. This is an example of acceptable writing.
    B. The word "occur" should be spelled "occurr."
    C. The word "appears" should be changed to "appear."
    D. The phrase "several times" should be changed to "from time to time."

KEY (CORRECT ANSWERS)

1.	B	6.	A
2.	A	7.	C
3.	B	8.	C
4.	D	9.	B
5.	C	10.	C

TEST 3

DIRECTIONS: Same as for Tests 1 and 2.

1. The clerk could have completed the assignment on time if he knows where these materials were located.

    A. This is an example of acceptable writing.
    B. The word "knows" should be replaced by "had known."
    C. The word "were" should be replaced by "had been."
    D. The words "where these materials were located" should be replaced by "the location of these materials."

    1.____

2. All employees should be given safety training. Not just those who have accidents.

    A. This is an example of acceptable writing.
    B. The period after the word "training" should be changed to a colon.
    C. The period after the word "training" should be changed to a semicolon, and the first letter of the word "Not" should be changed to a small "n."
    D. The period after the word "training" should be changed to a comma, and the first letter of the word "Not" should be changed to a small "n."

    2.____

3. This proposal is designed to promote employee awareness of the suggestion program, to encourage employee participation in the program, and to increase the number of suggestions submitted.

    A. This is an example of acceptable writing.
    B. The word "proposal" should be spelled "preposal."
    C. The words "to increase the number of suggestions submitted" should be changed to "an increase in the number of suggestions is expected."
    D. The word "promote" should be changed to "enhance" and the word "increase" should be changed to "add to."

    3.____

4. The introduction of inovative managerial techniques should be preceded by careful analysis of the specific circumstances and conditions in each department.

    A. This is an example of acceptable writing.
    B. The word "techniques" should be spelled "techneques."
    C. The word "inovative" should be spelled "innovative."
    D. A comma should be placed after the word "circumstances" and after the word "conditions."

    4.____

5. This occurrence indicates that such criticism embarrasses him.

    A. This is an example of acceptable writing.
    B. The word "occurrence" should be spelled "occurence."
    C. The word "criticism" should be spelled "critisism."
    D. The word "embarrasses" should be spelled "embarasses."

    5.____

KEY (CORRECT ANSWERS)

1. B
2. D
3. A
4. C
5. A

ARITHMETIC

EXAMINATION SECTION
TEST 1

DIRECTIONS: Each question or incomplete statement is followed by several suggested answers or completions. Select the one that BEST answers the question or completes the statement. *PRINT THE LETTER OF THE CORRECT ANSWER IN THE SPACE AT THE RIGHT.*

1. From 30983 subtract 29998. The answer should be   1.____
    A. 985   B. 995   C. 1005   D. 1015

2. From $2537.75 subtract $1764.28. The answer should be   2.____
    A. $763.58   B. $773.47   C. $774.48   D. $873.58

3. From 254211 subtract 76348. The answer should be   3.____
    A. 177863   B. 177963   C. 187963   D. 188973

4. Divide 4025 by 35. The answer should be   4.____
    A. 105   B. 109   C. 115   D. 125

5. Multiply 0.35 by 2764. The answer should be   5.____
    A. 997.50   B. 967.40   C. 957.40   D. 834.40

6. Multiply 1367 by 0.50. The answer should be   6.____
    A. 6.8350   B. 68.350   C. 683.50   D. 6835.0

7. Multiply 841 by 0.01. The answer should be   7.____
    A. 0.841   B. 8.41   C. 84.1   D. 841

8. Multiply 1962 by 25. The answer should be   8.____
    A. 47740   B. 48460   C. 48950   D. 49050

9. Multiply 905 by 0.05. The answer should be   9.____
    A. 452.5   B. 45.25   C. 4.525   D. 0.4525

10. Multiply 8.93 by 4.7. The answer should be   10.____
    A. 41.971   B. 40.871   C. 4.1971   D. 4.0871

11. Multiply 25 by 763. The answer should be   11.____
    A. 18075   B. 18875   C. 19075   D. 20965

12. Multiply 2530 by 0.10. The answer should be   12.____
    A. 2.5300   B. 25.300   C. 253.00   D. 2530.0

13. Multiply 3053 by 0.25. The answer should be   13._____

    A.   76.325   B.   86.315   C.   763.25   D.   863.15

14. Multiply 6204 by 0.35. The answer should be   14._____

    A.   2282.40   B.   2171.40   C.   228.24   D.   217.14

15. Multiply $.35 by 7619. The answer should be   15._____

    A. $2324.75   B. $2565.65   C. $2666.65   D. $2756.75

16. Multiply 6513 by 45. The answer should be   16._____

    A.   293185   B.   293085   C.   292185   D.   270975

17. Multiply 3579 by 70. The answer should be   17._____

    A.   25053.0   B.   240530   C.   250530   D.   259530

18. A class had an average of 24 words correct on a spelling test. The class average on this   18._____
spelling test was 80%.
The AVERAGE number of words missed on this test was

    A.   2   B.   4   C.   6   D.   8

19. In which one of the following is 24 renamed as a product of primes?   19._____

    A.   2 x 6 x 2   B.   8 x 3 x 1
    C.   2 x 2 x 3 x 2   D.   3 x 4 x 2

Questions 20-23.

DIRECTIONS: In answering Questions 20 through 23, perform the indicated operation. Select
the BEST answer from the choices below.

20. Add: 7068   20._____
             2807
             9434
             6179

    A.   26,488   B.   24,588   C.   25,488   D.   25,478

21. Divide: $75\sqrt{45555}$ 21._____

    A.   674   B.   607.4   C.   6074   D.   60.74

22. Multiply: 907   22._____
               x806

    A.   73,142   B.   13,202   C.   721,042   D.   731,042

23. Subtract: 60085   23._____
                -47194

    A.   12,891   B.   13,891   C.   12,991   D.   12,871

24. A librarian reported that 1/5% of all books taken out last school year had not been returned.
If 85,000 books were borrowed from the library, how many were not returned?

A. 170   B. 425   C. 1,700   D. 4,250

24.____

25. At 40 miles per hour, how many minutes would it take to travel 12 miles?

A. 30   B. 18   C. 15   D. 20

25.____

KEY (CORRECT ANSWERS)

1.	A	11.	C
2.	B	12.	C
3.	A	13.	C
4.	C	14.	B
5.	B	15.	C
6.	C	16.	B
7.	B	17.	C
8.	D	18.	C
9.	B	19.	C
10.	A	20.	C

21.	B
22.	D
23.	A
24.	A
25.	B

SOLUTIONS TO PROBLEMS

1. $30,983 - 29,998 = 985$

2. $\$2537.75 - \$1764.28 = \$773.47$

3. $254,211 - 76,348 = 177,863$

4. $4025 \div 35 = 115$

5. $(.35)(2764) = 967.4$

6. $(1367)(.50) = 683.5$

7. $(841)(.01) = 8.41$

8. $(1962)(25) = 49,050$

9. $(905)(.05) = 45.25$

10. $(8.93)(4.7) = 41.971$

11. $(25)(763) = 19,075$

12. $(2530)(.10) = 253$

13. $(3053)(.25) = 763.25$

14. $(6204)(.35) = 2171.4$

15. $(\$.35)(7619) = \$2666.65$

16. $(6513)(45) = 293,085$

17. $(3579)(70) = 250,530$

18. $24 \div .80 = 30$. Then, $30 - 24 = 6$ words

19. $24 = 2 \times 2 \times 3 \times 2$, where each number is a prime.

20. $7068 \div 2807 + 9434 + 6179 = 25,488$

21. $45,555 \div 75 = 607.4$

22. $(907)(806) = 731,042$

23. $60,085 - 47,194 = 12,891$

24. $(1/5\%)(85,000) = (.002)(85,000) = 170$ books

25. Let x = number of minutes. Then, $\frac{40}{60} = \frac{12}{x}$. Solving, x = 18

TEST 2

DIRECTIONS: Each question or incomplete statement is followed by several suggested answers or completions. Select the one that BEST answers the question or completes the statement. *PRINT THE LETTER OF THE CORRECT ANSWER IN THE SPACE AT THE RIGHT.*

1. The sum of 57901 + 34762 is   1.____

    A. 81663   B. 82663   C. 91663   D. 92663

2. The sum of 559 + 448 + 362 + 662 is   2.____

    A. 2121   B. 2031   C. 2021   D. 1931

3. The sum of 36153 + 28624 + 81379 is   3.____

    A. 136156   B. 146046   C. 146146   D. 146156

4. The sum of 742 + 9197 + 8972 is   4.____

    A. 19901   B. 18911   C. 18801   D. 17921

5. The sum of 7989 + 8759 + 2726 is   5.____

    A. 18455   B. 18475   C. 19464   D. 19474

6. The sum of $111.55 + $95.05 + $38.80 is   6.____

    A. $234.40   B. $235.30   C. $245.40   D. $254.50

7. The sum of 1302 + 46187 + 92610 + 4522 is   7.____

    A. 144621   B. 143511   C. 134621   D. 134521

8. The sum of 47953 + 58041 + 63022 + 22333 is   8.____

    A. 170248   B. 181349   C. 191349   D. 200359

9. The sum of 76563 + 43693 + 38521 + 50987 + 72723 is   9.____

    A. 271378   B. 282386   C. 282487   D. 292597

10. The sum of 85923 + 97211 + 11333 + 4412 + 22533 is   10.____

    A. 209302   B. 212422   C. 221412   D. 221533

11. The sum of 4299 + 54163 + 89765 + 1012 + 38962 is   11.____

    A. 188201   B. 188300   C. 188301   D. 189311

12. The sum of 48526 + 709 + 11534 + 80432 + 6096 is   12.____

    A. 135177   B. 139297   C. 147297   D. 149197

13. The sum of $407.62 + $109.01 + $68.44 + $378.68 is   13.____

    A. $963.75   B. $964.85   C. $973.65   D. $974.85

14. From 40614 subtract 4697. The answer should be   14.____

     A.   35917   B.   35927   C.   36023   D.   36027

15. From 81773 subtract 5717. The answer should be   15.____

     A.   75964   B.   76056   C.   76066   D.   76956

16. From $1755.35 subtract $1201.75. The answer should be   16.____

     A. $542.50   B. $544.50   C. $553.60   D. $554.60

17. From $2402.10 subtract $998.85. The answer should be   17.____

     A. $1514.35   B. $1504.25   C. $1413.25   D. $1403.25

18. Add: 12 1/2
           2 1/2
           3 1/2   18.____

     A.   17   B.   17 1/4   C.   17 3/4   D.   18

19. Subtract: 150
            -80   19.____

     A.   70   B.   80   C.   130   D.   150

20. After cleaning up some lots in the city dump, five cleanup crews loaded the following   20.____
amounts of garbage on trucks:
     Crew No. 1 loaded 2 1/4 tons
     Crew No. 2 loaded 3 tons
     Crew No. 3 loaded 1 1/4 tons
     Crew No. 4 loaded 2 1/4tons
     Crew No. 5 loaded 1/2 ton.
The TOTAL number of tons of garbage loaded was

     A.   8 1/4   B.   8 3/4   C.   9   D.   9 1/4

21. Subtract: 17 3/4
            -7 1/4   21.____

     A.   7 1/2   B.   10 1/2   C.   14 1/4   D.   17 3/4

22. Yesterday, Tom and Bill each received 10 leaflets about rat control. They were supposed   22.____
to distribute one leaflet to each supermarket in the neighborhood. When the day was
over, Tom had 8 leaflets left. Bill had no leaflets left.
How many supermarkets got leaflets yesterday?

     A.   8   B.   10   C.   12   D.   18

23. What is 2/3 of 1 1/8?   23.____

     A.   1 11/16   B.   3/4   C.   3/8   D.   4 1/3

24. A farmer bought a load of 120 bushels of corn.   24.____
After he fed 45 bushels to his hogs, what fraction of his supply remained?

     A.   5/8   B.   3/5   C.   3/8   D.   4/7

25. In the numeral 3,159,217, the 2 is in the _____ column.

    A. hundreds   B. units   C. thousands   D. tens

25._____

KEY (CORRECT ANSWERS)

1.	D	11.	A
2.	B	12.	C
3.	D	13.	A
4.	B	14.	A
5.	D	15.	B
6.	C	16.	C
7.	A	17.	D
8.	C	18.	D
9.	C	19.	A
10.	C	20.	D

21.	B
22.	C
23.	B
24.	A
25.	A

SOLUTIONS TO PROBLEMS

1. $57,901 + 34,762 = 92,663$

2. $559 + 448 + 362 + 662 = 2031$

3. $36,153 + 28,624 + 81,379 = 146,156$

4. $742 + 9197 + 8972 = 18,911$

5. $7989 + 8759 + 2726 = 19,474$

6. $\$111.55 + \$95.05 + \$38.80 = \$245.40$

7. $1302 + 46,187 + 92,610 + 4522 = 144,621$

8. $47,953 + 58,041 + 63,022 + 22,333 = 191,349$

9. $76,563 + 45,693 + 38,521 + 50,987 + 72,723 = 282,487$

10. $85,923 + 97,211 + 11,333 + 4412 + 22,533 = 221,412$

11. $4299 + 54,163 + 89,765 + 1012 + 38,962 = 188,201$

12. $48,526 + 709 + 11,534 + 80,432 + 6096 = 147,297$

13. $\$407.62 + \$109.01 + \$68.44 + \$378.68 = \$963.75$

14. $40,614 - 4697 = 35,917$

15. $81,773 - 5717 = 76,056$

16. $\$1755.35 - \$1201.75 = \$553.60$

17. $\$2402.10 - \$998.85 = \$1403.25$

18. $12\ 1/2 + 2\ 1/4 + 3\ 1/4 = 17\ 4/4 = 18$

19. $150 - 80 = 70$

20. $2\ 1/4 + 3 + 1\ 1/4 + 2\ 1/4 + 1/2 = 8\ 5/4 = 9\ 1/4$ tons

21. $17\ 3/4 - 7\ 1/4 = 10\ 2/4 = 10\ 1/2$

22. $10 + 10 - 8 - 0 = 12$ supermarkets

23. $\left(\dfrac{2}{3}\right)\left(1\dfrac{1}{8}\right) = \left(\dfrac{2}{3}\right)\left(\dfrac{9}{8}\right) = \dfrac{18}{24} = \dfrac{3}{4}$

24. $120 - 45 = 75$. Then, $\dfrac{75}{120} = \dfrac{5}{8}$

25. The number 2 is in the hundreds column of 3,159,217

TEST 3

DIRECTIONS: Each question or incomplete statement is followed by several suggested answers or completions. Select the one that BEST answers the question or completes the statement. *PRINT THE LETTER OF THE CORRECT ANSWER IN THE SPACE AT THE RIGHT.*

1. The distance covered in three minutes by a subway train traveling at 30 mph is _____ mile(s).   1._____

    A.   3   B.   2   C.   1 1/2   D.   1

2. A crate contains 3 pieces of equipment weighing 73, 84, and 47 pounds, respectively.   2._____
   The empty crate weighs 16 pounds.
   If the crate is lifted by 4 trackmen, each trackman lifting one corner of the crate, the AVERAGE number of pounds lifted by each of the trackmen is

    A.   68   B.   61   C.   55   D.   51

3. The weight per foot of a length of square-bar 4" x 4" in cross-section, as compared with   3._____
   one 2" x 2" in cross-section, is _____ as much.

    A.   twice   B.   2 1/2 times
    C.   3 times   D.   4 times

4. An order for 360 feet of 2" x 8" lumber is shipped in 20-foot lengths.   4._____
   The MAXIMUM number of 9-foot pieces that can be cut from this shipment is

    A.   54   B.   40   C.   36   D.   18

5. If a trackman gets $10.40 per hour and time and one-half for working over 40 hours, his   5._____
   gross salary for a week in which he worked 44 hours should be

    A. $457.60   B. $478.40   C. $499.20   D. $514.80

6. If a section of ballast 6'-0" wide, 8'-0" long, and 2'-6" deep is excavated, the amount of   6._____
   ballast removed is _____ cu. feet.

    A.   96   B.   104   C.   120   D.   144

7. The sum of 7'2 3/4", 0'-2 7/8", 3'-0", 4'-6 3/8", and 1'-9 1/4" is   7._____

    A.   16'-8 1/4"   B.   16'-8 3/4"   C.   16'-9 1/4"   D.   16' -9 3/4"

8. The sum of 3 1/16", 4 1/4", 2 5/8", and 5 7/16" is   8._____

    A.   15 3/16"   B.   15 1/4"   C.   15 3/8"   D.   15 1/2"

9. Add: $51.79, $29.39, and $8.98.   9._____
   The CORRECT answer is

    A. $78.97   B. $88.96   C. $89.06   D. $90.16

10. Add: $72.07 and $31.54. Then subtract $25.75.   10._____
    The CORRECT answer is

    A. $77.86   B. $82.14   C. $88.96   D. $129.36

11. Start with $82.47. Then subtract $25.50, $4.75, and 35¢. 11.____
    The CORRECT answer is

    A. $30.60   B. $51.87   C. $52.22   D. $65.25

12. Add: $19.35 and $37.75. Then subtract $9.90 and $19.80. 12.____
    The CORRECT answer is

    A. $27.40   B. $37.00   C. $37.30   D. $47.20

13. Add: $153 13.____
            114
            210
         +186

    A. $657   B. $663   C. $713   D. $757

14. Add: $64.91 14.____
            13.53
            19.27
            20.00
        +72.84

    A. $170.25   B. $178.35   C. $180.45   D. $190.55

15. Add: 1963 15.____
           1742
        +2497

    A.   6202   B.   6022   C.   5212   D.   5102

16. Add: 206 16.____
           709
         1342
        +2076

    A.   3432   B.   3443   C.   4312   D.   4333

17. Subtract: $190.76 17.____
          -   .99

    A. $189.97   B. $189.87   C. $189.77   D. $189.67

18. From 99876 subtract 85397. The answer should be 18.____

    A.   14589   B.   14521   C.   14479   D.   13589

19. From $876.51 subtract $92.89. The answer should be 19.____

    A. $773.52   B. $774.72   C. $783.62   D. $784.72

20. From 70935 subtract 49489. The answer should be 20.____

    A.   20436   B.   21446   C.   21536   D.   21546

21. From $391.55 subtract $273.45. The answer should be
   21._____

   A. $118.10   B. $128.20   C. $178.10   D. $218.20

22. When 119 is subtracted from the sum of 2016 + 1634, the answer is
   22._____

   A. 2460   B. 3531   C. 3650   D. 3769

23. Multiply 35 x 65 x 15. The answer should be
   23._____

   A. 2275   B. 24265   C. 31145   D. 34125

24. Multiply: 4.06
   24._____
             x.031

   A. 1.2586   B. .12586   C. .02586   D. .1786

25. When 65 is added to the result of 14 multiplied by 13, the answer is
   25._____

   A. 92   B. 182   C. 247   D. 16055

KEY (CORRECT ANSWERS)

1. C	11. B
2. C	12. A
3. D	13. B
4. C	14. D
5. B	15. A
6. C	16. D
7. C	17. C
8. C	18. C
9. D	19. C
10. A	20. B

21. A
22. B
23. D
24. B
25. C

SOLUTIONS TO PROBLEMS

1. Let x = distance. Then, $\frac{30}{60} = \frac{x}{3}$ Solving, x = 1 1/2 miles

2. $(73 + 84 + 47 + 16) \div 4 = 55$ pounds

3. $(4 \times 4) \div (2 \times 2) = $ a ratio of 4 to 1.

4. $20 \div 9 = 2\ 2/9$, rounded down to 2 pieces. Then, $(360 \div 20)(2) = 36$

5. Salary $= (\$10.40)(40) + (\$15.60)(4) = \$478.40$

6. $(6)(8)(2\ 1/2) = 120$ cu.ft.

7. $7'2\frac{3}{4}"+0'2\frac{7}{8}"+3'0"+4'6\frac{3}{8}"+1'9\frac{1}{4}"=15'19\frac{18}{8}"=15'21\frac{1}{4}"=16'9\frac{1}{4}"$

8. $3\frac{1}{16}"+4\frac{1}{4}"+2\frac{5}{8}"+5\frac{7}{16}"=14\frac{22}{16}"=15\frac{3}{8}"$

9. $\$51.79 + \$29.39 + \$8.98 = \$90.16$

10. $\$72.07 + \$31.54 = \$103.61$. Then, $\$103.61 - \$25.75 = \$77.86$

11. $\$82.47 - \$25.50 - \$4.75 - \$0.35 = \$51.87$

12. $\$19.35 + \$37.75 = \$57.10$. Then, $\$57.10 - \$9.90 - \$19.80 = \$27.40$

13. $\$153 + \$114 + \$210 + \$186 = \$663$

14. $\$64.91 + \$13.53 + \$19.27 + \$20.00 + \$72.84 = \$190.55$

15. $1963 + 1742 + 2497 = 6202$

16. $206 + 709 + 1342 + 2076 = 4333$

17. $\$190.76 - .99 = \$189.77$

18. $99,876 - 85,397 = 14,479$

19. $\$876.51 - \$92.89 = \$783.62$

20. $70,935 - 49,489 = 21,446$

21. $\$391.55 - \$273.45 = \$118.10$

22. $(2016 + 1634) - 119 = 3650 - 119 = 3531$

23. $(35)(65)(15) = 34,125$

24. $(4.06)(.031) = .12586$

25. $65 + (14)(13) = 65 + 182 = 247$

———————

EXAMINATION SECTION
TEST 1

DIRECTIONS: Each question or incomplete statement is followed by several suggested answers or completions. Select the one that BEST answers the question or completes the statement. *PRINT THE LETTER OF THE CORRECT ANSWER IN THE SPACE AT THE RIGHT.*

1. Which of the following fractions is the SMALLEST?   1.____

    A. 2/3   B. 4/5   C. 5/7   D. 5/11

2. 40% is equivalent to which of the following?   2.____

    A. 4/5   B. 4/6   C. 2/5   D. 4/100

3. How many 100's are in 10,000?   3.____

    A. 10   B. 100   C. 10,000   D. 100,000

4. $\frac{6}{7}+\frac{11}{12}$ is approximately   4.____

    A. 1   B. 2   C. 17   D. 19

5. The time required to heat water to a certain temperature is directly proportional to the volume of water being heated.   5.____
If it takes 12 minutes to heat 1 1/2 gallons of water, how many minutes will it take to heat 2 gallons of water?

    A. 12   B. 16   C. 18   D. 24

6. The cost of an item increased by 25%.   6.____
If the original cost was C dollars, identify the expression which gives the new cost of that item.

    A. C + 0.25   B. 1/4 C   C. 25C   D. 1.25C

7. Given the formula $PV = nRT$, all of the following are true EXCEPT   7.____

    A. $T = PV/nR$ B. $P = nRT/V$ C. $V = P/nRT$ D. $n = PV/RT$

8. If a Fahrenheit (F) temperature reading is 104, find its Celsius (C) equivalent, given that $C = i(F-32)$ 8.____

    A. 36   B. 40   C. 72   D. 76

9. If 40% of a graduating class plans to go directly to work after graduation, which of the following must be TRUE?   9.____

    A.   Less than half of the class plans to go directly to work.
    B.   Forty members of the class plan to enter the job market.
    C.   Most of the class plans to go directly to work.
    D.   Six in ten members of the class are expected not to graduate.

10. Given a multiple-choice test item which has 5 choices, what is the probability of guessing the correct answer if you know nothing about the item content?   10._____

    A. 5%   B. 10%   C. 20%   D. 25%

11. Which graph BEST represents the data shown in the table at the right?   11._____

S	T
0	80
5	75
10	65
15	50
20	30
25	5

A.
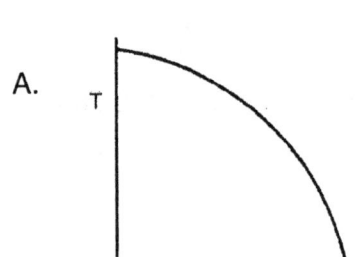

B.
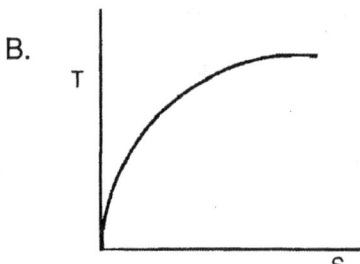

C.
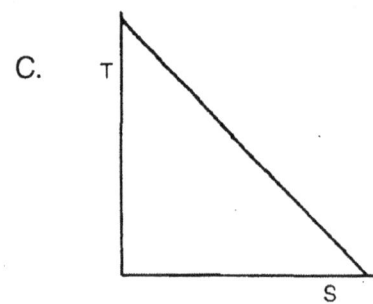

D.
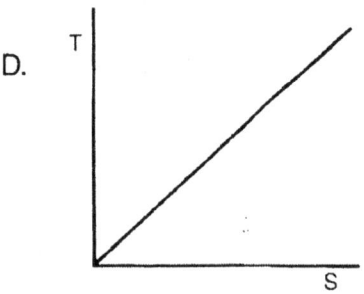

12. If 3(X + 5Y) = 24, find Y when X = 3.   12._____

    A. 1   B. 3   C. 33/5   D. 7

13. The payroll of a grocery store for its 23 clerks is $395,421. Which expression below shows the average salary of a clerk?   13._____

    A. 395,421 x 23   B. 23 ÷ 395,421

    C. (395,421x14) ÷ 23   D. 395,421 ÷ 23

14. If 12.8 pounds of coffee cost $50.80, what is the APPROXIMATE price per pound?   14._____

    A. $2.00   B. $3.00   C. $4.00   D. $5.00

15. A road map has a scale where 1 inch corresponds to 150 miles. A distance of 3 3/4 inches on the map corresponds to what actual distance?   15._____
    _____ miles

    A. 153.75   B. 375   C. 525   D. 562.5

16. How many square feet of plywood are needed to construct the back and 4 adjacent sides of the box shown at the right? _____ square feet.

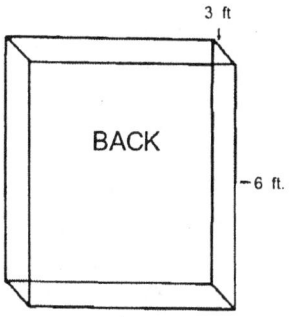

16._____

A. 63
B. 90
C. 96
D. 126

17. One thirty pound bag of lawn fertilizer costs $20.00 and will cover 600 square feet of lawn. Terry's lawn is a 96 foot by 75 foot rectangle. How much will it cost Terry to buy enough bags of fertilizer for her lawn?
Which of the following do you NOT need in order to solve this problem?
The

17._____

A. product of 96 and 75
B. fact that one bag weighs 30 pounds
C. fact that one bag covers 600 square feet
D. fact that one bag costs $20.00

18. On the graph shown at the right, between which hours was the drop in temperature GREATEST?

18._____

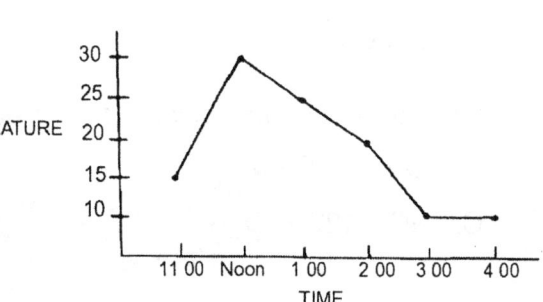

A. 11:00 - Noon
B. Noon - 1:00
C. 1:00 - 2:00
D. 2:00 - 3:00

19. If on a typical railroad track, the distance from the center of one railroad tie to the next is 30 inches, approximately how many ties would be needed for one mile of track?

19._____

A. 180   B. 2,110   C. 6,340   D. 63,360

20. Which of the following is MOST likely to be the volume of a wine bottle?

20._____

A. 750 milliliters   B. 7 kilograms
C. 7 milligrams   D. 7 liters

21. What is the reading on the gauge shown at the right?

21._____

A. -7
B. -3
C. 1
D. 3

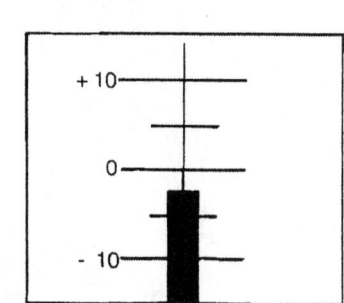

85

22. Which statement below disproves the assertion, *All students in Mrs. Marino's 10th grade   22.____
    geometry class are planning to go to college?*

    A. Albert is in Mrs, Marino's class, but he is not planning to take mathematics next
        year.
    B. Jorge is not in Mrs. Marino's class, but he is still planning to go to college.
    C. Pierre is in Mrs. Marino's class but says he will not be attending school anymore
        after this year.
    D. Crystal is in Mrs. Marino's class and plans to attend Yale University when she grad-
        uates.

23. A store advertisement reads, *Buy now while our prices are low. There will never be a bet-   23.____
    ter time to buy.* The customer reading this advertisement should assume that

    A. the prices at the store will probably never be lower
    B. right now, this store has the best prices in town
    C. prices are higher at other stores
    D. prices are always lowest at this store

24. *Given any positive integer A, there is always a positive number B such that A x B is less   24.____
    than 1.*
    Which statement below supports this generalization?

    A. 8 x 1/16 =1/2   B. 8x1/2 = 4
    C. 5/2 X 1/10= 1/4   D. 1/2x1/2 = 1/2

25. Of the following expressions, which is equivalent to 4C + D = 12E?   25.____

    A. C = 4(12E - D)   B. 4+ D = 12E - C

    C. 4C + 12E = -D   D. C $= \dfrac{12E-D}{4}$

KEY (CORRECT ANSWERS)

1.	D	11.	A
2.	C	12.	A
3.	B	13.	D
4.	B	14.	C
5.	B	15.	D
6.	D	16.	C
7.	C	17.	B
8.	B	18.	D
9.	A	19.	B
10.	C	20.	A

21.	B
22.	C
23.	A
24.	A
25.	D

SOLUTIONS TO PROBLEMS

1. Converting to decimals, we get $.\overline{6}$, .8, .714 (approx), $.\overline{45}$. The smallest is $.\overline{45}$ corresponding to 5/11.

2. 40% = 40/100 = 2/5

3. 10,000 ÷ 100 = 100

4. $\dfrac{6}{7} + \dfrac{11}{12} = (72 + 77) \div 84 = \dfrac{149}{84} \approx 1.77 \approx 2$

5. Let x = required minutes. Then, 12/1 1/2 = x/2 This reduces to 1 1/2x = 24. Solving, x = 16

6. New cost is C + .25C = 1.25C

7. For PV = nRT, V = nRT/P

8. C = 5/9 (104-32) = 5/9 (72) = 40

9. Since 40% is less than 50% (or half), we conclude that less than half of the class plans to go to work directly after graduation.

10. The probability of guessing right is 1/5 or 20%.

11. Curve A is most accurate since as S increases, we see that T decreases. Note, however, that the relationship is NOT linear. Although S increases in equal amounts, the decrease in T is NOT in equal amounts.

12. 3(3+5Y) = 24. This simplifies to 9 + 15Y = 24 Solving, Y = 1

13. The average salary is $395,421 ÷ 23

14. The price per pound is $50.80 ÷ 12.8 = $3.96875 or approximately $4.

15. Actual distance is (3 3/4)(l50) = 562.5 miles

16. The area of the back = (6)(5) = 30 sq.ft. The combined area of the two vertical sides is (2)(6)(3) = 36 sq.ft. The combined area of the horizontal sides is (2)(5)(3) = 30 sq.ft. Total area = 30 + 36 + 30 = 96 square feet.

17. Choice B is not relevant to solving the problem since the cost will be [(96)(75) / 600][$20] = $240. So, the weight per bag is not needed.

18. For the graph, the largest temperature drop was from 2:00 P.M. to 3:00 P.M. The temperature dropped 20 - 10 = 10 degrees.

19. 1 mile = 5280 feet = 63,360 inches. Then, 63,360 ÷ 30 = 2112 or about 2110 ties are needed.

20. Since 1 liter = 1.06 quarts, 750 milliliters = (750/1000)(1.06) = .795 quarts. This is a reasonable volume for a wine bottle.

21. The reading is -3.

22. Statement C contradicts the given information, since Pierre is in Mrs. Marino's class. Then he should plan to go to college.

23. Since there will never be a better time to buy at this particular store, the customer can assume the current prices will probably never be lower.

24. Statement A illustrates this concept. Note that in general, if n is a positive integer, then

$$(n)\left(\frac{1}{n+1}\right) < 1$$

Example: (100)(1/100)< 1

TEST 2

DIRECTIONS: Each question or incomplete statement is followed by several suggested answers or completions. Select the one that BEST answers the question or completes the statement. *PRINT THE LETTER OF THE CORRECT ANSWER IN THE SPACE AT THE RIGHT.*

1. Which of the following lists numbers in INCREASING order?   1.____

   A. 0.4, 0.04, 0.004   B. 2.71, 3.15, 2.996
   C. 0.7, 0.77, 0.777   D. 0.06, 0.5, 0.073

                                                                                                 2.____
2. $\dfrac{4}{10} + \dfrac{7}{100} + \dfrac{5}{1000} =$

   A. 4.75   B. 0.475   C. 0.0475   D. 0.00475

3. 700 times what number equals 7?   3.____

   A. 10   B. 0.1   C. 0.01   D. 0.001

4. 943 - 251 is approximately   4.____

   A. 600   B. 650   C. 700   D. 1200

5. The time needed to set up a complicated piece of machinery is inversely proportional to   5.____
   the number of years' experience of the worker.
   If a worker with 10 years' experience needs 6 hours to do the job, how long will it take
   a worker with 15 years' experience?

   A. 4   B. 5   C. 9   D. 25

6. Let W represent the number of waiters and D, the number of diners in a particular restau-   6.____
   rant.
   Identify the expression which represents the statement: There are 10 times as many
   diners as waiters.

   A. 10W = D   B. 10D = W
   C. 10D + 10W   D. 10 = D + W

7. Which of the following is equivalent to the formula F = XC + Y?   7.____

   A. F-C=X+Y   B. Y = F + XC

   C. $C = \dfrac{F\ Y}{X}$ D. $C = \dfrac{F\ X}{Y}$

8. Given the formula A = BC / D, if A = 12, B = 6, and D = 3, what is the value of C?   8.____

   A. 2/3   B. 6   C. 18   D. 24

9. 5 is to 7 as X is to 35. X =   9.____

   A. 7   B. 12   C. 25   D. 49

10. Kramer Middle School has 5 seventh grade mathematics teachers: two of the math teachers are women and three are men.
If you are assigned a teacher at random, what is the probability of getting a female teacher?

   A. 0.2   B. 0.4   C. 0.6   D. 0.8

10.____

11. Which statement BEST describes the graph shown at the right? Temperature

   A. and time decrease at the same rate
   B. and time increase at the same rate
   C. increases over time
   D. decreases over time

11.____

12. If 3X + 4 = 2Y, find Y when X = 2.

   A. 0   B. 3   C. 4 1/2   D. 5

12.____

13. A car goes 243 miles on 8.7 gallons of gas. Which numeric expression should be used to determine the car's miles per gallon?

   A. 243 x 87   B. 8.7 ÷ 243
   C. 243 ÷ 8.7   D. 243 - 8.7

13.____

14. What is the average cost per book if you buy six books at $4.00 each and four books at $5.00 each?

   A. $4.40   B. $4.50   C. $4.60   D. $5.40

14.____

15. A publisher's sale offers a 15% discount to anyone buying more than 100 workbooks. What will be the discount on 200 workbooks selling at $2.25 each?

   A. $15.00   B. $30.00   C. $33.75   D. $67.50

15.____

16. A road crew erects 125 meters of fencing in one workday. How many workdays are required to erect a kilometer of fencing?

   A. 0.8   B. 8   C. 80   D. 800

16.____

17. Last month Kim made several telephone calls to New York City totaling 45 minutes in all. What does Kim need in order to calculate the average duration of her New York City calls?
The

   A. total number of calls she made to New York City
   B. cost per minute of a call to New York City
   C. total cost of her telephone bill last month
   D. days of the week on which the calls were made

17.____

91

18.   18._____

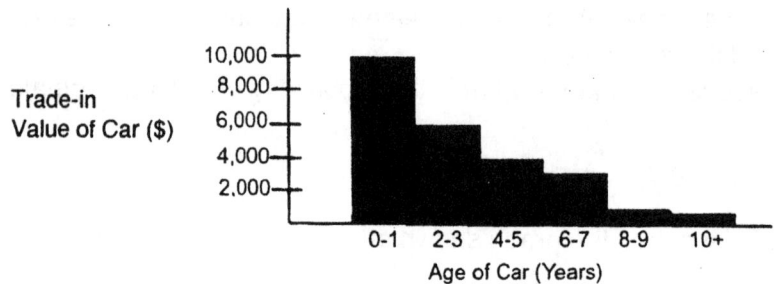

The chart above relates a car's age to its trade-in value. Based on the chart, which of the following is TRUE?

A. A 4- to 5-year old car has a trade-in value of about $2,000.
B. The trade-in value of an 8- to 9-year old car is about 1/3 that of a 2- to 3-year old car.
C. A 6- to 7-year old car has no trade-in value.
D. A 4- to 5-year old car's trade-in value is about $2,000 less than that of a 2- to 3-year old car.

19. Which of the following expressions could be used to determine how many seconds are in   19._____
     a 24-hour day?

A. 60 x 60 x 24   B. 60 x 12 x 24
C. 60 x 2 x 24   D. 60 x 24

20. For measuring milk, we could use each of the following EXCEPT   20._____

A. liters   B. kilograms
C. millimeters   D. cubic centimeters

21. What is the reading on the gauge shown at the right?   21._____

A. 51
B. 60
C. 62.5
D. 70

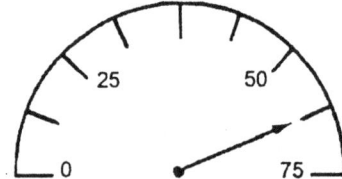

22. Bill is taller than Yvonne. Yvonne is shorter than Sue. Sue is 5'4" tall.   22._____
     Which of the following conclusions must be TRUE?

A. Bill is taller than Sue.
B. Yvonne is taller than 5'4".
C. Sue is taller than Bill.
D. Yvonne is the shortest.

23. The Bass family traveled 268 miles during the first day of their vacation and another 300 23._____
     miles on the next day. Maria Bass said they were 568 miles from home.
     Which of the following facts did Maria assume?

A. They traveled faster on the first day and slower on the second.
B. If she plotted the vacation route on a map, it would be a straight line.
C. Their car used more gasoline on the second day.
D. They traveled faster on the second day than they did on the first day.

24. *The word LEFT in a mathematics problem indicates that it is a subtraction problem.*   24.____
Which of the following mathematics problems proves this statement FALSE?

    A.   I want to put 150 bottles into cartons which hold 8 bottles each. After I completely fill as many cartons as I can, how many bottles will be left?
    B.   Sarah had 5 books but gave one to John. How many books did Sarah have left?
    C.   Carlos had $4.25 but spent $3.75. How much did he have left?
    D.   We had 38 models in stock but after yesterday's sale, only 12 are left. How many did we sell?

25. Let Q represent the number of miles Dave can jog in 15 minutes.   25.____
Identify the expression which represents the number of miles Dave can jog between 3:00 PM and 4:45 PM?

    A.   1 3/4 Q   B.   7Q

    C. $15 \times 1\frac{3}{4} \times Q$ D.   Q/7

KEY (CORRECT ANSWERS)

1.	C	11.	D
2.	B	12.	D
3.	C	13.	C
4.	C	14.	A
5.	A	15.	D
6.	A	16.	B
7.	C	17.	A
8.	B	18.	D
9.	C	19.	A
10.	B	20.	C

21.	C
22.	D
23.	B
24.	A
25.	B

SOLUTIONS TO PROBLEMS

1. Choice C is in ascending order since .7 < .77 < .777

2. Rewrite in decimal form: .4 + .07 + .005 = .475

3. Let x = missing number. Then, 700x = 7. Solving, x = 7/700 = .01

4. 943 - 251 = 692 ≈ 700

5. Let x = hours needed. Then, 10/15 = x/6. Solving, x = 4

6. The number of diners (D) is 10 times as many waiters (10W). So, D = 10W or 10W = D

7. Given F = XC + Y, subtract Y from each side to get F - Y = XC. Finally, dividing by X, we get (F-Y)/X = C

8. 12 = 6C/3. Then, 12 = 2C, so C = 6

9. 5/7 = X/35 Then, 7x = 175, so x = 25

10. Probability of a female teacher = 2/5 = .4

11. Statement D is best, since as time increases, the temperature decreases

12. (3)(2) + 4 = 2Y. Then, 10 = 2Y, so Y = 5

13. Miles per gallon = 243 / 8.7

14. Total purchase is (6)($4) + (4)($5) = $44. The average cost per book is $44 ÷ 10 = $4.40

15. (220)($2.25) = $450. The discount is (.15)($450) = $67.50

16. The number of workdays is 1000 ÷ 125 = 8

17. Choice A is correct because the average duration of the phone calls = total time ÷ total number of calls

18. Statement D is correct since a 4-5 year-old car's value is $4,000, whereas a 2-3 year-old car's value is $6000.

19. 60 seconds = 1 minute and 60 minutes = 1 hour. Thus, 24 hours = (24)(60)(60) or (60)(60)(24) seconds

20. We can't use millimeters in measuring milk since millimeters is a linear measurement

21. The reading shows the average of 50 and 75 = 62.5

22. Since Yvonne is shorter than both Bill and Sue, Yvonne is the shortest.

23. Statement B is assumed correct since 568 = 268 + 300 could only be true if the mileage traveled represents a straight line

24. To find the number of bottles left, we look only for the remainder when 150 is divided by 8 (which happens to be 6)

———

EXAMINATION SECTION
TEST 1

DIRECTIONS: Each question or incomplete statement is followed by several suggested answers or completions. Select the one that BEST answers the question or completes the statement. *PRINT THE LETTER OF THE CORRECT ANSWER IN THE SPACE AT THE RIGHT.*

1. At 7:00 A.M., a student leaves his home in his automobile to drive to school 28 miles away. He averages 50 mph until 7:30 A.M., when his car breaks down. The student has to walk and run the rest of the way.
   If he wants to arrive at school at 8:00 A.M., how fast, in mph, must he travel on foot?

   A. 3   B. 4   C. 5   D. 6   E. 7

   1.____

2. Express $1+\dfrac{1}{2+\dfrac{1}{3+\dfrac{1}{4}}}$ in simplest terms.

   A. 27/28   B. 30/43   C. 1 1/9   D. 1 1/27   E. 1 13/30

   2.____

3. A theater charges $5.00 admission for adults and $2.50 for children. At one showing, 240 admissions brought in a total of $800.
   How many adults attended the showing?

   A. 40   B. 80   C. 120   D. 160   E. 266

   3.____

4. $\sqrt{25 + ?} = 5 + 8$

   A. 8   B. 12   C. 64   D. 144   E. 169

   4.____

5. The perimeter of a square is 20.
   Which of the following represents the area?

   A. 5   B. 10   C. 20   D. 25   E. 100

   5.____

6. Evaluate the expression $\dfrac{1}{4} + \dfrac{3}{8} - \dfrac{6}{16} - \dfrac{8}{32}$

   A. 7/16   B. 1/32   C. 1/8   D. 1/4   E. 0

   6.____

7. Bill spent 20% of the money he initially had in his wallet on groceries and 25% on gas. He had $66.00 left. How much money did he have before he shopped?

   A. $85   B. $100   C. $110   D. $111   E. $120

   7.____

8. Express the product $(2x + 5y)^2$ in simple form.

   A. $4x^2 + 25y^2$ B. $4x^2 + 20xy + 25y^2$
   C. $4x^2 + 10y + 25y^2$ D. $4x^2 - 20xy + 25y^2$
   E. $4x + 25y$

   8.____

9. A student received test grades of 83, 90, and 88.   9.___
What was her grade on a fourth test if the average for the four tests is 84?

    A. 85   B. 80   C. 75   D. 70   E. 65

10. A rectangular room is 3 meters wide, 4 meters long, and 2 meters high.   10.___
How far is it from the northeast corner at the floor to the southwest corner at the ceiling?
_____ members.

    A. $\sqrt{29}$ B. $\sqrt{11}$ C. $\sqrt{9}$ D. 9   E. 5

11. If an electron has a mass of 9.109×10^{-31} kg. and a proton has a mass of 1.672×10^{-27} 11.___
kg., approximately how many electrons are required to have the same mass as one proton?

    A. 150,000   B. 1,800   C. 5.4×10^4
    D. 5.4×10^{-4} E. 15×10^{-58}

12. The introduction of a new manufacturing process will affect a saving of $1,450 per week   12.___
over the initial 8-week production period. New equipment, however, will cost 1/4 of the
total savings.
How much did the equipment cost?

    A. $11,600.00   B. $2,900.00   C. $725.00
    D. $362.50   E. $181.25

13. If P dollars is invested at r percent compounded annually, at the end of n years it will have   13.___
grown to $A = P(1 + r)^n$. An investment made at 16% compounded annually. It grows to
$1,740 at the end of one year.
How much was originally invested?

    A. $150   B. $278.40   C. $1,461.60
    D. $1,500   E. $1,700

14. What is 1/4% of 200?   14.___

    A. 0.05   B. 0.5   C. 5   D. 12.5   E. 50

15. Which of the following is .5% of .95?   15.___

    A. .000475   B. .00475   C. .0475   D. .475   E. 4.75

16. What is the value of (5 lbs. 1 oz)/(3 lbs. 6 oz.) in ounces?   16.___

    A. 22   B. 1.66   C. 1.5   D. 0.66   E. 0.28

17. If 1 inch = 2.54 centimeters, 3/8 centimeter equals which of the following in inches?   17.___

    A. 6.77   B. .95   C. .39   D. .38   E. .15

18. If $2x + y = 7$ and $x - 4y = 4$, then x equals which of the following?   18.___

    A. -15/9   B. - 1/9   C. 7/16   D. 11/9   E. 32/9

19. What part of an hour is 6 seconds?   19.___

    A. 1/600   B. 1/10   C. 1/360   D. 1/60   E. 1/5

20. If $1/3 + 5(x-1) = 8$, then which of the following is the value of x?   20.____

    A. 8/13   B. 8/5   C. 38/25   D. 38/15   E. 38

21. Which line is perpendicular to the x-axis?   21.____

    A. $x = 3$ B. $y = 3$ C. $x = y$
    D. $x = y/3$ E. $y = x/3$

22. If a dental hygienist at a certain office is paid H dollars a week, the dental assistant works   22.____
    36 hours a week at A dollars per hour, and the receptionist works 40 hours a week and
    receives R dollars every other week, which of the following represents the weekly payroll
    for these three employees?

    A. $H/3 + 36A + 40R/3$ B. $H + 36A + R/2$
    C. $H/3 + 12A + R/6$ D. $5H + 36 + 20R$
    E. $H/3 + 12A + 40R$

23. Company A ordered five units of anesthetic at $12.00 per unit. Company B ordered 10   23.____
    units at $13.00 per unit, and Company C ordered 4 at $10.00 per unit. Since all these
    companies were at one address, the three orders were put on one bill.
    Approximately what percent of the total bill did Company A have to pay?

    A. 5   B. 18   C. 26   D. 36   E. 55

24. Which of the following is the value of A, if $50(A/100) = 2A^2$?   24.____

    A. 25   B. 1   C. 5/2   D. 1/4   E. 1/2

25. Five-eighths of the employees in a certain company are male. One-fifth of these males   25.____
    are single.
    What percentage of the employees in the company are single males?

    A. 12.5   B. 20.0   C. 25.0   D. 32.0   E. 62.5

26. If x = 20% of y, and z = 35% of x, then z = _____% of y.   26.____

    A. 70   B. 57   C. 7   D. 1.75   E. .07

27. Which of the following is the value of the expression $\dfrac{|14-3|-|7-16|}{3|(-2)+1|}$?   27.____

    A. -20/3   B. -2/3   C. 0   D. 2/3   E. 20/3

28. A tank can be filled by a pipe in 30 minutes and emptied by another pipe in 50 minutes.   28.____
    How many minutes will it take to fill the tank if both pipes are open?

    A. 45   B. 60   C. 75   D. 80   E. 100

29. If $(4/5)x = (2/5)y$, then which of the following is equal to y/x?   29.____

    A. 1/2   B. 2/5   C. 25/8   D. 2   E. 3

30. Which of the following would NOT result in a straight line?   30.____
    x =

    A. 1/y   B. 2y + 5   C. (y+6)/(2)
    D. 5 - y   E. 4(x+3y)

31. $\dfrac{5}{4}+\dfrac{4}{5}+\dfrac{3}{2}-$ ____ = a positive integer.

31.____

    A. 10/20   B. 11/20   C. 71/20   D. 3/20   E. 4/20

32.____

32. If $\dfrac{2}{x}+\dfrac{3}{5}=\dfrac{4}{3}$, then which of the following is the value of x?

    A. 30/11   B. 30/29   C. 11/30   D. -11/6   E. -5/2

33. Optometry school applicants decreased by 25% during a 4-year period. During the same time, the number of first-year openings in optometry school increased by 12%. If the ratio of applicants to first-year student openings had been 3 to 1, then which of the following would be the APPROXIMATE ratio at the end of the 4-year period?

33.____

    A. 1.5 to 1   B. 2 to 1   C. 3 to 2
    D. 4 to 3   E. 6 to 5

34. If then which of the following is the value of x?

34.____

    A. 4   B. 27   C. 29   D. 49   E. 729

35. Two cars start at the same point and travel north and west at the rate of 24 and 32 mph, respectively.
How far apart are they at the end of 2 hours?

35.____

    A. 64   B. 80   C. 112   D. 116   E. 100

36. Right triangle ABC with right angle C and AB = 6, BC = 3, find AC.

36.____

    A. 3   B. 6   C. 27   D. 33   E. $3\sqrt{3}$

37. When each of the sides of a square is increased by 1 yard, the area of the new square is 53 square yards more than that of the original square.
What is the length of the sides of the original square?

37.____

    A. 25   B. 26   C. 27   D. 52   E. 54

38.____

38. Evaluate: $3(2)^2 + \sqrt{25} - (-2)^3$.

    A. 9   B. 24   C. 25   D. 33   E. 76

39. Which of the following is the length of the line segment BC if AB = 14, AD = 5, and angle BAD = 30°?

39.____

    A. $\sqrt{221}$

    B. $\sqrt{171}$

    C. $7\sqrt{3}$

    D. 7

    E. 9

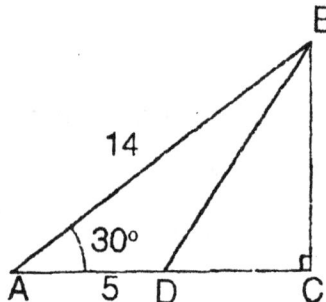

40. A bowl contains 7 green and 3 red marbles.
What is the probability that two marbles selected at random from this bowl without replacement are both red?

    A. 1/15   B. 9/100   C. 21/100   D. 47/90   E. 6/10

40.____

41. If x pens cost 75 cents and y pencils cost 57 cents, then which equation below can be used to find the cost of 2 pens and 3 pencils?

    A. 2(75/x) + 3(57/y)   B. 3x/75 + 2y/57
    C. 75/2x + 57/3y   D. 2(x/75) + 3(y/57)
    E. 3(75/x) + 2(57/y)

41.____

42. Maria has a number of dimes and quarters whose total value is less than $9.00. There are twice as many dimes as quarters.
At most, how many quarters could she have?

    A. 14   B. 15   C. 19   D. 20   E. 35

42.____

43. The number (1, 2, 3, 6) have an average (arithmetic mean) of 3 and a variance of 3.5.
What is the average (arithmetic mean) and variance of the set of numbers (3, 6, 9, 18)?

    A. 9, 31.5   B. 3, 10.5   C. 3, 31.5
    D. 6, 7.5   E. 9, 27.5

43.____

44. A fence encloses a triangular-shaped region whose sides are 20 feet, 20 feet, and 10 feet in length.
If the number of inches between fence posts (centers) is 30 inches, how many posts will be needed?

    A. 17   B. 20   C. 21   D. 22   E. 23

44.____

45. A ceiling 6 feet by 7 feet can be painted for $52. Find the cost of painting a ceiling 18 feet by 21 feet, all things being equal except the dimensions.

    A. $104   B. $126   C. $156   D. $378   E. $468

45.____

46. Three consecutive odd numbers have a sum of 51.
What is the LARGEST of these numbers?

    A. 15   B. 17   C. 18   D. 19   E. 21

46.____

47. It takes 5 hours for a qualified typist to complete a report. Coffee break begins at 10:15 A.M. It is now 9:55 A.M.
How much of the task can the typist be expected to complete by coffee break?

    A. 1/8   B. 1/25   C. 1/3   D. 1/5   E. 1/15

47.____

48. A container in the form of a rectangular solid is 10 feet long, 9 feet wide, and 2 feet deep.
The container is filled with a liquid weighing 100 pounds per cubic foot.
What is the weight of the liquid in the container in pounds?

    A. 90   B. 180   C. 1,800   D. 9,000   E. 18,000

48.____

49. The value of cos(π /3) equals the value of   49.____

    A.   - cos(2 π /3)   B.   cos(2 π /3)   C.   cos(6 π /3)

    D.   - cos(5 π /3)   E.   cos(4 π /3)

50. If $5 \leq x \leq 12$ and -2 y 9, then is as large as possible when x = _____ and y = _____.   50.____

    A.   12; 9   B.   12; 0   C.   12; -2   D.   0; 9   E.   0; 0

KEY (CORRECT ANSWERS)

1. D	11. B	21. A	31. B	41. A
2. E	12. B	22. B	32. A	42. C
3. B	13. D	23. C	33. B	43. A
4. D	14. B	24. D	34. C	44. B
5. D	15. B	25. A	35. B	45. E
6. E	16. C	26. C	36. E	46. D
7. E	17. E	27. D	37. B	47. E
8. B	18. E	28. C	38. C	48. E
9. C	19. A	29. D	39. D	49. A
10. A	20. D	30. A	40. A	50. B

SOLUTIONS TO PROBLEMS

1. Let x = rate of walking/running. Then, (50)(1/2) + (x)(1/2) = 28 Simplifying, 1/2x = 3. Solving, x = 6.

2. $3 + \frac{1}{4} = 3\frac{1}{4}$, $1/3\frac{1}{4} = \frac{4}{13}$, $2 + \frac{4}{13} = 2\frac{4}{13}$, $1/2\frac{4}{13} = \frac{13}{30}$.

   Finally, $1 + \frac{13}{30} = 1\frac{13}{30}$.

3. Let x = number of adults, 240-x = number of children.
   Then, 5x + 2.50(240-x) = 800. Simplifying, we get 5x + 600 - 2.50x = 800. This reduces to 2.50x = 200. Solving, x = 80.

4. $\sqrt{25+x} = 13$ Squaring both sides, 25 + x = 169. So, x = 144.

5. If the perimeter of a square is 20, each side must be 5.
   The area is $5^2 = 25$

6. Changing to a denominator of 32, we get 8/32 + 12/32 - 12/32 - 8/32 = 0/32 = 0

7. Let x = original amount. 100% - 20% - 25% = 55%
   Then, $66 = .55x. Solving, x = $120

8. $(2x+5y)^2 = 4x^2 + 10xy + 10xy + 25y^2 = 4x^2 + 20xy + 25y^2$

9. Let x = grade on her 4th test. Then, (83+90+88+x)/4 = 84 This becomes (261+x)/4 = 84. Further reduction leads to 261 + x = 336, so x = 75

10. The required distance is $\sqrt{3^2 + 4^2 + 2^2} = \sqrt{9+16+4} = \sqrt{29}$

11. $(1.672 \times 10^{-27}) \div (9.109 \times 10^{-31})$ .1836 x 10^4 ≈ 1800

12. Total savings is ($1450)(8) = $11,600.
    Equipment costs (1/4)($11,600) = $2900

13. $1740 = P(I + .16)'. Then, P = $1740 ÷ 1.16 = $1500

14. 1/4% of 200 is (.0025)(200) = .5

15. .5% of .95 is (.005)(.95) = .00475

16. 5 lbs. 1 oz. = 81 oz. and 3 lbs. 6 oz. = 54 oz.
    Then, 81 oz. ÷ 54 oz. = 1.5

17. 3/8 cm = 3/8 ÷ 2.54 = .375 ÷ 2.54 ≈ .1476 ≈ .15 inch

18. From equation 1, y = 7 - 2x. Substituting into equation 2, x - 4(7-2x) = 4. Simplifying, x - 28 + 8x = 4.
    This reduces to 9x = 32, so x = 32/9

19. Since there are 3600 seconds in 1 hour, 6 seconds would represent 6/3600 = 1/600 of an hour

20. 1/3 + 5(x-1) = 8. Simplify to 1/3 + 5x - 5 = 8.
    This will reduce to 5x = 12 2/3, so x = 38/15

21. A line perpendicular to the x-axis must have an undefined slope. The equation must be x = constant. The only choice fitting this format is x = 3

22. The receptionist works 40 hours at R/2 dollars per week.
    Thus, the weekly payroll for all three workers is H + 36A + R/2
    (The 40 hours is not used in computing.)

23. The total bill was (5)($12) + (10)($13) + (4)($10) = $230. Company A's bill was $60.
    Thus, $60/$230 $\approx$ 26.1% $\approx$ 26%

24. $50(A/100) = 2A^2$ becomes $A/2 = 2A^2$. Simplifying further, we get $A = 4A^2$ or $A(4A-1) = 0$.
    The two values of A are 0 and 1/4.

25. The number of single males is represented as (5/8) (1/5)(100)% = 12.5%

26. z = .35x and x = .20y. Thus, z = (.35)(.20)y = .07y.
    Then, z is 7% of y.

27. The numerator is |11|-|-9| = 11 - 9 = 2. The denominator is 3|-1| = 3. Thus, the fraction = 2/3

28. Let x = required number of minutes. Then, 1/30 x - 1/50 x = 1 Multiplying by 150, 5x - 3x = 150. Solving, x = 75

29. $\frac{4}{5}x = \frac{2}{5}y$. Then, $\frac{y}{x} = \frac{4}{5} \div \frac{2}{5} = 2$

30. $x = \frac{1}{y}$ becomes xy = 1, which represents a hyperbola.

31. $\frac{5}{4} + \frac{4}{5} + \frac{3}{2} = (25+16+30)/20 = 71/20$. If 71/20 - x = a positive integer, then the only correct values of x are 11/20, 31/20, 51/20.

32. Multiplying the equation by 15x, we get 30 + 9x = 20x. Then, 30 = 11x, so x = 30/11

33. Let 3x = number of applicants, x = 1st year student openings. Over the 4-year period, the number of applicants dropped to .75(3x) = 2.25x and the number of openings rose to 1.12x. Now, 2.25x $\div$ 1.12x $\approx$ 2 to 1

34. $\sqrt{x-25} = 2$. Squaring both sides, x - 25 = 4, so x = 29

35. At the end of 2 hours, their individual <u>distances</u> are 48 miles and 64 miles. Their distance apart is = 80 miles

36. $AC^2 + 3^2 = 6^2$. This simplifies to $AC^2 = 27$.
    Thus, $AC = \sqrt{27} = 3\sqrt{3}$

37. Let x = original length of each side, so that x + 1 = new length of each side of the square. Then, $(x+1)^2 = x^2 + 53$. This simplifies to $x^2 + 2x + 1 = x^2 + 53$. Then, 2x + 1 = 53, so x = 26

38. $3(2)^2 + \sqrt{25} - (-2)^3 = 12 + 5 + 8 = 25$

39. Sine 30° = BC/14 1/2 = BC/14, so BC = 7

40. Probability of 2 red marbles being drawn without replacement is (3/10)(2/9) = 1/15

41. Each pen costs 75/x cents and each pencil costs 57/y cents. Then, 2 pens and 3 pencils cost 2(75/x) + 3(57/y)

42. Let x = number of quarters, 2x = number of dimes.
    Then, .25x + .10(2x) < 9.00
    Solving, x < 20, so, x = 19

43. The new set of numbers is 3 times as large as the original set. Therefore, the mean is 3 times as big, which is 9, and the variance is 3^2 or 9 times as big, which is (9)(3.5) = 31.5

44. Using the diagram shown at the right, for the fence $\overline{BC}$, we'll need 5 posts whose distance from each other is 2 1/2'. (This includes a post at B and a post at C.) Now along $\overline{AB}$, since AB = 20' and $20 \div 2\frac{1}{2} = 8$, we'll need 8 posts (including a post at A). Finally, starting at A and ending at C, we need to place only 20 ÷ 2 1/2 - 1 = 7 posts since a post already exists at A and at C. Thus, the total number of posts is 5 + 8 + 7 = 20

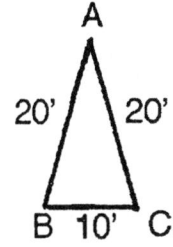

45. (6')(7') = 42 square feet costing $52, which means $52/$42 or $(26/21) per square foot. Now a ceiling 18 ft by 21 ft is 378 square feet and will cost (26/21)(378) = $468

46. Let x, x+2, x+4 represent the three odd numbers. Then, x + x+2 + x+4 = 51. This reduces to 3x + 6 = 51, from which x = 15. The three numbers are 15, 17, 19 and so the largest is 19.

47. From 9:55 AM to 10:15 AM represents 20 minutes.
    Then, 20 minutes/5 hours = 20 minutes/300 minutes, which reduces to 1/15.

48. Volume is (10)(9)(2) = 180 cu.ft. The weight of the liquid is (100)(180) = 18,000 lbs.

49. Cosine $\frac{\pi}{3}$ = .5, which is also the value of - Cosine $\frac{2\pi}{3}$

50. To make $(3x-4)/(4+5y^2)$ as large as possible, we maximize the numerator and minimize the denominator. Given the restriction $5 \leq x \leq 12$ use x = 12. Given the restriction use y = 0. (<u>Note carefully</u> that y = 0 yields a smaller value of $4 + 5y^2$ than y = -2)

———

Table of Contents

§ 2. Definitions

As used in this chapter,

1. "Hazardous employment" means a work or occupation described in section three of this chapter.

2. "Department" means the department of labor of the state of New York;

"Chairman" means the chairman of the workmen's compensation board of the state of New York;

"Commissioner" means the industrial commissioner of the state of New York;

"Board" means the workmen's compensation board of the state of New York;

"Commissioners" means the commissioners of the state insurance fund of the department of labor of the state of New York.

3. "Employer," except when otherwise expressly stated, means a person, partnership, association, corporation, and the legal representatives of a deceased employer, or the receiver or trustee of a person, partnership, association or corporation, having one or more persons in employment, including the state, a municipal corporation, fire district or other political subdivision of the state, and every authority or commission heretofore or hereafter continued or created by the public authorities law. For the purposes of this chapter only "employer" shall also mean a person, partnership, association, corporation, and the legal representatives of a deceased employer, or the receiver or trustee of a person, partnership, association or corporation who delivers or causes to be delivered newspapers or periodicals for delivering or selling and delivering by a newspaper carrier under the age of eighteen years as defined in section thirty-two hundred twenty-eight of the education law. For the purpose of this chapter only, "employer" shall also mean a person, partnership, association, or corporation who leases or otherwise contracts with an operator or lessee for the purpose of driving, operating or leasing a taxicab as so defined in section one hundred forty-eight-a of the vehicle and traffic law, except where such person is an owner-operator of such taxicab who personally regularly operates such vehicle an average of forty or more hours per week and leases such taxicab for some portion of the remaining time, and except if the taxicab is a livery subject to section eighteen-c of this chapter, in which case the livery driver's employer shall only be such employer as is defined in that section. For the purposes of this section only, such an owner-operator shall be deemed to be an employer if he controls, directs, supervises, or has the power to hire or terminate such other person who leases the vehicle.

Notwithstanding any other provision of this chapter and for purposes of this chapter only, "employer" shall mean, with respect to a jockey, apprentice jockey or exercise person licensed under article two or four of the racing, pari-mutuel wagering and breeding law performing services for an owner or trainer in connection with the training or racing of a horse at a facility of a racing association or corporation subject to article two or four of the racing, pari-mutuel wagering and breeding law and subject to the jurisdiction of the New York state racing and wagering board, The New York Jockey Injury Compensation Fund, Inc. and all owners and trainers who are licensed or required to be licensed under article two or four of the racing, pari-mutuel wagering and breeding law at the time of any occurrence for which benefits are payable pursuant to this chapter in respect to the injury or death of such jockey, apprentice jockey or exercise person.

Notwithstanding any other provision of this chapter, and for purposes of this chapter only, the employer of a black car operator, as defined in article six-F of the executive law, shall, on and after the fund liability date, as defined in such article, be the New York black car operators' injury compensation fund, inc. created pursuant to such article.

For the purpose of this chapter only, whether a livery base operating in any locality where liveries must register with a local taxi and limousine commission shall be deemed the "employer" of any livery driver engaging in covered services shall be determined in accordance with section eighteen-c of this chapter.

4. "Employee" means a person engaged in one of the occupations enumerated in section three of this article or who is in the service of an employer whose principal business is that of carrying on or conducting a hazardous employment upon the premises or at the plant, or in the course of his or her employment away from the plant of his or her employer; "employee" shall also mean for the purposes of this chapter any individual performing services in construction for a contractor who does not overcome the presumption of employment as provided under section eight hundred sixty-one-c of the labor law; "employee" shall also mean for the purposes of this chapter any individual performing

services in the commercial goods transportation industry for a commercial goods transportation contractor who does not overcome the presumption of employment as provided under section eight hundred sixty-two-b of the labor law; "employee" shall also mean for the purposes of this chapter civil defense volunteers who are personnel of volunteer agencies sponsored or authorized by a local office under regulations of the civil defense commission, to the extent of the provisions of groups seventeen and nineteen; "employee" shall at the election of a municipal corporation made pursuant to local law duly enacted also mean a member of an auxiliary police organization authorized by local law; and for the purposes of this chapter only a newspaper carrier under the age of eighteen years as defined in section thirty-two hundred twenty-eight of the education law, and shall not include domestic servants except as provided in section three of this chapter, and except where the employer has elected to bring such employees under the law by securing compensation in accordance with the terms of section fifty of this chapter. The term "employee" shall not include persons who are members of a supervised amateur athletic activity operated on a non-profit basis, provided that said members are not also otherwise engaged or employed by any person, firm or corporation participating in said athletic activity, nor shall it include the spouse or minor child of an employer who is a farmer unless the services of such spouse or minor child shall be engaged by said employer under an express contract of hire nor shall it include an executive officer of a corporation who at all times during the period involved owns all of the issued and outstanding stock of the corporation and holds all of the offices pursuant to paragraph (e) of section seven hundred fifteen of the business corporation law or two executive officers of a corporation who at all times during the period involved between them own all of the issued and outstanding stock of such corporation and hold all such offices except as provided in subdivision six of section fifty-four of this chapter provided, however, that where there are two executive officers of a corporation each officer must own at least one share of stock, nor shall it include a self-employed person or a partner of a partnership as defined in section ten of the partnership law who is not covered under a compensation insurance contract or a certificate of self-insurance as provided in subdivision eight of section fifty-four of this chapter, nor shall it include farm laborers except as provided in group fourteen-b of section three of this chapter. If a farm labor contractor recruits or supplies farm laborers for work on a farm, such farm laborers shall for the purposes of this chapter be deemed to be employees of the owner or lessee of such farm. The term "employee" shall not include baby sitters as defined in subdivision three of section one hundred thirty-one and subdivision three of section one hundred thirty-two of the labor law or minors fourteen years of age or over engaged in casual employment consisting of yard work and household chores in and about a one family owner-occupied residence or the premises of a non-profit, non-commercial organization, not involving the use of power-driven machinery. The term "employee" shall not include persons engaged by the owner in casual employment consisting of yard work, household chores and making repairs to or painting in and about a one-family owner-occupied residence. The term "employee" shall not include the services of a licensed real estate broker or sales associate if it be proven that (a) substantially all of the remuneration (whether or not paid in cash) for the services performed by such broker or sales associate is directly related to sales or other output (including the performance of services) rather than to the number of hours worked; (b) the services performed by the broker or sales associate are performed pursuant to a written contract executed between such broker or sales associate and the person for whom the services are performed within the past twelve to fifteen months; and (c) the written contract provided for in paragraph (b) of this subdivision was not executed under duress and contains the following provisions:

(i) that the broker or sales associate is engaged as an independent contractor associated with the person for whom services are performed pursuant to article twelve-A of the real property law and shall be treated as such for all purposes, including but not limited to federal and state taxation, withholding, unemployment insurance and workers' compensation;

(ii) that the broker or sales associate (A) shall be paid a commission on his or her gross sales, if any, without deduction for taxes, which commission shall be directly related to sales or other output; (B) shall not receive any remuneration related to the number of hours worked; and (C) shall not be treated as an employee with respect to such services for federal and state tax purposes;

(iii) that the broker or sales associate shall be permitted to work any hours he or she chooses;

(iv) that the broker or sales associate shall be permitted to work out of his or her own home or the office of the person for whom services are performed;

(v) that the broker or sales associate shall be free to engage in outside employment;

(vi) that the person for whom the services are performed may provide office facilities and supplies for the use of the broker or sales associate, but the broker or sales associate shall otherwise bear his or her own expenses, including but not limited to automobile, travel, and entertainment expenses;

(vii) that the person for whom the services are performed and the broker or sales associate shall comply with the requirements of article twelve-A of the real property law and the regulations pertaining thereto, but such compliance shall not affect the broker or sales associate's status as an independent contractor nor should it be construed as an indication that the broker or sales associate is an employee of the person for whom the services are performed for any purpose whatsoever;

(viii) that the contract and the association created thereby may be terminated by either party thereto at any time upon notice given to the other.

"Employee" shall also mean, for purposes of this chapter, an infant rendering services for the public good as prescribed in sections seven hundred fifty-eight-a and 353.6 of the family court act.

For the purpose of this chapter only, "employee" shall also mean a driver, operator or lessee who contracts with an owner, operator or lessor for the purpose of operating a taxicab as so defined in section one hundred forty-eight-a of the vehicle and traffic law, except where such person leases the taxicab from a person who personally, regularly operates such vehicle an average of forty or more hours per week, and except if the taxicab is a livery subject to section eighteen-c of this chapter, in which case the livery driver's employer shall only be such employer as is defined in that section. For the purposes of this section only, such person shall be deemed to be an employee of the owner-operator if the owner-operator controls, directs, supervises, or has the power to hire or terminate such person.

"Employee" shall also mean, for purposes of this chapter, a professional musician or a person otherwise engaged in the performing arts who performs services as such for a television or radio station or network, a film production, a theatre, hotel, restaurant, night club or similar establishment unless, by written contract, such musician or person is stipulated to be an employee of another employer covered by this chapter. "Engaged in the performing arts" shall mean performing service in connection with the production of or performance in any artistic endeavor which requires artistic or technical skill or expertise.

Notwithstanding any other provision of this chapter, and for purposes of this chapter only, a jockey, apprentice jockey or exercise person licensed under article two or four of the racing, pari-mutuel wagering and breeding law performing services for an owner or trainer in connection with the training or racing of a horse at a facility of a racing association or corporation subject to article two or four of the racing, pari-mutuel wagering and breeding law and subject to the jurisdiction of the New York state racing and wagering board shall be regarded as the "employee" not solely of such owner or trainer, but shall instead be conclusively presumed to be the "employee" of The New York Jockey Injury Compensation Fund, Inc. and also of all owners and trainers who are licensed or required to be licensed under article two or four of the racing, pari-mutuel wagering and breeding law at the time of any occurrence for which benefits are payable pursuant to this chapter in respect of the injury or death of such jockey, apprentice jockey or exercise person.

"Employee" shall also mean, for purposes of this chapter, a professional model, who:

(a) performs modeling services for; or

(b) consents in writing to the transfer of his or her exclusive legal right to the use of his or her name, portrait, picture or image, for advertising purposes or for the purposes of trade, directly to

a retail store, a manufacturer, an advertising agency, a photographer, a publishing company or any other such person or entity, which dictates such professional model's assignments, hours of work or performance locations and which compensates such professional model in return for a waiver of such professional model's privacy rights enumerated above, unless such services are performed pursuant to a written contract wherein it is stated that such professional model is the employee of another employer covered by this chapter. For the purposes of this paragraph, the term "professional model" means a person who, in the course of his or her trade, occupation or profession, performs modeling services. For purposes of this paragraph, the term "modeling services" means the appearance by a professional model in photographic sessions or the engagement of such model in live, filmed or taped modeling performances for remuneration.

Notwithstanding any other provision of this chapter, and for purposes of this chapter only, a black car operator, as defined in article six-F of the executive law, shall, on and after the fund liability date, as defined in such article, be an "employee" of the New York black car operators' injury compensation fund, inc. created pursuant to such article.

"Employee" shall not include, for the purposes of this chapter, the services of a licensed insurance agent or broker if it be proven that (a) substantially all of the remuneration (whether or not paid in cash) for the services performed by such agent or broker is directly related to sales or other output (including the performance of services) rather than to the number of hours worked; (b) such agent is not a life insurance agent receiving a training allowance subsidy described in paragraph three of subsection (e) of section four thousand two hundred twenty-eight of the insurance law; (c) the services performed by the broker or sales associate are performed pursuant to a written contract executed between such broker or sales associate and the person for whom the services are performed; and (d) the written contract provided for in clause (c) of this paragraph was not executed under duress and contains the following provisions:

(i) that the agent or broker is engaged as an independent contractor associated with the person for whom services are performed pursuant to article twenty-one of the insurance law and shall be treated as such for all purposes, including but not limited to federal and state taxation, withholding (other than federal insurance contributions act (FICA) taxes required for full time life insurance agents pursuant to section 3121(d)(3) of the federal internal revenue code), unemployment insurance and workers' compensation;

(ii) that the agent or broker (1) shall be paid a commission on his or her gross sales, if any, without deduction for taxes (other than federal insurance contributions act (FICA) taxes required for full time life insurance agents pursuant to section 3121(d)(3) of the federal internal revenue code), which commission shall be directly related to sales or other output; (2) shall not receive any remuneration related to the number of hours worked; and (3) shall not be treated as an employee with respect to such services for federal and state tax purposes (other than federal insurance contributions act (FICA) taxes required for full time life insurance agents pursuant to section 3121(d)(3) of the federal internal revenue code);

(iii) that the agent or broker shall be permitted to work any hours he or she chooses;

(iv) that the agent or broker shall be permitted to work out of his or her own office or home or the office of the person for whom services are performed;

(v) that the person for whom the services are performed may provide office facilities, clerical support, and supplies for the use of the agent or broker, but the agent or broker shall otherwise bear his or her own expenses, including but not limited to automobile, travel, and entertainment expenses;

(vi) that the person for whom the services are performed and the agent or broker shall comply with the requirements of article twenty-one of the insurance law and the regulations pertaining thereto, but such compliance shall not affect the agent's or broker's status as an independent contractor nor should it be construed as an indication that the agent or broker is an employee of the person for whom the services are performed for any purpose whatsoever;

(vii) that the contract and the association created thereby may be terminated by either party thereto at any time with notice given to the other.

"Employee" shall not include a media sales representative if it be proven that (a) substantially all of the compensation for the services performed by such media sales representative is directly related to sales or other productivity rather than to the number of hours worked; (b) the media sales representative must be incorporated under the laws of this state in order to be considered an independent contractor and shall be solely responsible for the payment of workers' compensation premiums; (c) the services performed by the media sales representative are performed pursuant to a written contract executed between such media sales representative and the person for whom the services are performed; and (d) the written contract provided for in subparagraph (c) of this paragraph was not executed under duress and contains the following provisions:

(i) that the media sales representative is engaged as an independent contractor associated with the person for whom services are performed and shall be treated as such for all purposes, including but not limited to federal and state taxation, withholdings, and workers' compensation;

(ii) that the media sales representative (A) shall be paid a commission based on a fixed fee rate outlined in the written contract, if any, without deduction for taxes, which commission shall be directly related to sales pursuant to price guidelines or other productivity within the sales area; (B) shall not receive any compensation related to the number of hours worked; and (C) shall not be treated as an employee with respect to such services for federal and state tax purposes;

(iii) that the media sales representative shall be permitted to work any hours he or she chooses subject to the restrictions in section three hundred ninety-nine-p of the general business law;

(iv) that the media sales representative may work at any site other than on the premises of the person for whom services are performed;

(v) that the person for whom the services are performed shall not be responsible for any reimbursement expenses other than those outlined in the written contract;

(vi) that the person for whom the services are performed and the media sales representative shall comply with all articles of the labor law that apply to such work other than article eighteen of the labor law, but such compliance shall not affect the media sales representative's status as an independent contractor nor shall it be construed as an indication that the media sales representative is an employee of the person for whom the services are performed for any purpose whatsoever; and

(vii) that the contract and the association created thereby may be terminated by the media sales representative thereto at any time with two weeks' notice given to the person for whom the services are performed.

For the purposes of this subdivision, "media sales representative" shall include any contractor engaged in the sale or renewal of magazine subscriptions or the sale or renewal of magazine advertising space who (i) receives no direction or control on the methods by which they perform services other than training on product characteristics, (ii) are solely in control of their work schedule, and (iii) may refuse any work assignment.

For the purpose of this chapter only, whether a livery driver dispatched by an independent livery base, as those terms are defined in article six-G of the executive law, is an "employee" shall be determined in accordance with section eighteen-c of this chapter.

5. "Employment" includes employment in a trade, business or occupation carried on by the employer for pecuniary gain, or in connection therewith, except where the employer elects to bring his employees within the provisions of this chapter as provided in section three, and except employment as a domestic worker as provided in section three, and except where a town elects to have the provisions of this chapter apply to the town superintendent of highways. "Employment" shall also include, in connection with the civil defense effort and for purposes of this chapter the service of a civil defense volunteer in authorized activities of a volunteer agency sponsored or authorized by a local office as defined in a state defense emergency act. "Employment" shall also include participation with an auxiliary police effort made within a municipal corporation which elected to include auxiliary policemen within the definition of "employee" as authorized by subdivision four of this section and for purposes of this chapter, the services of members or volunteers in activities authorized by local law. The service of a civil defense volunteer who is also an employee recompensed by an employer for service to such employer, shall not be deemed to be in employment of a local office when he is performing civil defense service in his employment or in relation thereto. For the purposes of this chapter only "employment" shall also include the delivery or sale and delivery of newspapers or periodicals by a newspaper carrier as defined in section thirty-two hundred twenty-eight of the education law. The term "employment" shall not include the services of a licensed real estate broker or sales associate if it be proven that (a) substantially all of the remuneration (whether or not paid in cash) for the services performed by such broker or sales associate is directly related to sales or other output (including the performance of services) rather than to the number of hours worked; (b) the services performed by the broker or sales associate are performed pursuant to a written contract executed between such broker or sales associate and the person for whom the services are performed within the past twelve to fifteen months;

and (c) the written contract provided for in paragraph (b) herein was not executed under duress and contains the following provisions:

(i) that the broker or sales associate is engaged as an independent contractor associated with the person for whom services are performed pursuant to article twelve-A of the real property law and shall be treated as such for all purposes, including but not limited to federal and state taxation, withholding, unemployment insurance and workers' compensation;

(ii) that the broker or sales associate (A) shall be paid a commission on his or her gross sales, if any, without deduction for taxes, which commission shall be directly related to sales or other output; (B) shall not receive any remuneration related to the number of hours worked; and (C) shall not be treated as an employee with respect to such services for federal and state tax purposes;

(iii) that the broker or sales associate shall be permitted to work any hours he or she chooses;

(iv) that the broker or sales associate shall be permitted to work out of his or her own home or the office of the person for whom services are performed;

(v) that the broker or sales associate shall be free to engage in outside employment;

(vi) that the person for whom the services are performed may provide office facilities and supplies for the use of the broker or sales associate, but the broker or sales associate shall otherwise bear his or her own expenses, including but not limited to automobile, travel, and entertainment expenses;

(vii) that the person for whom the services are performed and the broker or sales associate shall comply with the requirements of article twelve-A of the real property law and the regulations pertaining thereto, but such compliance shall not affect the broker or sales associate's status as an independent contractor nor should it be construed as an indication that the broker or sales associate is an employee of the person for whom the services are performed for any purpose whatsoever;

(viii) that the contract and the association created thereby may be terminated by either party thereto at any time upon notice given to the other.

For the purpose of this chapter only, "employment" shall also include the service of a driver, operator or lessee of a taxicab as so defined in section one hundred forty-eight-a of the vehicle and traffic law, except where a person leases a taxicab from an owner-operator of a taxicab who, regularly operates the vehicle an average of forty or more hours per week. Such a lessee shall be deemed to be in employment if the lessor controls, directs, supervises, or has the power to hire or terminate the lessee.

Notwithstanding any other provision of this chapter, and for purposes of this chapter only, a jockey, apprentice jockey or exercise person licensed under article two or four of the racing, pari-mutuel wagering and breeding law performing services for an owner or trainer in connection with the training or racing of a horse at a facility of a racing association or corporation subject to article two or four of the racing, pari-mutuel wagering and breeding law and subject to the jurisdiction of the New York state racing and wagering board shall be regarded as in the "employment" not solely of such owner and trainer, but shall instead be conclusively presumed to be in the "employment" of The New York Jockey Injury Compensation Fund, Inc. and of all owners and trainers who are licensed or required to be licensed under article two or four of the racing, pari-mutuel wagering and breeding law, at the time of any occurrence for which benefits are payable pursuant to this chapter in respect of the injury or death of such jockey, apprentice jockey or exercise person. For the purpose of this chapter only, whether a livery driver's performance of covered services, as those terms are defined in article six-G of the executive law, constitutes "employment" shall be determined in accordance with section eighteen-c of this chapter.

Notwithstanding any other provision of this chapter, and for purposes of this chapter only, a black car operator, as that term is defined in article six-F of the executive law, shall, on and after the fund liability date, as that term is defined in such article, be regarded as in the "employment" of the New York black car operators' injury compensation fund, inc. created pursuant to such article.

"Employment" shall not include, for the purposes of this chapter, the services of a licensed insurance agent or broker if it be proven that (a) substantially all of the remuneration (whether or not paid in cash) for the services performed by such agent or broker is directly related to sales or other output (including the performance of services) rather than to the number of hours worked; (b) such agent is not a life insurance agent receiving a training allowance subsidy described in paragraph three of subsection (e) of section four thousand two hundred twenty-eight of the insurance law; (c) the services performed by the agent or broker are performed pursuant to a written contract executed between such agent or broker and the person for whom the services are performed; and (d) the written contract provided for in clause (c) of this paragraph was not executed under duress and contains the following provisions:

(i) that the agent or broker is engaged as an independent contractor associated with the person for whom services are performed pursuant to article twenty-one of the insurance law and shall be treated as such for all purposes, including but not limited to federal and state taxation, withholding (other than federal insurance contributions act (FICA) taxes required for full time life insurance agents pursuant to section 3121(d)(3) of the federal internal revenue code), unemployment insurance and workers' compensation;

(ii) that the agent or broker (1) shall be paid a commission on his or her gross sales, if any, without deduction for taxes (other than federal insurance contributions act (FICA) taxes required for full time life insurance agents pursuant to section 3121(d)(3) of the federal internal revenue code), which commission shall be directly related to sales or other output; (2) shall not receive any remuneration related to the number of hours worked; and (3) shall not be treated as an employee with respect to such services for federal and state tax purposes (other than federal insurance contributions act (FICA) taxes required for full time life insurance agents pursuant to section 3121(d)(3) of the federal internal revenue code);

(iii) that the agent or broker shall be permitted to work any hours he or she chooses;

(iv) that the agent or broker shall be permitted to work out of his or her own office or home or the office of the person for whom services are performed;

(v) that the person for whom the services are performed may provide office facilities, clerical support, and supplies for the use of the agent or broker, but the agent or broker shall otherwise bear his or her own expenses, including but not limited to automobile, travel, and entertainment expenses;

(vi) that the person for whom the services are performed and the agent or broker shall comply with the requirements of article twenty-one of the insurance law and the regulations pertaining thereto, but such compliance shall not affect the agent's or broker's status as an independent contractor nor should it be construed as an indication that the agent or broker is an employee of the person for whom the services are performed for any purpose whatsoever;

(vii) that the contract and the association created thereby may be terminated by either party thereto at any time with notice given to the other.

"Employment" shall not include the services of a media sales representative if it be proven that (A) substantially all of the compensation for the services performed by such media sales representative is directly related to sales or other productivity rather than to the number of hours worked; (B) the media sales representative must be incorporated under the laws of this state in order to be considered an independent contractor and shall be solely responsible for the payment of workers' compensation premiums; (C) the services performed by the media sales representative are performed pursuant to a written contract executed between such media sales representative and the person for whom the services are performed; and (D) the written contract provided for in subparagraph (C) of this paragraph was not executed under duress and contains the following provisions:

(i) that the media sales representative is engaged as an independent contractor associated with the person for whom services are performed and shall be treated as such for all purposes, including but not limited to federal and state taxation, withholdings, and workers' compensation;

(ii) that the media sales representative (A) shall be paid a commission, based on a fixed fee rate outlined in the written contract, if any, without deduction for taxes, which commission shall be directly related to sales pursuant to price guidelines or other productivity within the sales area; (B) shall not receive any compensation related to the number of hours worked; and (C) shall not be treated as an employee with respect to such services for federal and state tax purposes;

(iii) that the media sales representative shall be permitted to work any hours he or she chooses subject to the restrictions in section three hundred ninety-nine-p of the general business law;

(iv) that the media sales representative may work at any site other than on the premises of the person for whom services are performed;

(v) that the person for whom the services are performed shall not be responsible for any reimbursement expenses other than those outlined in the written contract;

(vi) that the person for whom the services are performed and the media sales representative shall comply with all articles of the labor law that apply to such work other than article eighteen of the labor law, but such compliance shall not affect the media sales representative's status as an independent contractor nor shall it be construed as an indication that the media sales representative is an employee of the person for whom the services are performed for any purpose whatsoever; and

(vii) that the contract and the association created thereby may be terminated by the media sales representative thereto at any time with two weeks' notice given to the person for whom the services are performed.

For the purposes of this subdivision, "media sales representative" shall include any contractor engaged in the sale or renewal of magazine subscriptions or the sale or renewal of magazine advertising space who (i) receives no direction or control on the methods by which they perform services other than training on product characteristics, (ii) are solely in control of their work schedule, and (iii) may refuse any work assignment.

6. "Compensation" means the money allowance payable to an employee or to his dependents as provided for in this chapter, and includes funeral benefits provided therein.

7. "Injury" and "personal injury" mean only accidental injuries arising out of and in the course of employment and such disease or infection as may naturally and unavoidably result therefrom. The terms "injury" and "personal injury" shall not include an injury which is solely mental and is based on workrelated stress if such mental injury is a direct consequence of a lawful personnel decision involving a disciplinary action, work evaluation, job transfer, demotion, or termination taken in good faith by the employer.

8. "Death" when mentioned as a basis for the right to compensation means only death resulting from such injury.

9. "Wages" means the money rate at which the service rendered is recompensed under the contract of hiring in force at the time of the accident, including the reasonable value of board, rent, housing, lodging or similar advantage received from the employer, or in the case of (a) a civil defense volunteer, (b) a volunteer worker in a state department as provided in group sixteen of subdivision one of section three of this chapter, (c) a volunteer worker for a social services district as provided in group seventeen of subdivision one of section three of this chapter, (d) a county fire coordinator, a deputy county fire coordinator or a comparable county official to whom the provisions of group fifteen-a of subdivision one of section three of this chapter are applicable, who is also a volunteer firefighter or ambulance worker, (e) a fire district officer whether elective or appointive and whether or not he is compensated for his services or a paid fire or ambulance district employee, (f) a state fire instructor whose compensation is paid in whole or in part by the state, (g) an enrolled member of a fire company who, is not a volunteer firefighter, receives compensation for his services and is not a full-time fireman, known as a "call fireman", (h) persons who are performing services for a public or not-for-profit corporation, association, institution or agency organized as an unincorporated association or duly incorporated under the laws of this state in fulfillment of a sentence of probation or of conditional discharge, or persons performing such services pursuant to the provisions of section 170.55 or 170.56 of the criminal procedure law, (i) an auxiliary policeman in a municipal corporation which elected to include such persons within the definition of "employee" as authorized by subdivision four of this section, or (j) a duly appointed member of a regional hazardous materials incidents team recognized under section two hundred nine-y of the general municipal law, such money rate applying in his regular vocation or the amount of the regular earnings of such volunteer, coordinator, instructor, or comparable officer, fire or ambulance district officer or employee or call fireman, or team member as the case may be, in his regular vocation, plus any amount earned as such a coordinator, instructor or comparable officer, or as such a fire or ambulance district officer or employee or call fireman or team member, provided, however, that in no event shall the average weekly wage be fixed at less than thirty dollars regardless of whether or not such volunteer, coordinator, instructor or comparable officer or fire or ambulance district officer or employee or call fireman or team member had gainful employment elsewhere at the time of the injury.

The wages of a livery driver, as defined in article six-G of the executive law, shall be calculated in accordance with this paragraph. The chair shall promulgate regulations, in consultation with the independent livery driver benefit fund, and all local taxi and limousine commissions, as defined in article six-G of the executive law, establishing amounts that livery drivers are presumptively deemed to receive in annual wages, and may vary such presumptive wage by such geographic region or political subdivision of the state as the chair may set. Such regulations may establish other factors or criteria for determining the presumptive wage. The presumptive wage shall be set based on the chair's findings as to the amount earned by livery drivers, and their expenses. A livery driver or the livery driver's employer, including the independent livery driver benefit fund, may rebut the presumptive wage by competent evidence that the driver's actual wages for covered services, as defined in article six-G of the executive law, were different. The chair shall promulgate such other rules as are necessary to compute livery driver wages in accordance with this paragraph.

10. "State fund" means the state insurance fund provided for in article five of this chapter.

11. "Child" shall include a posthumous child, a child legally adopted prior to the injury of the employee; and a step-child or child born out of wedlock dependent upon the deceased.

12. "Insurance carrier" shall include the state fund, stock corporations, mutual corporations or reciprocal insurers with which employers have insured, and employers permitted to pay compensation directly under the provisions of subdivisions three, three-a or four of section fifty of this chapter. For purposes of this chapter, a nonprofit property/casualty insurance company which is licensed pursuant to subsection (b) of section six thousand seven hundred four of the insurance law shall be deemed a stock corporation and a nonprofit property/casualty insurance company which is licensed as a reciprocal insurer pursuant to subsection (c) of section six thousand seven hundred four of the insurance law shall be deemed a reciprocal insurer.

13. "Manufacture," "construction," "operation" and "installation" shall include "repair," "demolition," "fabrication" and "alteration" and shall include all work done in connection with the repair of plants, buildings, grounds and approaches of all places where any of the hazardous employments are being carried on, operated or conducted.

14. "Minor" means a person who has not attained the age of eighteen years.

15. "Occupational disease" means a disease resulting from the nature of employment and contracted therein.

16. "New York state average weekly wage" shall mean the average weekly wage of the state of New York for the previous calendar year as reported by the commissioner of labor to the superintendent of financial services on March thirty-first.

17. A "substantially owned affiliated entity" of any person means the parent company of the person, any subsidiary of the person, or any entity in which the parent of the person owns more than fifty percent of the voting stock, or an entity in which one or more of the top five shareholders of the person individually or collectively also owns a controlling share of the voting stock, or an entity which exhibits any other indicia of control over the person or over which the person exhibits control, regardless of whether or not the controlling party or parties have any identifiable or documented ownership interest. Such indicia shall include: power or responsibility over employment decisions; access to and/or use of the relevant entity's assets or equipment; power or responsibility over contracts of the person; responsibility for maintenance or submission of certified payroll records; and influence over the business decisions of the relevant entity.

18. [Repealed]

19. A "claim for reimbursement" from the special disability fund means an application to the board under paragraph (f) of subdivision eight of section fifteen of this chapter for a determination that the special disability fund is liable in the first instance for any reimbursement to the insurance carrier, self-insured employer or state insurance fund.

20. A "request for reimbursement" from the special disability fund means an application to the special disability fund for reimbursement for specific costs, subsequent to a determination by the board that the special disability fund is liable to provide reimbursement on the claim.

21. The "workers' compensation rating board" or the "New York workers' compensation rating board" shall mean the compensation insurance rating board until February first, two thousand eight, and thereafter the[1]superintendent of financial services or other entity designated by the superintendent of financial services for collection and analysis of data or such other purposes as set forth in this chapter.

22. "Cost of compensation" means the amount that an employer must pay to secure compensation as calculated in accordance with regulation of the board or, in the absence of such regulation, based on average market rates for a comparable employer.

23. "Special disability fund advisory committee" shall mean an advisory committee to the workers' compensation board, acting by a majority thereof, solely with respect to the special fund entitled the special disability fund, composed of the director of the budget, the commissioner of labor, the commissioner of taxation and finance, the chair of the workers' compensation board, and the superintendent of financial services.

§ 13. Treatment and care of injured employees

(a) The employer shall promptly provide for an injured employee such medical, dental, surgical, optometric or other attendance or treatment, nurse and hospital service, medicine, optometric services, crutches, eye-glasses, false teeth, artificial eyes, orthotics, prosthetic devices, functional assistive and adaptive devices and apparatus for such period as the nature of the injury or the process of recovery may require. The employer shall be liable for the payment of the expenses of medical, dental, surgical, optometric or other attendance or treatment, nurse and hospital service, medicine, optometric services, crutches, eye-glasses, false teeth, artificial eyes, orthotics, prosthetic devices, functional assistive and adaptive devices and apparatus, as well as artificial members of the body or other devices or appliances necessary in the first instance to replace, support or relieve a portion or part of the body resulting from and necessitated by the injury of an employee, for such period as the nature of the injury or the process of recovery may require, and the employer shall also be liable for replacements or repairs of such artificial members of the body or such other devices, eye-glasses, false teeth, artificial eyes, orthotics, prosthetic devices, functional assistive and adaptive devices or appliances necessitated by ordinary wear or loss or damage to a prosthesis, with or without bodily injury to the employee. Damage to or loss of a prosthetic device shall be deemed an injury except that no disability benefits shall be payable with respect to such injury under section fifteen of this article. Such a replacement or repair of artificial members of the body or such other devices, eye-glasses, false teeth, artificial eyes, orthotics, prosthetic devices, functional assistive and adaptive devices or appliances or the providing of medical treatment and care as defined herein shall not constitute the payment of compensation under section twenty-five-a of this article. All fees and other charges for such treatment and services shall be limited to such charges as prevail in the same community for similar treatment of injured persons of a like standard of living.

The chair shall prepare and establish a schedule for the state, or schedules limited to defined localities, of charges and fees for such medical treatment and care, and including all medical, dental, surgical, optometric or other attendance or treatment, nurse and hospital service, medicine, optometric services, crutches, eye-glasses, false teeth, artificial eyes, orthotics, prosthetic devices, functional assistive and adaptive devices and apparatus in accordance with and to be subject to change pursuant to rules promulgated by the chair. Before preparing such schedule for the state or schedules for limited localities the chair shall request the president of the medical society of the state of New York and the president of the New York state osteopathic medical society to submit to him or her a report on the amount of remuneration deemed by such society to be fair and adequate for the types of medical care to be rendered under this chapter, but consideration shall be given to the view of other interested parties. In the case of physical therapy fees schedules the chair shall request the president of a recognized professional association representing physical therapists in the state of New York to submit to him or her a report on the amount of remuneration deemed by such association to be fair and reasonable for the type of physical therapy services rendered under this chapter, but consideration shall be given to the views of other interested parties. The chair shall also prepare and establish a schedule for the state, or schedules limited to defined localities, of charges and fees for outpatient hospital services not covered under the medical fee schedule previously referred to in this subdivision, to be determined in accordance with and to be subject to change pursuant to rules promulgated by the chair. Before preparing such schedule for the state or schedules for limited localities the chair shall request the president of the hospital association of New York state to submit to him or her a report on the amount of remuneration deemed by such association to be fair and adequate for the types of hospital outpatient care to be rendered under this chapter, but consideration shall be given to the views of other interested parties. In the case of occupational therapy fees schedules the chair shall request the president of a recognized professional association representing occupational therapists in the state of New York to submit to him or her a report on the amount of remuneration deemed by such association to be fair and reasonable for the type of occupational therapy services rendered under this chapter, but consideration shall be given to the views of other interested parties. The amounts payable by the employer for such treatment and services shall be the fees and charges established by such schedule. Nothing in this schedule, however, shall prevent voluntary payment of amounts higher or lower than the fees and charges fixed therein, but no physician rendering medical treatment or care, and no physical or occupational therapist rendering their respective physical or occupational therapy services may receive payment in any higher amount unless such increased amount has been authorized by the employer, or by decision as provided in section thirteen-g of this article. Nothing in this section shall be construed as preventing the employment of a duly authorized physician on a salary basis by an authorized compensation medical bureau or laboratory.

 (b) In the case of persons, injured outside of this state, but entitled to compensation or benefits under this chapter, the provisions as to selection of authorized physicians shall be inapplicable. In such cases the employer shall promptly provide all necessary medical treatment and care but if the employer fail to provide the same, after request by the injured employee such injured employee may do so at the expense of the employer. The employee shall not be entitled to recover any amount expended by him for such treatment or services unless he shall have requested the employer to furnish the same and the employer shall have refused or neglected to do so, or unless the nature of the injury required such treatment and services and the employer or his superintendent or foreman having knowledge of such injury shall have neglected to provide the same; nor shall any claim for medical or surgical treatment be valid and enforceable, as against such employer, unless within twenty days following the first treatment, the physician giving such treatment, furnish to the employer and the chairman a report of such injury and treatment, on a form prescribed by the chairman. The board may, however, by the unanimous vote of a panel of not less than three members qualified to act, excuse the failure to give such notice within twenty days when it finds it to be in the interest of justice to do so, and may, subject to the limitations contained in section twenty-eight of this chapter, make an award for the reasonable value of such medical or surgical treatment. All fees and other charges for such treatment and services, whether furnished by the employer or otherwise, shall be subject to regulation by the board as provided in section twenty-four of this chapter, and shall be limited to such charges as prevail in the same community for similar treatment of injured persons of a like standard of living.

(c) The liability of an employer for medical treatment as herein provided shall not be affected by the fact that his employee was injured through the fault or negligence of a third party, not in the same employ. The employer shall, however, have an additional cause of action against such third party to recover any amounts paid by him for such medical treatment, in like manner as provided in section twenty-nine of this chapter.

(d) (1) In the event that an insurer or health benefits plan makes payments for medical and/or hospital services for or on behalf of an injured employee they shall be entitled to be reimbursed for such payments by the carrier or employer within the limits of the medical and hospital fee schedules if the board determines that the claim is compensable. For the purposes of this section, an insurer or health benefits plan includes a medical expense indemnity corporation, a health or hospital service corporation, a commercial insurance company licensed to write accident and health insurance in the state of New York, a health maintenance organization operating in accordance with article forty-three of the insurance law or article forty-four of the public health law, or a self-insured or self-funded health care benefits plan operated by, or on behalf of, any business, municipality or other entity (including an employee welfare fund as defined in article forty-four of the insurance law or any other union trust fund or union health benefits plan). Notwithstanding any other provision of law, in no event shall the carrier or employer be required to reimburse the insurer or health benefits plan in an amount greater than the amount paid for medical and hospital services for or on behalf of the injured employee by such corporation or company; provided, however, if the carrier or employer does not reimburse the insurer or health benefits plan within thirty days after the board determines that the claim is compensable, the carrier or employer shall reimburse the insurer or health benefits plan at the amount the carrier or employer would be obligated to reimburse the hospital or other provider of medical services if the carrier or employer made payment directly to the provider of medical and/or hospital services pursuant to this chapter (or, in the case of inpatient hospital services, pursuant to paragraphs (b) and (b-1) of subdivision one of section twenty-eight hundred seven-c of the public health law). Upon reimbursement to the insurer or health benefits plan pursuant to this subdivision, the carrier or employer shall be relieved of liability for the medical and/or hospital services for which payment has been made by the insurer or health benefits plan.

(2) An insurer or health benefits plan entitled to reimbursement pursuant to paragraph one of this subdivision shall receive copies of the hearing and decision notices and shall develop with the carrier or employer its own mechanisms and standard operating procedures for payment of undisputed claims for reimbursement. In cases of disputed claims for reimbursement that are filed with the board within three years of the date of payment for services rendered by the health care provider or within ninety days of the effective date of a chapter of the laws of nineteen hundred ninety-two, entitled "AN ACT to amend the workers' compensation law, in relation to reimbursement of insurers and health benefit plans", whichever is later, the sole remedy of the insurer or health benefit plan to recover on a claim arising pursuant to this subdivision shall be the submission of the controversy to mandatory arbitration or other alternative dispute resolution procedures as defined by rules and regulations promulgated by the chair in accordance with subdivision (h) of this section.

(e) The board, on its own motion, or a referee, upon the recommendation of the compensation medical director for the board, hearing a claim for compensation may require examination of any claimant, or of the testimony, reports and exhibits, or both, by a physician especially qualified with respect to the diagnosis or treatment of the disability for which compensation is claimed; and may require a report from such physician on the diagnosis, the causal relationship between the alleged injury and subsequent disability or death, proper treatment, and the extent of the disability of such claimant. The employer or his or her insurance carrier shall pay for such examination in an amount to be directed by the chairman.

The chairman may in his discretion designate physicians of outstanding qualifications in such fields of medicine as he deems essential in order to ascertain the diagnosis, the causal relationship between the alleged injury and subsequent disability, the type of medical care and operative procedure requisite in particular cases where such matters are not readily determinable by the regularly employed medical examiners of the board. Each of such physicians shall have had, prior to his or her designation, at least five years of practice in the field with respect to which he or she is designated, and shall receive a fee for each case, or shall be paid on a per diem basis, as determined by the chairman. Claimants may be required to submit to examination by such physicians in the manner hereinbefore specified. The contents of reports of designated physicians when introduced in evidence shall constitute prima facie evidence of fact as to the matter contained therein, and the makers of such reports shall be subject to examination upon demand and shall be paid an additional fee, as determined by the chairman, for testifying in each case.

(f) Copies of medical reports of claimant's attending physician or medical consultant, made pursuant to this chapter subsequent to the date of the request provided for in this subdivision and antedating not more than thirty days, shall be transmitted by the physician or consultant to the claimant's licensed representative or attorney representing the claimant before the board upon his written request therefor accompanied by a notice of his retainer and consent to such transmittal signed by the claimant.

(g) Every hospital operating in the state shall, within twenty days of receiving a written request by a claimant, claimant's representative, employer, carrier or special fund created under this chapter, provide to such claimant, claimant's representative, employer, carrier or special fund for use in board proceedings the medical records of an employee who has received treatment in such hospital and who is claiming benefits under this chapter. Each hospital shall designate at least one officer or employee who shall be responsible for provision of such records on written request, and to whom the board, claimant, claimant's, employer, carrier representative or special fund may address informal inquiries regarding provision of such records.

No hospital shall be required to produce the records of any claimant pursuant to this section without receiving the cost of copying such records as determined by the chair. Such cost shall be paid by the requesting party except that the employer or carrier or special fund shall reimburse a claimant or claimant's representative the cost of an initial set of such records where the request is made by a claimant or claimant's representative. Should the hospital not be able to provide the requested records within twenty days, they shall notify in writing the party requesting the records of the reason why the records were not provided and the date on which they will be provided. Such date shall be within a reasonable period of time, but shall not exceed thirty days. Failure to either provide the records within twenty days or to provide a reason why the records have not been provided shall subject the hospital to a fine of two hundred dollars, which shall be imposed by the chair payable to the board upon finding that this subdivision has not been complied with. No hospital shall be required to produce the records of any claimant without receiving its customary fees or charges for reproduction of such records.

(h) (1) The chair shall require the performance of computer searches to identify injured employees who, with respect to the same injury or illness, have filed claims under the provisions of this chapter and made claims to, or on their behalf with, a payor of medical payments eligible for reimbursement pursuant to this section. Such searches shall be done at least quarterly upon request of payors and upon submission to the board of computer tapes containing the information the chair shall need to identify injured employees who file dual claims under this section. At least quarterly, the chair shall identify injured employees who have filed dual claims by social security number and workers' compensation board number and shall notify the payor of such results.

(2) Such payor shall use the information of dual filings solely for the purpose of reimbursement from the carrier or employer. The chair, upon a finding that such entity has used the information for purposes other than reimbursement from the carrier or employer, may, after hearing, impose a penalty of not more than ten thousand dollars and may prohibit such entity from receiving information under this subdivision for up to three years.

(3) The chair shall adopt rules and regulations to carry out the provisions of this section, which rules and regulations shall provide for alternative dispute resolution procedures for settlement of disputed claims for reimbursement under subdivision (d) of this section including but not limited to referral and submission of disputed claims to mandatory arbitration with private arbitration associations. Such rules and regulations may provide for a reasonable fee to be charged to payors for computer searches. Claims for computer searches submitted to the board prior to March thirty-first, nineteen hundred ninety-two, may be submitted with a payment date on or after April first, nineteen hundred eighty-eight. Claims for reimbursement submitted after March thirty-first, nineteen hundred ninety-two, shall have a payment date that is no later than three years prior to the date of submission of the claim for matching purposes to the board. If disputed, these claims shall be resolved through the dispute resolution procedures set forth in this section. Upon resolution of the reimbursement dispute in accordance with this section, the amount paid to the prevailing party shall be increased by the amount of any fee paid to the arbitrator or incurred by reason of any other alternate dispute resolution procedure.

(i) (1) When a claimant or pharmacy submits a claim to the employer or its carrier for payment of prescribed medicine or for reimbursement of the cost of prescribed medicine which the employer is required to provide under this section, the employer or carrier shall pay the amount prescribed by the fee schedule adopted under section thirteen-o of this article, or if the prescribed medicine is not included on the current fee schedule, the usual and customary charges for such prescribed medicine, within forty-five days of receipt of the claim, unless the liability of the employer or carrier on the claim for which the claimant seeks payment or reimbursement of payment for the prescribed medicine is not established, or the prescribed medicine is not for a causally related condition.

(2) Where the liability of the employer or carrier on the claim for which the claimant seeks payment or reimbursement of payment for the prescribed medicine or reimbursement for payment of prescribed medicine is not established, or is not for a causally related condition, the employer or carrier shall pay any undisputed portion of the claim in accordance with this section and notify the claimant or pharmacy, as appropriate, in writing within forty-five days of receipt of the claim:

(i) that the claim is not being paid and explaining the reasons for nonpayment; or

(ii) to request all additional information reasonably needed to determine the employer's or carrier's liability for the claim. Upon receipt of the information requested in this subparagraph, the employer or carrier shall comply with paragraph one of this subdivision.

(3) Each claim for payment of prescribed medicine or reimbursement for payment of prescribed medicine that is processed in violation of this section shall constitute a separate violation. In addition to the other penalties provided in this chapter, any employer or carrier that fails to reimburse the claimant or pay the pharmacy, as appropriate and as required in this section shall be obligated to pay to the claimant or pharmacy the amount prescribed on the fee schedule adopted under section thirteen-o of this article, or if the prescribed medicine is not included on the current fee schedule, the usual and customary charges for the prescribed medicine plus simple interest at the rate set forth in section five thousand four of the civil practice law and rules.

(4) Nothing in this subdivision shall prohibit employers or carriers from agreeing to or arranging for direct billing by the pharmacy to the employer or carrier for the cost of prescribed medicine, in order for claimants to more promptly receive prescribed medicine for which employers and carriers are liable under this section.

(5) Notwithstanding any other provision of this chapter, if an employer or carrier has contracted with a pharmacy to provide prescribed medicine to claimants, then such employer or carrier may require claimants to obtain all prescribed medicines from the pharmacy with which it has contracted, except if a medical emergency occurs and it would not be reasonably possible to obtain immediately required prescribed medicine from the pharmacy with which the employer or carrier has a contract. An employer or carrier that requires claimants to obtain prescribed medicines from a pharmacy with which it has a contract must notify claimants of the pharmacy or pharmacies with which it has a contract, the locations and addresses of the pharmacy or pharmacies, if applicable, how to initially fill and refill prescriptions through the mail, internet, telephone or other means, and any other required information that must be supplied to the pharmacy or pharmacies. If the pharmacy or pharmacies with which the employer or carrier contracts does not offer mail order service and does not have a physical location within a reasonable distance from the claimant, as defined by regulation of the board, the claimant may obtain prescribed medicines at the pharmacy or pharmacies of his or her choice and the employer or carrier will be liable for such charges in accordance with the fee schedule prescribed in section thirteen-o of this chapter.

§ 13-a. Selection of authorized physician by employee.

(1) An injured employee may, when care is required, select to treat him or her any physician authorized by the chair to render medical care, as hereafter provided. If for any reason during the period when medical treatment and care is required, the employee wishes to transfer his or her treatment and care to another authorized physician, he or she may do so, in accordance with rules prescribed by the chair. In such instance the remuneration of the physician whose services are being dispensed with shall be limited to the value of treatment rendered at fees as established in the schedule for his or her location, unless payment in higher amounts has been approved as authorized in section thirteen, paragraph a. If a claimant shall receive treatment in any hospital or other institution

operated in whole or in part by the state of New York, the employer shall be liable for food, clothing and maintenance furnished by the hospital or other institution to such employee. If the employee is unable due to the nature of the injury to select such authorized physician and the emergency nature of the injury requires immediate medical treatment and care, or if he or she does not desire to select a physician, and in writing so advises the employer, the employer shall promptly provide him or her with the necessary medical care, provided however, that nothing herein contained shall operate to prevent such employee, when subsequently able to do so, from selecting for continuance of any medical treatment or care required, any physician authorized by the chair to render medical care as hereinafter provided.

(2) The chairman shall prescribe the form of a notice informing employees of their privilege under this chapter, and such notice shall be posted and maintained by the employer in a conspicuous place or places in and about his place or places of business.

(3) The employer shall have the right to transfer the care of an injured employee from the attending physician, whether chosen originally by the employee or by the employer, to another authorized physician (1) if the interest of the injured employee necessitates the transfer or (2) if the physician has not been authorized to treat injured employees under this act or (3) if he has not been authorized under this act to treat the particular injury or condition as provided by section thirteen-b (2). An authorized physician from whom the case has been transferred shall have the right of appeal to an arbitration committee as provided in subdivision two of section thirteen-g and if said arbitration committee finds that the transfer was not authorized by this section, said employer shall pay to the physician a sum equal to the total fee earned by the physician to whom the care of the injured employee has been transferred, or such proportion of said fee as the arbitration committee shall deem adequate.

(4) (a) No claim for medical or surgical treatment shall be valid and enforceable, as against such employer, or employee, unless within forty-eight hours following the first treatment the physician giving such treatment furnishes to the employer and directly to the chair a preliminary notice of such injury and treatment, within fifteen days thereafter a more complete report and subsequent thereto progress reports if requested in writing by the chair, board, employer or insurance carrier at intervals of not less than three weeks apart or at less frequent intervals if requested on forms prescribed by the chair. The board may excuse failure to give such notices within the designated periods when it finds it to be in the interest of justice to do so.

(b) Upon receipt of the notice provided for by paragraph (a) of this subdivision, the employer, the carrier, and the claimant each shall be entitled to have the claimant examined by a physician authorized by the chair in accordance with sections thirteen-b and one hundred thirty-seven of this chapter, at a medical facility convenient to the claimant and in the presence of the claimant's physician, and refusal by the claimant to submit to such independent medical examination at such time or times as may reasonably be necessary in the opinion of the board, shall bar the claimant from recovering compensation for any period during which he or she has refused to submit to such examination. No hospital shall be required to produce the records of any claimant without receiving its customary fees or charges for reproduction of such records.

(c) Where it would place an unreasonable burden upon the employer or carrier to arrange for, or for the claimant to attend, an independent medical examination by an authorized physician, the employer or carrier shall arrange for such examination to be performed by a qualified physician in a medical facility convenient to the claimant.

(d) The independent medical examiner shall provide such reports and shall submit to investigation as required by the chair.

(e) In order to qualify as admissible medical evidence, for purposes of adjudicating any claim under this chapter, any report submitted to the board by an independent medical examiner licensed by the state of New York shall include the following:

(i) a signed statement certifying that the report is a full and truthful representation of the independent medical examiner's professional opinion with respect to the claimant's condition:

(ii) such examiner's board issued authorization number;

(iii) the name of the individual or entity requesting the examination;

(iv) if applicable, the registration number as required by section thirteen-n of this article; and

(v) such other information as the chair may require by regulation.

Any report by an independent medical examiner who is not authorized and who performs an independent medical examination in accordance with paragraph (c) of this subdivision, which is to be used as medical evidence under this chapter, shall include in the report such information as the chair may require by regulation.

(5) No claim for specialist consultations, surgical operations, physiotherapeutic or occupational therapy procedures, x-ray examinations or special diagnostic laboratory tests costing more than one thousand dollars shall be valid and enforceable, as against such employer, unless such special services shall have been authorized by the employer or by the board, or unless such authorization has been unreasonably withheld, or withheld for a period of more than thirty calendar days from receipt of a request for authorization, or unless such special services are required in an emergency, provided, however, that the basis for a denial of such authorization by the employer must be based on a conflicting second opinion rendered by a physician authorized by the board. The board, with the approval of the superintendent of financial services, shall issue and maintain a list of pre-authorized procedures under this section.

(6) Any interference by any person with the selection by an injured employee of an authorized physician to treat him, except when the selection is made pursuant to article ten-A of this chapter, and the improper influencing or attempt by any person improperly to influence the medical opinion of any physician who has treated or examined an injured employee, shall be a misdemeanor; provided, however, that it shall not constitute interference or improper influence if, in the presence of such injured employee's physician, an employer, his carrier or agent should recommend or provide information concerning rehabilitation services or the availability thereof to an injured employee or his family.

(7)(a) Notwithstanding any other provision of this chapter to the contrary, any insurance carrier authorized to transact the business of workers' compensation insurance in this state, self-insurer or the state insurance fund may contract with a network or networks, legally and properly organized, to perform diagnostic tests, x-ray examinations, magnetic resonance imaging, or other radiological examinations or tests of claimants and may require claimant to obtain or undergo such diagnostic test, x-ray examinations, magnetic resonance imaging or other radiological examinations or tests with a provider or at a facility that is affiliated with the network or networks with which the carrier contracts, except if a medical emergency occurs requiring an immediate diagnostic test, x-ray examination, magnetic resonance imaging or other radiological examination or test or if the network with which the insurance carrier, self-insurer or the state insurance fund contracts does not have a provider or facility able to perform the examination or test within a reasonable distance from the claimant's residence or place of employment, as defined by regulation of the board.

(b) Any insurance carrier, self-insurer or the state insurance fund which requires claimants to obtain or undergo diagnostic tests, x-ray examinations, magnetic resonance imaging or other radiological examinations or tests with a provider or at a facility affiliated with a network or networks with which it contracts, must notify the claimant of the name and contact information for the network or networks at the same time the written statement of the claimant's rights as required by subdivision two of section one hundred ten of this chapter or immediately after imposing such requirement if the time period within which the written statement of the claimant's rights as required by subdivision two of section one hundred ten of this chapter has expired.

(c) At the time a request for authorization for special diagnostic tests, x-ray examinations, magnetic resonance imaging or other radiological examinations or tests costing more than one thousand dollars as required by subdivision five of this section is approved, the insurance carrier, self-insurer or state insurance fund, or if so delegated the network with which the insurance carrier, self-insurer or state insurance fund has contracted, shall notify the physician requesting authorization of the requirement that the claimant obtain or undergo the special diagnostic test, x-ray examination, magnetic resonance imaging or other radiological examination or test with a provider or at a facility affiliated with the network or networks with which it has contracted, the contact information for the network and a list of the providers and facilities within the claimant's geographic location, as defined by regulation of the board. The claimant, in consultation with the provider who requested the special diagnostic test, x-ray examination, magnetic resonance imaging or other radiological test or exam, will determine the provider or facility from within the network which will perform such diagnostic test, x-ray examination, magnetic resonance imaging or other radiological examination or test.

(d) The results of the special diagnostic test, x-ray examination, magnetic resonance imaging or other radiological test or exam must be sent to the physician who requested the test or exam immediately upon completion of the report detailing the results.

§ 14. Weekly wages basis of compensation

Except as otherwise provided in this chapter, the average weekly wages of the injured employee at the time of the injury shall be taken as the basis upon which to compute compensation or death benefits, and shall be determined as follows:

1. If the injured employee shall have worked in the employment in which he was working at the time of the accident, whether for the same employer or not, during substantially the whole of the year immediately preceding his injury, his average annual earnings shall consist of three hundred times the average daily wage or salary for a six-day worker, and two hundred sixty times the average daily wage or salary for a five-day worker, which he shall have earned in such employment during the days when so employed;

2. If the injured employee shall not have worked in such employment during substantially the whole of such year, his average annual earnings, if a six-day worker, shall consist of three hundred times the average daily wage or salary, and, if a five-day worker, two hundred and sixty times the average daily wage or salary, which an employee of the same class working substantially the whole of such immediately preceding year in the same or in a similar employment in the same or a neighboring place shall have earned in such employment during the days when so employed;

3. If either of the foregoing methods of arriving at the annual average earnings of an injured employee cannot reasonably and fairly be applied, such annual average earnings shall be such sum as, having regard to the previous earnings of the injured employee and of other employees of the same or most similar class, working in the same or most similar employment, or other employment as defined in this chapter, in the same or neighboring locality, shall reasonably represent the annual earning capacity of the injured employee in the employment in which he was working at the time of the accident, provided, however, his average annual earnings shall consist of not less than two hundred times the average daily wage or salary which he shall have earned in such employment during the days when so employed, further provided, however, that if the injured employee shall have been in the military or naval service of the United States or of the state of New York within twelve months prior to his injury, and his average annual earnings cannot be fairly determined under subdivisions one and two, then the average annual earnings shall be determined by multiplying his average daily wage during the days so employed by not less than two hundred and forty;

4. The average weekly wages of an employee shall be one-fifty-second part of his average annual earnings;

5. If it be established that the injured employee was under the age of twenty-five when injured, and that under normal conditions his wages would be expected to increase, that fact may be considered in arriving at his average weekly wages.

6. If the injured employee is concurrently engaged in more than one employment at the time of injury, the employee's average weekly wages shall be calculated upon the basis of wages earned from all concurrent employments covered under this chapter. The employer in whose employment the employee was injured shall be liable for the benefits that would have been payable if the employee had had no other employment. Any additional benefits resulting from the increase in average weekly wages due to the employee's concurrent employments shall be payable in the first instance by the employer in whose employment the employee was injured and shall be reimbursed by the special disability fund created under subdivision eight of section fifteen of this article, but only if such claim is presented in

accordance with subparagraph two of paragraph (h) of subdivision eight of section fifteen of this article. The employer in whose employment the employee was injured shall be liable for all medical costs.

7. The average weekly wages of a jockey, apprentice jockey or exercise person licensed under article two or four of the racing, pari-mutuel wagering and breeding law shall be computed based upon all of the earnings of such jockey, apprentice jockey or exercise person, including those derived from outside of the state.

§ 14-a. Double compensation and death benefits when minors illegally employed

1. Compensation, death benefits, and awards to the commissioner of taxation and finance in accordance with subdivision nine of section fifteen and section twenty-five-a, as provided in this article, shall be double the amount otherwise payable if the injured employee at the time of the accident is a minor employed, permitted or suffered to work in violation of any provision of the labor law or in violation of any rule heretofore or hereafter adopted by the board of standards and appeals pursuant to subdivision four of section one hundred thirty-three of said law.

An employer who knowingly permits or suffers a newspaper carrier to work in violation of section thirty-two hundred twenty-eight of the education law, shall be liable for the increased awards provided by this section.

2. The employer alone and not the insurance carrier shall be liable for the increased compensation, increased death benefits, or awards to the commissioner of taxation and finance provided for by this section. Any provision in an insurance policy undertaking to relieve an employer from such increased liability shall be void.

3. A person over eighteen years of age may apply for a certificate of age to the superintendent of schools or to an employment certificating officer. Upon such application a certificate of age, signed by the officer issuing it and containing the name, date of birth, address and signature of the applicant shall be issued to him if he furnishes evidence that he is over eighteen years of age such as is required for the issuance of an employment certificate. Such a certificate of age shall be conclusive evidence for an employer that the person has reached the age certified to therein, and the provisions of this section shall not apply to the employer of such person while the person is engaged in employment lawful for the age and sex as certified to in the certificate of age.

4. With respect to a jockey, apprentice jockey or exercise person licensed under article two or four of the racing, pari-mutuel wagering and breeding law who, pursuant to section two of this chapter, is an employee of all owners and trainers licensed or required to be licensed under article two or four of the racing, pari-mutuel wagering and breeding law and The New York Jockey Injury Compensation Fund, Inc., the owner or trainer for whom such jockey, apprentice jockey or exercise person was performing services at the time of the accident shall be solely responsible for the double payments described in subdivision one of this section, to the extent that such payments exceed any amounts otherwise payable with respect to such jockey, apprentice jockey or exercise person under any other section of this chapter, and the New York Jockey Injury Compensation Fund, Inc. shall have no responsibility for such excess payments, unless there shall be a failure of the responsible owner or trainer to pay such award within the time provided under this chapter. In the event of such failure to pay and the board requires the fund to pay the award on behalf of such owner or trainer who has been found to have violated this section, the fund shall be entitled to an award against such owner or trainer for the amount so paid which shall be collected in the same manner as an award of compensation.

5. With respect to a black car operator who, pursuant to section two of this chapter, is an employee of the New York black car operators' injury compensation fund, inc., the central dispatch facility for which the black car operator was performing services at the time of the accident shall be solely responsible for the double payments described in subdivision one of this section, to the extent that such payments

exceed any amounts otherwise payable with respect to such black car operator under any other section of this chapter, and the New York black car operators' injury compensation fund, inc. shall have no responsibility for such excess payments, unless there shall be a failure of the responsible central dispatch facility to pay such award within the time provided under this chapter. In the event of such failure to pay, the board may require the fund to pay the award on behalf of the central dispatch facility that is found to have violated this section. In such a case, the fund shall be entitled to an award against the central dispatch facility for the excess amount paid by the fund, which shall be collected in the same manner as an award of compensation.

§ 15. Schedule in case of disability
The following schedule of compensation is hereby established:

1. Permanent total disability. In case of total disability adjudged to be permanent sixty-six and two-thirds per centum of the average weekly wages shall be paid to the employee during the continuance of such total disability. Loss of both hands, or both arms, or both feet, or both legs, or both eyes, or of any two thereof shall, in the absence of conclusive proof to the contrary, constitute permanent total disability. In all other cases permanent total disability shall be determined in accordance with the facts. Notwithstanding any other provision of this chapter, an injured employee disabled due to the loss or total loss of use of both eyes, or both hands, or both arms, or both feet, or both legs, or of any two thereof shall not suffer any diminution of his compensation by engaging in business or employment provided his earnings or wages, when combined with his compensation, shall not be in excess of the wage base on which the maximum weekly compensation benefit is computed under the law in effect at time of such earning; further provided, that if the combination exceeds such wage base, the compensation shall be diminished to an amount which, together with his earnings or wages, shall equal the wage base; and further provided that the application of this subdivision shall not result in reduction of compensation which an injured employee who is disabled due to the loss or total loss of use of both eyes, or both hands, or both arms, or both feet, or both legs or of any two thereof, would otherwise be entitled to under any other provision of this section.

2. Temporary total disability. In case of temporary total disability, sixty-six and two-thirds per centum of the average weekly wages shall be paid to the employee during the continuance thereof, except as otherwise provided in this chapter.

3. Permanent partial disability. In case of disability partial in character but permanent in quality the compensation shall be sixty-six and two-thirds per centum of the average weekly wages and shall be paid to the employee for the period named in this subdivision, as follows:

Member lost	Number of weeks' compensation
a. Arm	312
b. Leg	288
c. Hand	244
d. Foot	205
e. Eye	160
f. Thumb	75
g. First finger	46
h. Great toe	38
i. Second finger	30
j. Third finger	25
k. Toe other than great toe	16
l. Fourth finger	15

m. Loss of hearing. Compensation for the complete loss of the hearing of one ear, for sixty weeks, for the loss of hearing of both ears, for one hundred and fifty weeks.

n. Phalanges. Compensation for the loss of more than one phalange of a digit shall be the same as for loss of the entire digit. Compensation for loss of the first phalange shall be one-half of the compensation for loss of the entire digit.

o. Amputated arm or leg. Compensation for an arm or a leg, if amputated at or above the wrist or ankle, shall be for the proportionate loss of the arm or leg.

p. Binocular vision or per centum of vision. Compensation for loss of binocular vision or for eighty per centum or more of the vision of an eye shall be the same as for loss of the eye.

q. Two or more digits. Compensation for loss or loss of use of two or more digits, or one or more phalanges of two or more digits, of a hand or foot may be proportioned to the loss of use of the hand or foot occasioned thereby but shall not exceed the compensation for loss of a hand or foot.

r. Total loss of use. Compensation for permanent total loss of use of a member shall be the same as for loss of the member.

s. Partial loss or partial loss of use. Compensation for permanent partial loss or loss of use of a member may be for proportionate loss or loss of use of the member. Compensation for permanent partial loss or loss of use of an eye shall be awarded on the basis of uncorrected loss of vision or corrected loss of vision resulting from an injury whichever is the greater.

t. Disfigurement.

1. The board may award proper and equitable compensation for serious facial or head disfigurement, not to exceed twenty thousand dollars, including a disfigurement continuous in length which is partially in the facial area and also extends into the neck region as described in paragraph two hereof.

2. The board, if in its opinion the earning capacity of an employee has been or may in the future be impaired, may award compensation for any serious disfigurement in the region above the sterno clavicular articulations anterior to and including the region of the sterno cleido mastoid muscles on either side, but no award under subdivisions one and two shall, in the aggregate, exceed twenty thousand dollars.

3. Notwithstanding any other provision hereof, two or more serious disfigurements, not continuous in length, resulting from the same injury, if partially in the facial area and partially in the neck region as described in paragraph two hereof, shall be deemed to be a facial disfigurement.

u. Total or partial loss or loss of use of more than one member or parts of members. In any case in which there shall be a loss or loss of use of more than one member or parts of more than one member set forth in paragraphs a through t, inclusive, of this subdivision, but not amounting to permanent total disability, the board shall award compensation for the loss or loss of use of each such member or part thereof, which awards shall be fully payable in one lump sum upon the request of the injured employee.

v. Additional compensation for impairment of wage earning capacity in certain permanent partial disabilities. Notwithstanding any other provision of this subdivision, additional compensation shall be payable for impairment of wage earning capacity for any period after the termination of an award under paragraphs a, b, c, or d, of this subdivision for the loss or loss of use of fifty per centum or more of a member, provided such impairment of earning capacity shall be due solely thereto. Such additional compensation shall be determined in accordance with paragraph w of this subdivision. The additional compensation shall be reduced by fifty per centum of any amount of disability benefits which the disabled employee is receiving or entitled to receive for the same period under the social security act, and shall cease on the date the disabled employee receives or is entitled to receive old-age insurance benefits under the social security act. As soon as practicable after the injury, the worker shall be required to participate in a board approved rehabilitation program; or shall have demonstrated cooperation with efforts to institute such a board approved program and shall have been determined by the board not to be a feasible candidate for rehabilitation; such rehabilitation shall constitute treatment and care as provided in this chapter.

w. Other cases. In all other cases of permanent partial disability, the compensation shall be sixty-six and two-thirds percent of the difference between the injured employee's average weekly wages and his or her wage-earning capacity thereafter in the same employment or otherwise. Compensation under this paragraph shall be payable during the continuance of such permanent partial disability, but subject to reconsideration of the degree of such impairment by the board on its own motion or upon application of any party in interest however, all compensation payable under this paragraph shall not exceed (i) five hundred twenty-five weeks in cases in which the loss of wage-earning capacity is greater than ninety-five percent; (ii) five hundred weeks in cases in which the loss of wage-earning capacity is greater than ninety percent but not more than ninety-five percent; (iii) four hundred seventy-five weeks in cases in which the loss of wage-earning capacity is greater than eighty-five percent but not more than ninety percent; (iv) four hundred fifty weeks in cases in which the loss of wage-earning capacity is greater than eighty percent but not more than eighty-five percent; (v) four hundred twenty-five weeks in cases in which the loss of wage-earning capacity is greater than seventy-five percent but not more than eighty percent; (vi) four hundred weeks in cases in which the loss of wage-earning capacity is greater than seventy percent but not more than seventy-five percent; (vii) three hundred seventy-five weeks in cases in which the loss of wage-earning capacity is greater than sixty percent but not more than seventy percent; (viii) three hundred fifty weeks in cases in which the loss of wage-earning capacity is greater than fifty percent but not more than sixty percent; (ix) three hundred weeks in cases in which the loss of wage-earning capacity is greater than forty percent but not more than fifty percent; (x) two hundred seventy-five weeks in cases in which the loss of wage earning capacity is greater than thirty percent but not more than forty percent; (xi) two hundred fifty weeks in cases in which the loss of wage-earning capacity is greater than fifteen percent but not more than thirty percent; and (xii) two hundred twenty-five weeks in cases in which the loss of wage-earning capacity is fifteen percent or less. For those claimants classified as permanently partially disabled who no longer receive indemnity payments because they have surpassed their number of maximum benefit weeks, the following provisions will apply:

(1) There will be a presumption that medical services shall continue notwithstanding the completion of the time period for compensation set forth in this section and the burden of going forward and the burden of proof will lie with the carrier, self-insured employer or state insurance fund in any application before the board to discontinue or suspend such services. Medical services will continue during the pendency of any such application and any appeals thereto.

(2) The board is directed to promulgate regulations that establish an independent review and appeal by an outside agent or entity of the board's choosing of any administrative law judge's determination to discontinue or suspend medical services before a final determination of the board.

4. Effect of award. An award made to a claimant under subdivision three shall in case of death arising from causes other than the injury be payable to and for the benefit of the persons following:

a. If there be a surviving spouse and no child of the deceased under the age of eighteen years, to such spouse.

b. If there be a surviving spouse and surviving child or children of the deceased under the age of eighteen years, one-half shall be payable to the surviving spouse and the other half to the surviving child or children.

The board may in its discretion require the appointment of a guardian for the purpose of receiving the compensation of the minor child. In the absence of such a requirement by the board the appointment for such a purpose shall not be necessary.

c. If there be a surviving child or children of the deceased under the age of eighteen years, but no surviving spouse then to such child or children.

d. If there be no surviving spouse and no surviving child or children of the deceased under the age of eighteen years, then to such dependent or dependents as defined in section sixteen of this chapter, as directed by the board; and if there be no such dependents, then to the estate of such deceased in an amount not exceeding reasonable funeral expenses as provided in subdivision one of section sixteen of this chapter, or, if there be no estate, to the person or persons paying the funeral expenses of such deceased in an amount not exceeding reasonable funeral expenses as provided in subdivision one of section sixteen of this chapter.

An award for disability may be made after the death of the injured employee.

4-a. Protracted temporary total disability in connection with permanent partial disability. In case of temporary total disability and permanent partial disability both resulting from the same injury, if the temporary total disability continues for a longer period than the number of weeks set forth in the following schedule, the period of temporary total disability in excess of such number of weeks shall be added to the compensation period provided in subdivision three of this section: Arm, thirty-two weeks; leg, forty weeks; hand, thirty-two weeks; foot, thirty-two weeks; ear, twenty-five weeks; eye, twenty weeks; thumb, twenty-four weeks; first finger, eighteen weeks; great toe, twelve weeks; second finger, twelve weeks; third finger, eight weeks; fourth finger, eight weeks; toe other than great toe, eight weeks.

In any case resulting in loss or partial loss of use of arm, leg, hand, foot, ear, eye, thumb, finger or toe, where the temporary total disability does not extend beyond the periods above mentioned for such injury, compensation shall be limited to the schedule contained in subdivision three.

5. Temporary partial disability. In case of temporary partial disability resulting in decrease of earning capacity, the compensation shall be two-thirds of the difference between the injured employee's average weekly wages before the accident and his wage earning capacity after the accident in the same or other employment.

5-a. Determination of wage earning capacity. The wage earning capacity of an injured employee in cases of partial disability shall be determined by his actual earnings, provided, however, that if he has no such actual earnings the board may in the interest of justice fix such wage earning capacity as shall be reasonable, but not in excess of seventy-five per centum of his former full time actual earnings, having due regard to the nature of his injury and his physical impairment.

5-b. Non-schedule adjustments. Notwithstanding any other provision of this chapter, in any case coming within the provisions of subdivisions three or five of this section, in which the right to compensation has been established and compensation has been paid for not less than three months, in which the continuance of disability and of future earning capacity cannot be ascertained with reasonable certainty, the board may, in the interest of justice, approve a non-schedule adjustment agreed to between the claimant and the employer or his insurance carrier. The board shall require, before approving any such agreement, that there be an examination of the claimant in accordance with section nineteen of this chapter, and such approval shall only be given when it is found that the adjustment is fair and in the best interest of the claimant. The board may, in such case, order all future compensation to be paid in one or more lump sums or periodically, and any such adjustment shall be regarded as a closing of the claim unless the board find upon proof that there has been a change in condition or in the degree of disability of claimant not found in the medical evidence and, therefore, not contemplated at the time of the adjustment.

6. Maximum and minimum compensation for disability.

(a) Compensation for permanent or temporary total disability due to an accident or disablement resulting from an occupational disease that occurs, (1) on or after January first, nineteen hundred seventy-eight, shall not exceed one hundred twenty-five dollars per week, that occurs (2) on or after July first, nineteen hundred seventy-eight, shall not exceed one hundred eighty dollars per week, that occurs (3) on or after January first, nineteen hundred seventy-nine, shall not exceed two hundred fifteen dollars per week, that occurs (4) on or after July first, nineteen hundred eighty-three, shall not exceed two hundred fifty-five dollars per week, that occurs (5) on or after July first, nineteen hundred eighty-four, shall not exceed two hundred seventy-five dollars per week, that occurs (6) on or after July first, nineteen hundred eighty-five, shall not exceed three hundred dollars per week, that occurs (7) on or after July first, nineteen hundred ninety, shall not exceed three hundred forty dollars per week; and in the case of temporary total disability shall not be less than thirty dollars per week and in the case of permanent total disability shall not be less than twenty dollars per week except that if the employee's wages at the time of injury are less than thirty or twenty dollars per week respectively, he or she shall receive his or her full weekly wages. Compensation for permanent or temporary partial disability due to an accident or disablement resulting from an occupational disease that occurs (1) on or after January first, nineteen hundred seventy-eight, shall not exceed one hundred five dollars per week, that occurs (2) on or after July first, nineteen hundred eighty-three, shall not exceed one hundred twenty-five dollars per week, that occurs (3) on or after July first, nineteen hundred eighty-four, shall not exceed one hundred thirty-five dollars per week, that occurs (4) on or after July first, nineteen hundred eighty-five, shall not exceed one hundred fifty dollars per week, that occurs (5) on or after July first, nineteen hundred ninety, shall not exceed two hundred eighty dollars per week; nor be less than twenty dollars per week; except that if the employee's wages at the time of injury are less than twenty dollars per week, he or she shall receive his or her full weekly wages. In no event shall compensation when combined with decreased earnings or earning capacity exceed the amount of wages which the employee was receiving at the time the injury occurred. Compensation for permanent or temporary partial disability, or for permanent or temporary total disability due to an accident or disablement resulting from an occupational disease that occurs (1) on or after July first, nineteen hundred ninety-one and prior to July first, nineteen hundred ninety-two, shall not exceed three hundred fifty dollars per week; (2) on or after July first, nineteen hundred ninety-two, shall not exceed four hundred dollars per week; nor be less than forty dollars per week except that if the employee's wages at the time of injury are less than forty dollars per week, the employee shall receive his or her full wages. Compensation for permanent or temporary partial disability, or for permanent or temporary total disability due to an accident or disablement resulting from an occupational disease that occurs (1) on or after July first, two thousand seven shall not exceed five hundred dollars per week, (2) on or after July first, two thousand eight shall not exceed five hundred fifty dollars per week, (3) on or after July first, two thousand nine shall not exceed six hundred dollars per week, and (4) on or after July first, two thousand ten, and on or after July first of each succeeding year, shall not exceed two-thirds of the New York state average weekly wage for the year in which it is reported. Compensation for permanent or temporary partial disability, or for permanent or temporary total disability due to an accident or disablement resulting from an occupational disease that occurs on or after July first, two thousand seven shall not be less than one hundred dollars per week except that if the employee's wages at the time of injury are less than one hundred dollars per week, the employee shall receive his or her full wages. Compensation for permanent or temporary partial disability, or for permanent or temporary total disability due to an accident or disablement resulting from an occupational disease that occurs on or after May first, two thousand thirteen shall not be less than one hundred fifty dollars per week except that if the employee's wages at the time of injury are less than one hundred fifty dollars per week, the employee shall receive his or her full wages. In no event shall compensation when combined with decreased earnings or earning capacity exceed the amount of wages the employee was receiving at the time the injury occurred. Compensation for permanent or temporary partial disability, or for permanent or temporary total disability due to an accident or disablement resulting from an occupational disease or injury that occurred as a result of World Trade Center rescue activity by an employee of a private voluntary hospital, who passed a physical examination upon employment as a rescue worker that failed to reveal evidence of a condition that was the proximate cause of disablement or occupational disease or injury, shall not exceed three-quarters of a claimant's wage on September eleventh, two thousand one. In no event shall compensation when combined with decreased earnings or earning capacity exceed the amount of wages the employee was receiving on September eleventh, two thousand one.

(b) Compensation for temporary total disability due to an accident or disablement resulting from an occupational disease that occurs on or after July first, nineteen hundred seventy-four, and prior to July first, nineteen hundred seventy-eight, shall not exceed one hundred twenty-five dollars per week nor be less than thirty dollars per week; except that if the employee's wages at the time of injury are less than thirty dollars per week, he shall receive his full weekly wages. Compensation for permanent total disability or for permanent or temporary partial disability due to an accident or disablement resulting from an occupational disease that occurs on or after July first, nineteen hundred seventy-four, and prior to January first, nineteen hundred seventy-eight, shall not exceed ninety-five dollars per week; nor be less than twenty dollars per week; except that if the employee's wages at the time of injury are less than twenty dollars per week, he shall receive his full weekly wages. In no event shall compensation when combined with decreased earnings or earning capacity exceed the amount of wages which the employee was receiving at the time the injury occurred.

(c) Compensation for temporary total disability due to an accident or disablement resulting from an occupational disease that occurs on or after July first, nineteen hundred seventy and prior to July first, nineteen hundred seventy-four, shall not exceed ninety-five dollars per week nor be less than thirty dollars per week; except that if the employee's wages at the time of injury are less than thirty dollars per week, he shall receive his full weekly wages. Compensation for permanent total disability or for permanent or temporary partial disability due to an accident or disablement resulting from an occupational disease that occurs on or after July first, nineteen hundred seventy and prior to July first, nineteen hundred seventy-four, shall not exceed eighty dollars per week; nor be less than twenty dollars per week; except that if the employee's wages at the time of injury are less than twenty dollars per week, he shall receive his full weekly wages. In no event shall compensation when combined with decreased earnings or earning capacity exceed the amount of wages which the employee was receiving at the time the injury occurred.

(d) Compensation for temporary total disability due to an accident or disablement resulting from an occupational disease that occurs on or after July first, nineteen hundred sixty-eight, and prior to July first, nineteen hundred seventy, shall not exceed eighty-five dollars per week nor be less than thirty dollars per week; except that if the employee's wages at the time of injury are less than thirty dollars per week, he shall receive his full weekly wages. Compensation for permanent total disability or for permanent or temporary partial disability due to an accident or disablement resulting from an occupational disease that occurs on or after July first, nineteen hundred sixty-eight, and prior to July first, nineteen hundred seventy, shall not exceed seventy dollars per week; nor be less than twenty dollars per week; except that if the employee's wages at the time of injury are less than twenty dollars per week, he shall receive his full weekly wages. In no event shall compensation when combined with decreased earnings or earning capacity exceed the amount of wages which the employee was receiving at the time the injury occurred.

(e) Compensation for permanent or temporary partial disability, or for permanent or temporary total disability due to an accident or disablement resulting from an occupational disease that occurs on or after July first, nineteen hundred sixty-five, and prior to July first, nineteen hundred sixty-eight, shall not exceed sixty dollars per week; nor be less than twenty dollars per week; except that if the employee's wages at the time of injury are less than twenty dollars per week, he shall receive his full weekly wages. In no event shall compensation when combined with decreased earnings or earning capacity exceed the amount of wages which the employee was receiving at the time the injury occurred.

(f) Compensation for permanent or temporary partial disability, or for permanent or temporary total disability due to an accident or disablement resulting from an occupational disease that occurs on or after July first, nineteen hundred sixty-two and prior to July first nineteen hundred sixty-five, shall not exceed fifty-five dollars per week; nor be less than twenty dollars per week; except that if the employee's wages at the time of injury are less than twenty dollars per week, he shall receive his full weekly wages. In no event shall compensation when combined with decreased earnings or earning capacity exceed the amount of wages which the employee was receiving at the time the injury occurred.

(g) Compensation for permanent or temporary partial disability, or for permanent or temporary total disability due to an accident or disablement resulting from an occupational disease that occurs on or after July first, nineteen hundred sixty and prior to July first nineteen hundred sixty-two, shall not exceed fifty dollars per week; nor be less than twenty dollars per week, except that if the employee's wages at the time of injury are less than twenty dollars per week, he shall receive his full weekly wages. In no event shall compensation when combined with decreased earnings or earning capacity exceed the amount of wages which the employee was receiving at the time the injury occurred.

(h) Compensation for permanent or temporary partial disability, or for permanent or temporary total disability due to an accident or disablement resulting from an occupational disease that occurs on or after July first, nineteen hundred fifty-eight and prior to July first, nineteen hundred sixty, shall not exceed forty-five dollars per week; nor, except in cases of permanent total disability, be less than twenty dollars per week; except that if the employee's wages at the time of injury are less than twenty dollars per week, he shall receive his full weekly wages; further provided, that in each case of permanent total disability minimum compensation shall not be less than twenty dollars per week, except that where the employee's wages at the time of injury are less than twenty dollars per week he shall receive his full weekly wages. In no event shall compensation when combined with decreased earnings or earning capacity exceed the amount of wages which the employee was receiving at the time the injury occurred.

(i) Compensation for permanent or temporary partial disability, or for permanent or temporary total disability due to an accident or disablement resulting from an occupational disease that occurs on or after July first, nineteen hundred fifty-four and prior to July first, nineteen hundred fifty-eight, shall not exceed thirty-six dollars per week; nor, except in cases of permanent total disability, be less than twelve dollars per week; except that if the employee's wages at the time of injury are less than twelve dollars per week, he shall receive his full weekly wages; further provided, that in each case of permanent total disability minimum compensation shall not be less than fifteen dollars per week, except that where the employee's wages at the time of injury are less than fifteen dollars per week he shall receive his full weekly wages. In no event shall compensation when combined with decreased earnings or earning capacity exceed the amount of wages which the employee was receiving at the time the injury occurred.

(j) Compensation for permanent or temporary partial disability, or for permanent or temporary total disability due to an accident or disablement resulting from an occupational disease that occurs on or after July first, nineteen hundred forty-eight and prior to July first, nineteen hundred fifty-four, shall not exceed thirty-two dollars per week and compensation for permanent or temporary partial disability, or for permanent or temporary total disability due to an accident or disablement resulting from an occupational disease that occurs on or after June first, nineteen hundred forty-six, and prior to July first, nineteen hundred forty-eight, shall not exceed twenty-eight dollars per week; nor, except in cases of permanent total disability, be less than twelve dollars per week; except that if the employee's wages at the time of injury are less than twelve dollars per week, he shall receive his full weekly wages; further provided, that in each case of permanent total disability minimum compensation shall not be less than fifteen dollars per week, except that where the employee's wages at the time of injury are less than fifteen dollars per week, he shall receive his full weekly wages but in no event shall compensation when combined with decreased earnings or earning capacity exceed the amount of wages which the employee was receiving at the time the injury occurred; further provided, that compensation may be in excess of twenty-five dollars but shall not exceed twenty-eight dollars per week for permanent or temporary total disability due to an accident or disablement resulting from an occupational disease that occurred on or after June first, nineteen hundred forty-four, and prior to July first, nineteen hundred forty-eight, and in each case of temporary total disability minimum compensation shall not be less than twelve dollars per week, except that where the employee's wages at the time of injury are less than twelve dollars per week, he shall receive his full weekly wages; and further provided that, because of existing conditions due to the war compensation for permanent or temporary total disability may be in excess of twenty-five dollars but shall not exceed twenty-eight dollars per week for any period of disability arising out of claims accruing during the three year period commencing June first, nineteen hundred forty-four.

6-a. Reclassification of disabilities. Subject to the limitations set forth in sections twenty-five-a and one hundred twenty-three of this chapter, the board may, at any time, without regard to the date of accident, upon its own motion, or on application of any party in interest, reclassify a disability upon proof that there has been a change in condition, or that the previous classification was erroneous and not in the interest of justice.

7. Previous disability. The fact that an employee has suffered previous disability or received compensation therefor shall not preclude him from compensation for a later injury nor preclude compensation for death resulting therefrom; but in determining compensation for the later injury or death his average weekly wages shall be such sum as will reasonably represent his earning capacity at the time of the later injury, provided, however, that an employee who is suffering from a previous disability shall not receive compensation for a later injury in excess of the compensation allowed for such injury when considered by itself and not in conjunction with the previous disability except as hereinafter provided in subdivision eight of this section.

8. Disability following previous permanent physical impairment.

(a) Declaration of policy and legislative intent. As a guide to the interpretation and application of this subdivision, the policy and intent of this legislature is declared to be as follows:

First: That every person in this state who works for a living is entitled to reasonable opportunity to maintain his independence and self-respect through self-support even after he/she has been physically handicapped by injury or disease;

Second: That any plan which will reasonably, equitably and practically operate to break down hindrances and remove obstacles to the employment of partially disabled persons honorably discharged from our armed forces, or any other physically handicapped persons, is of vital importance to the state and its people and is of concern to this legislature;

Third: That it is the considered judgment of this legislature that the system embodied in this subdivision, which makes a logical and equitable adjustment of the liability under the workers' compensation law which an employer must assume in hiring employees, constitutes a practical and reasonable approach to a solution of the problem for the employment of physically handicapped persons.

Moreover, because of the insidious nature of slowly developing diseases such as silicosis and other dust diseases and because of the reluctance on the part of employers to employ persons previously exposed to silica or other harmful dust, means should also be provided whereby employers will be encouraged to employ and to continue the employment of such persons, by apportioning liability fairly between the employer and industry as a whole without at the same time removing any incentive for the prevention of harmful dust diseases.

(b) Definition. As used in this subdivision, "permanent physical impairment" means any permanent condition due to previous accident or disease or any congenital condition which is or is likely to be a hindrance or obstacle to employment.

(c) Permanent total disability after permanent partial disability. Notwithstanding the provisions of paragraph (d) of this subdivision, if an employee who has previously incurred permanent partial disability through the loss of one hand, one arm, one foot, one leg, or one eye, incurs permanent total disability through the loss of another member or organ, he/she shall be paid, in addition to the compensation for permanent partial disability provided in this section and after the cessation of the payments for the prescribed period of weeks special additional compensation during the continuance of such total disability to the amount of sixty-six and two-thirds per centum of the average weekly wage earned by him/her at the time the total permanent disability was incurred. If such employee shall establish an earning capacity by employment he shall be paid during the period of such employment, instead of the additional compensation above provided, two-thirds of the difference between his average weekly wages at the time the total disability was incurred and his wage earning capacity as determined by his actual earnings in such employment, subject to the limitations in subdivision six of this section. Such additional compensation, and expense as in this subdivision provided, shall be paid out of the special disability fund and in the manner as hereinafter in this subdivision provided.

(d) If an employee of an employer who has secured the payment of compensation as required under the provisions of section fifty of this chapter, who had a total or partial loss or loss of use of one hand, one arm, one foot, one leg or one eye, or who has other permanent physical impairment incurs a subsequent disability by accident arising out of and in the course of his employment or an occupational disease arising therefrom, resulting in a permanent disability caused by both conditions that is materially and substantially greater than that which would have resulted from the subsequent injury or occupational disease alone, the employer or his insurance carrier shall in the first instance pay all awards of compensation and all medical expense provided by this chapter, but such employer or his insurance carrier, except as specifically provided in paragraph (ee) of this subdivision, shall be reimbursed from the special disability fund created by this subdivision for all compensation and medical benefits subsequent to those payable for the first one hundred four weeks of disability for claims where the date of accident or date of disablement occurred prior to August first, nineteen hundred ninety-four, and two hundred sixty weeks of disability for claims where the date of accident or date of disablement occurred on or after August first, nineteen hundred ninety-four, regardless of knowledge on the part of the employer as to the existence of such pre-existing permanent physical impairment.

Notwithstanding anything to the contrary in this chapter, there may be apportionment of liability for the special disability fund under this subdivision within a single claim by disposition between the fund, carriers, self-insurers or employers.

(e) If the subsequent injury of such an employee resulting from an accident arising out of and in the course of his employment or an occupational disease resulting therefrom, as set forth in paragraph (d) of this subdivision, shall result in the death of the employee and it shall be determined that either the injury or death would not have occurred except for such pre-existing permanent physical impairment, the employer or his insurance carrier shall in the first instance pay the funeral expenses and the death benefits prescribed by this chapter, but he or his insurance carrier, except as specifically provided in paragraph (ee) of this subdivision, shall be reimbursed from the special disability fund created by this subdivision for all death benefits payable in excess of one hundred four weeks of disability for claims where the date of accident or date of disablement occurred prior to August first, nineteen hundred ninety-four, and two hundred sixty weeks of disability for claims where the date of accident or date of disablement occurred on or after August first, nineteen hundred ninety-four, regardless of knowledge on the part of the employer as to the existence of such pre-existing permanent physical impairment.

(ee) If an employee of an employer who has secured the payment of compensation as required under the provisions of section fifty of this chapter is disabled from silicosis or other dust disease, or in the event of death, death was due to silicosis or other dust disease, and if such an employee has been subject to an injurious exposure in an employment defined under paragraph twenty-nine of subdivision two of section three of this chapter, the provisions of this subdivision shall apply except as hereinafter stated; and it shall not be required that the employee had, either at the time of hiring or during the employment, any previous physical condition or disability which may result in such disability or death. In all such cases the employer or his insurance carrier shall in the first instance pay all awards of compensation and all medical expense provided by this chapter; and in the event of death, the employer or his insurance carrier shall also in the first instance pay the funeral expenses and the death benefits prescribed by this chapter; but such employer or his insurance carrier shall subject to the limitations of subparagraphs two and three of paragraph (h) of this subdivision be reimbursed from the special disability fund created by this subdivision for all compensation and medical benefits subsequent to those payable for the first one hundred four weeks of disability for claims where the date of accident or date of disablement occurred prior to August first, nineteen hundred ninety-four, and two hundred sixty weeks of disability for claims where the date of accident or date of disablement occurred on or after August first, nineteen hundred ninety-four, and, in the event of death, the employer or his insurance carrier shall be reimbursed from the special disability fund created by this subdivision for all death benefits payable in excess of one hundred four weeks for claims where the date of accident or date of disablement occurred prior to August first, nineteen hundred ninety-four, and two hundred sixty weeks for claims where the date of accident or date of disablement occurred on or after August first, nineteen hundred ninety-four; provided, however, that when total disability or death occurred after July first, nineteen hundred forty-seven, and prior to July first, nineteen hundred seventy-four, the employer or his insurance carrier shall be reimbursed from the special disability fund created by this subdivision for all compensation and medical benefits including funeral expenses and death benefits subsequent to those payable for the first two hundred sixty weeks of disability and death benefits combined; and further provided, however, that in the event of death due to silicosis or other dust disease on or after July first, nineteen hundred forty-seven, of such an employee who shall have been totally disabled from silicosis or other dust disease prior to such date, the employer or his insurance carrier shall be reimbursed from the special disability fund created by this subdivision for death benefits subsequent to those payable for the first one hundred four weeks.

The compensation of an employee who has heretofore been found to be totally and permanently disabled from silicosis or other dust disease and whose disablement occurred prior to July first, nineteen hundred forty-seven, shall be continued or resumed, as the case may be, after June first, nineteen hundred fifty-one, and payments shall be made during continuance of such disability at his/her regular weekly rate, notwithstanding the fact that such compensation is in excess of the maximum provided for his/her case under former article four-a of this chapter; but such compensation in excess of the maximum so provided shall be paid from the special fund created by this subdivision.

(f) Any award under this subdivision shall be made against the employer or his or her insurance carrier, but if such employer or insurance carrier be entitled to reimbursement as provided in this subdivision, notice or claim of the right to such reimbursement shall be filed with the board in writing prior to the final determination that the resulting disability is permanent, but in no case more than one hundred four weeks after the date of disability or death or fifty-two weeks after the date that a claim for compensation is filed with the chair, whichever is later, or in the event of the reopening of a case theretofore closed, no later than the determination of permanency upon such reopening. In no event shall such a notice of claim be filed beyond the dates set forth in subparagraph two of paragraph (h) of this subdivision.

The employer or his or her insurance carrier shall in the first instance make the payments of compensation and medical expenses provided by this subdivision. Whenever for any reason payments are not made by the employer or his or her insurance carrier at any time after the payments have been made for the first one hundred four weeks for claims where the date of accident or date of disablement occurred prior to August first, nineteen hundred ninety-four, and two hundred sixty weeks for claims where the date of accident or date of disablement occurred on or after August first, nineteen hundred ninety-four, the payments of subsequent compensation and medical expenses shall be made out of the special disability fund by the commissioner of taxation and finance upon vouchers approved by the chair of the workers' compensation board. In case any payments prior to the expiration of the first one hundred four weeks for claims where the date of accident or date of disablement occurred prior to August first, nineteen hundred ninety-four, and two hundred sixty weeks for claims where the date of accident or date of disablement occurred on or after August first, nineteen hundred ninety-four are not made by the employer or his or her insurance carrier by reason of the insolvency of such carrier, the payments until the expiration of one hundred four weeks for claims where the date of accident or date of disablement occurred prior to August first, nineteen hundred ninety-four, and two hundred sixty weeks for claims where the date of accident or date of disablement occurred on or after August first, nineteen hundred ninety-four shall be made out of the stock workers' compensation security fund created by the provisions of section one hundred seven of this chapter if the insolvent carrier be a stock company, or out of the mutual workers' compensation security fund created under the provisions of section one hundred nine-d of this chapter if the carrier be a mutual company. If any such payments are not made by an employer permitted to secure the payment of compensation pursuant to the provisions of subdivision three of section fifty of this chapter, the payments shall be made out of the proceeds of the sale of any securities deposited by the employer with the chair, upon vouchers approved by the chair, until such payments have been made for one hundred four weeks for claims where the date of accident or date of disablement occurred prior to August first, nineteen hundred ninety-four, and two hundred sixty weeks for claims where the date of accident or date of disablement occurred on or after August first, nineteen hundred ninety-four, from the date of disability, after which date they shall be made out of the special disability fund in the manner above provided.

In all cases in which awards have been made and charged against the special fund or injuries have occurred which would require payments to be made in accordance with the provisions of former subdivision eight of this section as it existed immediately prior to the time this subdivision, as hereby added, takes effect, the compensation so awarded or that shall be awarded in such cases shall continue to be paid out of the special disability fund by the commissioner of taxation and finance upon vouchers approved by the chair of the workers' compensation board, as though this subdivision had not been enacted.

(g) Upon the making of a determination that an employer or insurance carrier is entitled to reimbursement from the special disability fund in any case where the employer or insurance carrier has made payment into the aggregate trust fund, as provided in section twenty-seven of this chapter, or where payment of compensation has been commuted into one or more lump sum payments, the employer or insurance carrier shall be reimbursed forthwith for the sums paid in excess of those payable for one hundred four weeks for claims where the date of accident or date of disablement occurred prior to August first, nineteen hundred ninety-four, two hundred sixty weeks for claims where the date of accident or date of disablement occurred on or after August first, nineteen hundred ninety-four or two hundred sixty weeks in a silicosis or other dust disease case as otherwise provided in paragraph (ee) of this subdivision, exclusive of administrative and loading charges paid pursuant to section twenty-seven, in accordance with the decision and order of the board. In all other cases such employer or insurance carrier shall, periodically every six months from the decision and order of the board, be reimbursed from such special disability fund for all compensation and medical expense in accordance with the provisions of paragraph (f) of this subdivision.

(h) Special disability fund.

(1) The fund heretofore maintained and provided for by and pursuant to former subdivision eight of this section, is hereby continued and shall retain the liabilities heretofore charged or chargeable thereto under the provisions of such former subdivision eight of this section as it existed immediately prior to the time this subdivision, as hereby added, takes effect, and the liabilities chargeable thereto under the provisions of former subdivision eight-a of this section as added by chapter seven hundred forty-nine of the laws of nineteen hundred forty-four and repealed at the same time this subdivision, as heretofore added, takes effect, and payments therefrom on account of such liabilities shall continue to be made as provided herein. The said fund shall be known as the special disability fund and shall be available only for the purposes stated in this subdivision, and the assets thereof shall not at any time be appropriated or diverted to any other use or purpose.

(2) (A) No carrier or employer, or the state insurance fund, may file a claim for reimbursement from the special disability fund, for an injury or illness with a date of accident or date of disablement on or after July first, two thousand seven. No carrier or employer, or the state insurance fund, may file a claim for reimbursement from the special disability fund after July first, two thousand ten, and no written submissions or evidence in support of such a claim may be submitted after that date.

(B) All requests for reimbursement from the special disability fund with a date of injury or date of disablement prior to July first, two thousand seven as to which the board has determined that the special disability fund is liable must be submitted to the special disability fund by the later of (i) one year after the expense has been paid, or (ii) one year from the effective date of this paragraph.

(3) Effective the first day of January, two thousand fourteen, and annually thereafter, the chair of the board shall collect from all affected employers (A) a sum equal to one hundred fifty per centum of the total expected disbursements made from the special disability fund during the year (not including any disbursements made on account of anticipated liabilities or waiver agreements funded by bond proceeds and related earnings), less the estimated amount of the net assets in such fund expected as of December thirty-first and (B) a sum sufficient to cover debt service, and associated costs (the "debt service assessment") to be paid during the calendar year by the dormitory authority, as calculated in accordance with subparagraph four of this paragraph. Such assessments shall be included in the assessment rate established pursuant to subdivision two of section one hundred fifty-one of this chapter. Such assessments shall be deposited with the commissioner of taxation and finance and transferred to the benefit of such fund following payment of debt service and associated costs, if any, pursuant to section one hundred fifty-one of this chapter.

(4) The chair and the commissioner of taxation and finance are authorized and directed to enter into a financing agreement with the dormitory authority, to be known as the "special disability fund financing agreement." Such agreement shall set forth the process for calculating the annual debt service of the bonds issued by the dormitory authority and any other associated costs. For purposes of this section, "associated costs" may include a coverage factor, reserve fund requirements, all costs of any nature incurred by the dormitory authority in connection with the special disability fund financing agreement or pursuant thereto, the operating costs of the waiver agreement management office, the costs of any independent audits undertaken under this section, and any other costs for the implementation of this subparagraph and the issuance of bonds by the dormitory authority, including interest rate exchange payments, rebate payments, liquidity fees, credit provider fees, fiduciary fees, remarketing, dealer, auction agent and related fees and other similar bond-related expenses, unless otherwise funded. By January first of each year, the dormitory authority shall provide to the chair the calculation of the amount expected to be paid by the dormitory authority in debt service and associated costs for purposes of calculating the debt service assessment as set forth in subparagraph three of this paragraph. All monies received on account of any assessment under subparagraph three of this paragraph and this subparagraph shall be applied in accordance with this subparagraph and in accordance with the financing agreement until the financial obligations of the dormitory authority in respect to its contract with its bondholders are met and all associated costs payable to the dormitory authority have been paid, notwithstanding any other provision of law respecting secured transactions. This provision may be included by the dormitory authority in any contract of the dormitory authority with its bondholders.

The special disability fund financing agreement may restrict disbursements, investments, or rebates, and may prescribe a system of accounts applicable to the special disability fund, including custody of an account with a trust indenture trustee that may be prescribed by the dormitory authority as part of its contract with the bondholders. For purposes of this paragraph, the term "bonds" shall include notes issued in anticipation of the issuance of bonds, or notes issued pursuant to a commercial paper program.

(5) The commissioner of taxation and finance is hereby authorized to receive and credit to such special disability fund any sum or sums that may at any time be contributed to the state by the United States of America under any act of congress, or otherwise, to which the state may be or become entitled by reason of any payments made out of such fund.

(6) The commissioner of taxation and finance shall be the custodian of said fund and, unless otherwise provided for in the special disability fund financing agreement, shall invest any surplus or reserve moneys thereof in securities which constitute legal investments for savings banks under the laws of this state and in interest bearing certificates of deposit of a bank or trust company located and authorized to do business in this state or of a national bank located in this state secured by a pledge of direct obligations of the United States or of the state of New York in an amount equal to the amount of such certificates of deposit, and may sell any of the securities or certificates of deposit in which such fund is invested if necessary for the proper administration or in the best interest of such fund. Disbursements from such fund as provided by this subdivision shall be made by the commissioner of taxation and finance upon vouchers signed by the chair of the board unless the financing agreement provides for some other means of authorizing such disbursements that is no less protective of the fund.

The commissioner of taxation and finance, as custodian of such fund, annually as soon as practicable after January first, shall furnish to the chair of the workers' compensation board a statement of the fund, setting forth the balance of moneys in the said fund as of the beginning of the calendar year, the income of the fund, the summary of payments out of the fund on account of reimbursements and other charges ordered to be paid by the board, and all other charges against the fund, and setting forth the balance of the fund remaining to its credit on December thirty-first. Such statement shall be open to public inspection in the office of the secretary of the board. The chair, not less than ninety days after the issuance of the dormitory authority's annual audit, shall furnish to the temporary president of the senate and the speaker of the assembly the following reports on the special disability fund: a revenue and operating expense statement; a financing plan; a report concerning the assets and liabilities; the number of waiver agreements entered into by the waiver agreement management office; the number of claimants remaining in the fund; the estimated current unfunded liability of the fund with respect to such claims; and a debt issuance report including but not limited to (i) pledged assessment revenue and securitization coverage, (ii) debt service maturities, (iii) interest rate exchange or similar agreements, and (iv) financing and issuance costs.

The commissioner of taxation and finance may establish within the special disability fund such accounts and sub-accounts as he or she deems useful for the operation of the fund, or as necessary to segregate moneys within the fund, subject to the provisions of the financing agreement. The waiver agreement management office, as defined in section thirty-two of this article, shall make application to the chair on a quarterly basis for any administrative costs incurred by the office.

(i) When an application for apportionment of compensation is made under this subdivision, the chair of the workers' compensation board shall appoint an attorney to represent and defend such fund in such proceedings. Such attorney shall thereafter be given notice of all proceedings involving the rights or obligations of such fund. Such attorney may apply to the chair of the board for authority to hire such medical and other experts and to defray the expense thereof and of such witnesses as may be necessary to a proper defense of any claim, within an amount in the discretion of the chair and, if authorized, such amount shall be a charge against such special disability fund.

The provisions of this chapter with respect to procedure, except as may be otherwise provided in this subdivision, and the right of appeal shall be preserved to the claimant and to the employer or his insurance carrier and to such fund through its attorney as herein provided.

(j) The provisions of this subdivision, except as herein otherwise provided, shall not be applicable to any case where the accident causing the subsequent injury or death or the disablement or death from a subsequent occupational disease shall have occurred prior to the time this subdivision, as hereby added, takes effect, provided, however, that any rights that have accrued under former subdivision eight or eight-a of this section prior to the time this subdivision, as hereby added, takes effect shall continue to inure to the benefit of any persons affected thereby as though such subdivisions had not been repealed.

(k) The additional compensation required to be paid by an employer in the case of the injury of a minor illegally employed, in accordance with the provisions of subdivisions one and two of section fourteen-a of this chapter, shall not be reimbursable under the provisions of this subdivision.

(l) Notwithstanding anything to the contrary in this subdivision, when an employer or carrier shall have paid additional benefits to an employee pursuant to subdivision six of section fourteen of this article as a result of the employee's increased average weekly wages from wages earned in concurrent employment, reimbursement for all such additional benefits shall be made to the employer or carrier from the special disability fund created by this subdivision. It shall not be required that the employee had, either at the time of hiring or during the employment, any previous physical condition or disability, nor shall it be required that the employee's disability be permanent in nature. Notice of the right to reimbursement shall be filed with the board in writing prior to the decision making an award, and reimbursement shall be made periodically, every six months from the decision of the board.

9. Expenses for rehabilitating injured employees.

An employee, who as a result of injury is or may be expected to be totally or partially incapacitated for a remunerative occupation and who, under the direction of the state education department is being rendered fit to engage in a remunerative occupation, may receive additional compensation necessary for his rehabilitation, not more than thirty dollars per week of which may be expended for maintenance. Such expense and such of the administrative expenses of the state education department as are properly assignable to the expenses of rehabilitating employees entitled to compensation as a result of injuries under this chapter, shall be paid out of a special fund created in the following manner: The employer, or if insured, his insurance carrier, shall pay into the vocational rehabilitation fund for every case of injury causing death, in which there are no persons entitled to compensation, the sum of five hundred dollars where such injury occurred prior to July first, nineteen hundred sixty-three and the sum of one thousand dollars where such injury shall occur on or after July first, nineteen hundred sixty-three and the sum of two thousand dollars where such injury shall occur on or after September first, nineteen hundred seventy-eight. The commissioner of taxation and finance and the state comptroller shall be the joint custodians of this special fund and may invest any surplus moneys thereof in securities which constitute legal investments for savings banks under the laws of this state and in interest bearing certificates of deposit of a bank or trust company located and authorized to do business in this state or of a national bank located in this state secured by a pledge of direct obligations of the United States or of the state of New York in an amount equal to the amount of such certificates of deposit. He may also sell any of the securities or certificates of deposit in which such fund is invested if necessary for the proper administration or in the best interests of such fund. The provisions of this paragraph shall not apply with respect to policies containing coverage pursuant to subdivision four-a of section one hundred sixty-seven of the insurance law relating to every policy providing comprehensive personal liability insurance on a one, two, three or four family owner-occupied dwelling.

Disbursements from the vocational rehabilitation fund for the additional compensation provided for by this section shall be paid by the commissioner of taxation and finance on warrants drawn by the state comptroller upon vouchers signed by the commissioner of education or the deputy commissioner of education provided that the compensation claim number of an injured employee undergoing vocational rehabilitation has been verified by the chairman.

Disbursements from the vocational rehabilitation fund for administrative expenses of the state education department shall be paid by the commissioner of taxation and finance on warrants drawn by the state comptroller upon vouchers signed by the commissioner of education or the deputy commissioner of education.

§ 16. Death benefits

If the injury causes death, the compensation shall be known as a death benefit and shall be payable in the amount and to or for the benefit of the persons following:

1. Funeral expenses. The chair shall prepare and establish a schedule for the state or schedules limited to defined localities of maximum charges and fees for such funeral expenses, to be determined in accordance with, and to be subject to change pursuant to, rules promulgated by the chair. Before preparing such schedule for the state or schedules for limited localities, the chair shall request the president of the New York state funeral directors' association to submit to the chair a report on the amount of remuneration deemed by such association to be fair and adequate for the types of funeral services rendered under this chapter, but consideration shall also be given to the views of other interested parties. The amounts payable by the employer for such services shall be the actual fees and charges up to the maximum established by such schedule. Provided, however, no such schedule of charges and fees shall apply where a firefighter dies from injuries received in the line of duty as a direct result of firefighting or where a police officer dies from injuries received in the line of duty as a direct result of law enforcement activities, where such funeral expenses are reasonable. If such funeral expenses shall have been paid by the claimants entitled to compensation under this section or by others, the funeral expenses awarded shall be made payable to such claimants or others, otherwise they shall be made payable to the undertaker who shall have provided burial. Funeral expenses shall be awarded in case of all injuries causing death including cases in which there are no persons entitled to other compensation under this chapter.

1-a. For the purpose of this section, (1) the term dependent blind or physically disabled as used herein in relation to dependent children shall be deemed to mean totally blind or physically disabled children whose disablement is total and permanent, (2) the term surviving spouse shall be deemed to mean the legal spouse but shall not include a spouse who has abandoned the deceased, and (3) the term abandoned shall be deemed to mean such an abandonment as would be sufficient under section two hundred of the domestic relations law to sustain a judgment of separation on that ground.

1-b. If there be a surviving spouse and no child of the deceased under the age of eighteen years and no child of any age dependent blind or physically disabled, and the death occurs on or after July first, nineteen hundred forty-eight, and prior to January first, nineteen hundred seventy-eight, to such spouse forty per centum of the average wages of the deceased during widowhood or widowerhood with two years' compensation in one sum, upon remarriage; and where the death occurred prior to July first, nineteen hundred forty-eight, to such wife (or dependent husband) thirty per centum of such wages during widowhood (or dependent widowerhood) with two years' compensation in one sum, upon remarriage.

1-c. If there be a surviving spouse and no child of the deceased under the age of eighteen years or under the age of twenty-three years if enrolled and attending as a full time student in an accredited educational institution and such enrollment and full time attendance is certified by such institution and no child of any age dependent blind or physically disabled, and the death occurs on or after January first, nineteen hundred seventy-eight, to such spouse sixty-six and two-thirds per centum of the average wages of the deceased during widowhood or widowerhood with two years' compensation, in one sum, upon remarriage. Where the death occurs on or after January first, nineteen hundred seventy-eight, and the spouse is receiving the survivors insurance benefits under the social security act, the death benefit payable under this section shall be reduced in accordance with the provisions of table No. 1 below by five per centum of the spouse's share of the survivor's insurance benefits under the social security act for each ten dollars of deceased's average weekly wage in excess of one hundred dollars provided that in no case shall such reduction exceed fifty per centum of said spouse's share of the survivors insurance benefits under the social security act.

TABLE No. I
Offset provisions applicable in death benefits where there is a sole surviving spouse

AVERAGE WEEKLY WAGE	PERCENTAGE OF SPOUSE'S SHARE OF SURVIVORS INSURANCE BENEFITS
over $100 up to and including $110	5
over $110 up to and including $120	10
over $120 up to and including $130	15
over $130 up to and including $140	20
over $140 up to and including $150	25
over $150 up to and including $160	30
over $160 up to and including $170	35
over $170 up to and including $180	40
over $180 up to and including $190	45
over $190 up to and including $200	50
over $200	50

1-d. If there be a surviving spouse of an employee of a private voluntary hospital killed in a World Trade Center rescue, who passed a physical examination upon employment as a rescue worker that failed to reveal evidence of a condition that was the proximate cause of death, and no child of the deceased under the age of eighteen years, or under the age of twenty-three years if enrolled and attending as a full-time student in an accredited educational institution and such enrollment and full-time attendance is certified by such institution, and no child of any age dependent blind or physically disabled, to such spouse seventy-five per centum of the average wages of the deceased during widowhood or widowerhood, with two years' compensation, in one sum, upon remarriage. Where such death occurs, and the spouse is receiving the survivors insurance benefits under the social security act, the death benefit payable under this section shall be reduced in accordance with the provisions of table No. I in subdivision one-c of this section by five per centum of the spouse's share of the survivor's insurance benefits under the social security act for each ten dollars of deceased's average weekly wage in excess of one hundred dollars; provided that in no case shall such reduction exceed fifty per centum of such spouse's share of the survivors insurance benefits under the social security act.

2. If there be a surviving spouse and a surviving child or children of the deceased under the age of eighteen years or a surviving child or children of any age dependent blind or physically disabled, and the death occurs on or after July first, nineteen hundred forty-eight, and prior to January first, nineteen hundred seventy-eight, to such spouse thirty per centum of the average wages of the deceased during widowhood or widowerhood with two years' compensation in one sum, upon remarriage; and the additional amount of twenty per centum of such wages for each such child until the age of eighteen years or until the removal of the dependency of the blind or physically disabled child or children; in case of the subsequent death or remarriage of such surviving spouse any surviving child of the deceased employee, at the time under eighteen years of age or dependent through mental or physical infirmity, shall have his compensation increased to thirty per centum of such wages, and the same shall be payable until he shall reach the age of eighteen years or until such dependent blind or physically disabled condition shall have been removed; provided that the total amount payable shall in no case exceed sixty-six and two-thirds per centum of such wages. Upon statutory termination of compensation payments to all such children, the compensation of the surviving spouse shall be increased to forty per centum of such wages with two years' compensation, at such rate, in one sum, upon remarriage.

If there be a surviving wife (or dependent husband) and any of the aforementioned surviving children, and the death occurred prior to July first, nineteen hundred forty-eight, to such wife (or dependent husband) thirty per centum of the average wages of the deceased during widowhood (or dependent widowerhood) with two years' compensation in one sum, upon remarriage; and the additional amount of ten per centum of such wages for each such child until eighteen years of age or until the removal of the dependency of the blind or physically disabled child or children; in case of the subsequent death or remarriage of such surviving wife (or dependent husband) any surviving child of the deceased shall have his compensation increased to fifteen per centum of such wages until he shall reach the age of eighteen years or until such dependent blind or physically disabled condition shall have been removed; provided that the total amount payable shall in no case exceed sixty-six and two-thirds per centum of such wages.

The board may in its discretion require the appointment of a guardian for the purpose of receiving the compensation of a minor child or a dependent blind or physically disabled child. In the absence of such a requirement by the board the appointment of a guardian for such purposes shall not be necessary.

2-a. If there be a surviving spouse and a surviving child under the age of eighteen years or under the age of twenty-three years if enrolled and attending as a full time student in an accredited educational institution and such enrollment and full time attendance is certified by such institution or a surviving child of any age dependent blind or physically disabled and the death occurs on or after January first, nineteen hundred seventy-eight, to such spouse thirty-six and two-thirds per centum of the average wages of the deceased during widowhood or widowerhood with two years' compensation in one sum, upon remarriage; and thirty per centum of such wages to such child under the age of eighteen years or under the age of twenty-three years if enrolled and attending as a full time student in an accredited educational institution and such enrollment and full time attendance is certified by such institution or a surviving child of any age dependent blind or physically disabled; in the case of the subsequent death of such surviving spouse the surviving child shall have his compensation increased to sixty-six and two-thirds per centum of such wages and the same shall be payable so long as he is under the age of eighteen years or under the age of twenty-three years if enrolled and attending as a full time student in an accredited educational institution and such enrollment and full time attendance is certified by such institution or a surviving child of any age dependent blind or physically disabled; upon statutory termination of compensation payable to such child, the compensation of the surviving spouse shall be increased to sixty-six and two-thirds per centum of such wages with two years' compensation, at such rate, in one sum, upon remarriage. Upon remarriage of such surviving spouse, the surviving child shall continue to receive thirty per centum of such wages. Where the death occurs on or after January first, nineteen hundred seventy-eight and the spouse is receiving survivors insurance benefits under the social security act, the death benefit payable under this section shall be reduced by five per centum of the spouse's share of the survivors insurance benefits under the social security act for each ten dollars of deceased's average weekly wage in excess of one hundred dollars provided that in no case shall such reduction exceed fifty per centum of said spouse's share of the survivors insurance benefits under the social security act as set forth in table No. I below.

TABLE No. I
Offset provisions applicable in death benefits where there is a surviving spouse and one child

AVERAGE WEEKLY WAGE	PERCENTAGE OF SPOUSE'S SHARE OF SURVIVORS INSURANCE BENEFITS
over $100 up to and including $110	5
over $110 up to and including $120	10
over $120 up to and including $130	15
over $130 up to and including $140	20
over $140 up to and including $150	25
over $150 up to and including $160	30
over $160 up to and including $170	35
over $170 up to and including $180	40
over $180 up to and including $190	45
over $190 up to and including $200	50
over $200	50

If there be a surviving spouse and two or more surviving children under the age of eighteen years or under the age of twenty-three years if enrolled and attending as a full time student in an accredited educational institution and such enrollment and full time attendance is certified by such institution or a surviving child or children of any age dependent blind or physically disabled and a death occurs on or after January first, nineteen hundred seventy-eight, to such spouse thirty-six and two-thirds per centum of the average wage of the deceased during widowhood or widowerhood with two years' compensation in one sum upon remarriage; and thirty per centum of such wages to such children under the age of eighteen years or under the age of twenty-three years if enrolled and attending as a full time student in an accredited educational institution and such enrollment and full time attendance is certified by such institution or a surviving child or children of any age dependent blind or physically disabled, share and share alike; in case of the subsequent death of such surviving spouse the surviving children shall have their compensation increased to sixty-six and two-thirds per centum of such wages and the aggregate sum shall be payable, share and share alike, so long as they are under the age of eighteen years or under the age of twenty-three years if enrolled and attending as a full time student in an accredited educational institution and such enrollment and full time attendance is certified by such institution or a surviving child or children of any age dependent blind or physically disabled. Upon remarriage of such surviving spouse, if there be two surviving children each shall receive twenty-five per centum of such wages, and if there are surviving more than two children under the age of eighteen years or under the age of twenty-three if enrolled and attending as a full time student in an accredited educational institution and such enrollment and full time attendance is certified by such institution or a surviving child or children of any age dependent blind or physically disabled sixty-six and two-thirds per centum of such wages share and share alike. Upon statutory termination of compensation payable to such children, the compensation of the surviving spouse shall be increased to sixty-six and two-thirds per centum of such wages with two years' compensation, at such rate, in one sum, upon remarriage. Where the death occurs on or after January first, nineteen hundred seventy-eight, and the spouse is receiving survivors insurance benefits under the social security act, the death benefits payable under this section shall be reduced by five per centum of the spouse's share of the survivors insurance benefits under the social security act for each ten dollars of deceased's average weekly wage in excess of one hundred fifty dollars provided that in no case shall such reduction exceed fifty per centum of said spouse's share of the survivors insurance benefits under the social security act as set forth in table No. II below.

TABLE No. II
Offset provisions applicable in death benefit where there is a surviving spouse and two or more children

AVERAGE WEEKLY WAGE	PERCENTAGE OF SPOUSE'S SHARE OF SURVIVORS INSURANCE BENEFITS
over $150 up to and including $160	5
over $160 up to and including $170	10
over $170 up to and including $180	15
over $180 up to and including $190	20
over $190 up to and including $200	25
over $200 up to and including $210	30
over $210 up to and including $220	35
over $220 up to and including $230	40
over $230 up to and including $240	45
over $240 up to and including $250	50
over $250	50

2-b. If there be a surviving spouse of an employee of a private voluntary hospital killed in a World Trade Center rescue, who passed a physical examination upon employment as a rescue worker that failed to reveal evidence of a condition that was the proximate cause of death, and a surviving child under the age of eighteen years, or under the age of twenty-three years if enrolled and attending as a full-time student in an accredited educational institution and such enrollment and full-time attendance is certified by such institution, or a surviving child of any age dependent blind or physically disabled, to such spouse forty per centum of the average wages of the deceased during widowhood or widowerhood, with two years' compensation in one sum, upon remarriage; and thirty-five per centum of such wages to such child under the age of eighteen years, or under the age of twenty-three years if enrolled and attending as a full-time student in an accredited educational institution and such enrollment and full-time attendance is certified by such institution, or a surviving child of any age dependent blind or physically disabled; in the case of the subsequent death of such surviving spouse the surviving child shall have his or her compensation increased to seventy-five per centum of such wages and the same shall be payable so long as he or she is under the age of eighteen years, or under the age of twenty-three years if enrolled and attending as a full-time student in an accredited educational institution and such enrollment and full-time attendance is certified by such institution, or a surviving child of any age dependent blind or physically disabled; upon statutory termination of compensation payable to such child, the compensation of the surviving spouse shall be increased to seventy-five per centum of such wages with two years' compensation, at such rate, in one sum, upon remarriage. Upon remarriage of such surviving spouse, the surviving child shall continue to receive thirty-five per centum of such wages. Where such death occurs, and the spouse is receiving survivors insurance benefits under the social security act, the death benefit payable under this section shall be reduced by five per centum of the spouse's share of the survivors insurance benefits under the social security act for each ten dollars of deceased's average weekly wage in excess of one hundred dollars; provided that in no case shall such reduction exceed fifty per centum of such spouse's share of the survivors insurance benefits under the social security act as set forth in table No. I in subdivision one-c of this section. If there be a surviving spouse of an employee of a private voluntary hospital killed in a World Trade Center rescue, who passed a physical examination upon employment as a rescue worker that failed to reveal evidence of a condition that was the proximate cause of death, and two or more surviving children under the age of eighteen years, or under the age of twenty-three years if enrolled and attending as a full-time student in an accredited educational institution and such enrollment and full-time attendance is certified by such institution, or a surviving child or children of any age dependent blind or physically disabled and a death occurs on or after September eleventh, two thousand one, to such spouse forty per centum of the average wage of the deceased during widowhood or widowerhood with two years' compensation in one sum upon remarriage; and thirty-five per centum of such wages to such children under the age of eighteen years, or under the age of twenty-three years if enrolled and attending as a full-time student in an accredited educational institution and such enrollment and full-time attendance is certified by such institution, or a surviving child or children of any age dependent blind or physically disabled, share and share alike; in case of the subsequent death of such surviving spouse the surviving children shall have their compensation increased to seventy-five per centum of such wages and the aggregate sum shall be payable, share and share alike, so long as they are under the age of eighteen years, or under the age of twenty-three years if enrolled and attending as a full-time student in an accredited educational institution and such enrollment and full-time attendance is certified by such institution, or a surviving child or children of any age dependent blind or physically disabled. Upon remarriage of such surviving spouse, if there be two surviving children each shall receive thirty-seven and one-half per centum of such wages, and if there are surviving more than two children under the age of eighteen years, or under the age of twenty-three if enrolled and attending as a full-time student in an accredited educational institution and such enrollment and full-time attendance is certified by such institution, or a surviving child or children of any age dependent blind or physically disabled, seventy-five per centum of such wages share and share alike. Upon statutory termination of compensation payable to such children, the compensation of the surviving spouse shall be increased to seventy-five per centum of such wages with two years' compensation, at such rate, in one sum, upon remarriage. Where the death occurs on or after September eleventh, two thousand one, and the spouse is receiving survivors insurance benefits under the social security act, the death benefits payable under this section shall be reduced by five per centum of the spouse's share of the survivors insurance benefits under the social security act for each ten dollars of deceased's average weekly wage in excess of one hundred fifty dollars; provided that in no case shall such reduction exceed fifty per centum of said spouse's share of the survivors insurance benefits under the social security act as set forth in table No. II in subdivision two-a of this section.

3. If there be a surviving child or children of the deceased under the age of eighteen years or a dependent blind or physically disabled child or children of any age, but no surviving spouse then where the death occurs on or after July first, nineteen hundred forty-eight, and prior to January first, nineteen hundred seventy-eight, for the support of each such child until the age of eighteen years, or until the removal of the dependency of such blind or physically disabled child or children, thirty per centum of the wages of the deceased, and where the death occurred prior to July first, nineteen hundred forty-eight, for the support of each such child until the age of eighteen years, or until the removal of the dependency of such blind or physically disabled child or children, fifteen per centum of the wages of the deceased; provided that the aggregate shall in no case exceed sixty-six and two-thirds per centum of such wages.

3-a. If there be a surviving child or children of the deceased under the age of eighteen years or under the age of twenty-three years if enrolled and attending as a full time student in an accredited educational institution and such enrollment and full time attendance is certified by such institution or a dependent blind or physically disabled child or children of any age, but no surviving spouse then where the death occurs on or after January first, nineteen hundred seventy-eight, for the support of such child or children until the age of eighteen years, or under the age of twenty-three years if enrolled and attending as a full time student in an accredited educational institution and such enrollment and full time attendance is certified by such institution or until the removal of the dependency of such blind or physically disabled child or children, sixty-six and two-thirds per centum of the wages of the deceased. Where there are two or more children, the compensation payable shall be divided among such children share and share alike.

3-b. If there be a surviving child or children, of an employee of a private voluntary hospital killed in a World Trade Center rescue, who passed a physical examination upon employment as a rescue worker that failed to reveal evidence of a condition that was the proximate cause of death, under the age of eighteen years, or under the age of twenty-three years if enrolled and attending as a full-time student in an accredited educational institution and such enrollment and full-time attendance is certified by such institution, or a dependent blind or physically disabled child, or children of any age, but no surviving spouse then, where such death occurs, for the support of each such child until the age of eighteen years, or under the age of twenty-three years if enrolled and attending as a full-time student in an accredited educational institution and such enrollment and full-time attendance is certified by such institution or until the removal of the dependency of such blind or physically disabled child or children, seventy-five per centum of the wages of the deceased. Where there are two or more children, the compensation payable shall be divided among such children share and share alike.

4. If there be no surviving spouse or child under the age of eighteen years, or dependent blind or physically disabled child of any age, or if the amount payable to surviving spouse and to children under the age of eighteen years or such dependent blind or physically disabled children shall be less in the aggregate than sixty-six and two-thirds per centum of the average wages of the deceased, then where the death occurs on or after July first, nineteen hundred forty-eight, and prior to January first, nineteen hundred seventy-eight, for the support of grandchildren or brothers and sisters under the age of eighteen years, if dependent upon the deceased at the time of the accident, twenty-five per centum of such wages for the support of each such person until the age of eighteen years; and for the support of each parent, or grandparent, of the deceased if dependent upon him at the time of the accident, forty per centum of such wages during such dependency; and where the death occurred prior to July first, nineteen hundred forty-eight, to such dependent grandchildren or brothers and sisters, fifteen per centum of such wages until eighteen years of age, and to such dependent parent or grandparent, twenty-five per centum of such wages during dependency. But in no case shall the aggregate amount payable under this subdivision exceed the difference between sixty-six and two-thirds per centum of

such wages, and the amount payable as hereinbefore provided to surviving spouse or for the support of surviving child or children.

4-a. If there be no surviving spouse or child under the age of eighteen years or under the age of twenty-three years if enrolled and attending as a full time student in an accredited educational institution and such enrollment and full time attendance is certified by such institution or dependent blind or physically disabled child of any age, then where the death occurs on or after January first, nineteen hundred seventy-eight, for the support of grandchildren or brothers and sisters if dependent upon the deceased at the time of the accident, under the age of eighteen years, or under the age of twenty-three years if enrolled and attending as a full time student in an accredited educational institution and such enrollment and full time attendance is certified by such institution, or blind or physically disabled grandchildren or brothers and sisters of any age, twenty-five per centum of such wages for the support of each such person until the age of eighteen years; or until the age of twenty-three years if enrolled and attending as a full time student in an accredited educational institution or until the removal of the dependency of such blind or physically disabled grandchildren or brothers and sisters, and such enrollment and full time attendance is certified by such institution and for the support of each parent, or grandparent, of the deceased if dependent upon him or her at the time of the accident, forty per centum of such wages during such dependency. But in no case shall the aggregate amount payable under this subdivision exceed sixty-six and two-thirds per centum of such wages.

4-b. If there be no surviving spouse or child under the age of eighteen years or under the age of twenty-three years if enrolled and attending as a full time student in an accredited educational institution and such enrollment and full time attendance is certified by such institution or dependent blind or physically disabled child of any age or grandchildren or brothers and sisters if dependent upon the deceased at the time of the accident, under the age of eighteen years, or under the age of twenty-three years if enrolled and attending as a full time student in an accredited educational institution and such enrollment and full time attendance is certified by such institution or disabled blind or physically disabled grandchildren or brothers and sisters of any age, then a sum of fifty thousand dollars shall be paid to the deceased's surviving parents or if there be no surviving parents to the deceased's estate.

4-c. If there be no surviving spouse or child, or children of an employee of a private voluntary hospital killed in a World Trade Center rescue, who passed a physical examination upon employment as a rescue worker that failed to reveal evidence of a condition that was the proximate cause of death, under the age of eighteen years, or under the age of twenty-three years if enrolled and attending as a full-time student in an accredited educational institution and such enrollment and full-time attendance is certified by such institution, or dependent blind or physically disabled child of any age, then where the death occurs on or after September eleventh, two thousand one, for the support of grandchildren or brothers and sisters if dependent upon the deceased at the time of the accident, under the age of eighteen years, or under the age of twenty-three years if enrolled and attending as a full-time student in an accredited educational institution and such enrollment and full-time attendance is certified by such institution, or blind or physically disabled grandchildren or brothers and sisters of any age, twenty-five per centum of such wages for the support of each such person until the age of eighteen years; or until the age of twenty-three years if enrolled and attending as a full-time student in an accredited educational institution, or until the removal of the dependency of such blind or physically disabled grandchildren or brothers and sisters, and such enrollment and full-time attendance is certified by such institution and for the support of each parent, or grandparent, of the deceased if dependent upon him or her at the time of the accident, forty per centum of such wages during such dependency. But in no case shall the aggregate amount payable under this subdivision exceed seventy-five per centum of such wages.

4-d. If there be no surviving spouse or child, or children of an employee of a private voluntary hospital killed in a World Trade Center rescue, who passed a physical examination upon employment as a rescue worker that failed to reveal evidence of a condition that was the proximate cause of death, under the age of eighteen years, or under the age of twenty-three years if enrolled and attending as a full-time student in an accredited educational institution and such enrollment and full-time attendance is certified by such institution, or dependent blind or physically disabled child of any age, or grandchildren or brothers and sisters if dependent upon the deceased at the time of the accident, under the age of eighteen years, or under the age of twenty-three years if enrolled and attending as a full-time student in an accredited educational institution and such enrollment and full-time attendance is certified by such institution, or disabled blind or physically disabled grandchildren or brothers and sisters of any age, then a sum of fifty thousand dollars shall be paid to the deceased's surviving parents or if there be no surviving parents to the deceased's estate.

5. Any excess of wages over: (1) seven hundred fifty dollars shall not be taken into account in computing compensation under this section in cases where the death occurs on or after July first, two thousand seven, (2) eight hundred twenty-five dollars shall not be taken into account in computing compensation under this section in cases where the death occurs on or after July first, two thousand eight, (3) nine hundred dollars shall not be taken into account in computing compensation under this section in cases where the death occurs on or after July first, two thousand nine, and (4) where the death occurs on or after July first, two thousand ten, or when the death occurs on or after July first of each succeeding year, an amount equal to the New York state average weekly wage for the year in which it is reported shall not be taken into account in computing compensation under this section. Any excess of wages over five hundred ten dollars and five cents per week shall not be taken into account in computing compensation under this section in cases where the death occurs on or after July first, nineteen hundred ninety, nor shall any excess of wages over five hundred twenty-five dollars per week be taken into account in computing compensation pursuant to this section in cases where death occurs on or after July first, nineteen hundred ninety-one, nor shall any excess of wages over six hundred dollars per week be taken into account in computing compensation pursuant to this section in cases where death occurs on or after July first, nineteen hundred ninety-two with the exception that wages earned over six hundred dollars per week shall be taken into account in computing compensation under this section in cases involving an employee of a private voluntary hospital resulting from a World Trade Center rescue, who passed a physical examination upon employment as a rescue worker that failed to reveal evidence of a condition that was the proximate cause of death; nor shall any excess of wages over three hundred eighty-two dollars and fifty cents per week be taken into account in computing compensation under this section in cases where the death occurs on or after July first, nineteen hundred eighty-three, nor shall any excess of wages over four hundred twelve dollars and fifty cents per week be taken into account in computing compensation under this section in cases where the death occurs on or after July first, nineteen hundred eighty-four, nor shall any excess of wages over four hundred fifty dollars per week be taken into account in computing compensation under this section in cases where the death occurs on or after July first, nineteen hundred eighty-five; nor shall any excess of wages over one hundred eighty-seven dollars and fifty cents per week on or after January first, nineteen hundred seventy-eight or over two hundred seventy dollars per week on or after July first, nineteen hundred seventy-eight or over three hundred twenty-two dollars and fifty cents per week on or after January first, nineteen hundred seventy-nine, and prior to July first, nineteen hundred eighty-three, be taken into account in computing compensation under this section nor shall any excess of wages over six hundred and seventeen dollars and fifty cents a month be taken into account in computing compensation under this section in cases where the death occurred on or after July first, nineteen hundred seventy-four, and prior to January first, nineteen hundred seventy-eight, nor shall any excess of wages over five hundred and twenty dollars a month be taken into account in computing compensation in cases where death occurred on or after July first, nineteen hundred seventy and prior to July first, nineteen hundred seventy-four, nor shall any excess of wages over four hundred and fifty-five dollars a month be taken into account in computing compensation in cases where death occurred on or after July first, nineteen hundred sixty-eight and prior to July first, nineteen hundred seventy, nor shall any excess of wages over three hundred and ninety dollars a month be taken into account in computing compensation in cases where death occurred on or after July first, nineteen hundred sixty-five and prior to July first, nineteen hundred sixty-eight, nor shall any excess of wages over three hundred and fifty-seven dollars and fifty cents a month be taken into account in computing

compensation in cases where death occurred on or after July first, nineteen hundred sixty-two and prior to July first, nineteen hundred sixty-five, nor shall any excess of wages over three hundred and twenty-five dollars a month be taken into account in computing compensation in cases where death occurred on or after July first, nineteen hundred sixty and prior to July first, nineteen hundred sixty-two, nor shall any excess of wages over two hundred and ninety-two dollars and fifty cents a month be taken into account in computing compensation where death occurred on or after July first, nineteen hundred fifty-eight and prior to July first, nineteen hundred sixty, nor shall any excess of wages over two hundred and sixty dollars a month be taken into account in computing compensation where death occurred on or after July first, nineteen hundred fifty-four and prior to July first, nineteen hundred fifty-eight, nor shall any excess of wages over two hundred and twenty-seven dollars and fifty cents a month be taken into account in computing compensation where death occurred on or after July first, nineteen hundred forty-eight and prior to July first, nineteen hundred fifty-four, nor shall any excess of wages over one hundred and eighty-two dollars a month be taken into account in computing compensation where the death occurred on or after June first, nineteen hundred forty-six and prior to July first, nineteen hundred forty-eight. When death occurred on or after July first, nineteen hundred forty-eight and prior to January first, nineteen hundred seventy-eight, computing compensation to the widow or widower and children of a deceased employee in no event shall wages be deemed to be less than one hundred and thirty dollars a month. All questions of dependency shall be determined as of the time of the accident. When death occurred on or after January first, nineteen hundred seventy-eight, in no event shall wages be deemed to be less than forty-five dollars a week in computing compensation to the widow or widower and/or children of the deceased employee.

6. If there be a person entitled to death benefits under the provisions of this section, who shall be under the age of eighteen years, and who shall be an inmate of any institution and a public charge upon the department of social services of the city of New York, or any other department or body, the benefits allowed hereunder shall be payable to the said department of public welfare of the city of New York or any other department or body to the extent of the reasonable charges for the care and maintenance, during the continuance as a public charge in said institution, of said beneficiary and until the said person shall have attained the age of eighteen years. Any sum or sums remaining after the said payment out of the benefits shall be distributed as provided by the other subdivisions of this section.

7. In computing the offsets under subdivisions one-c and two-a of this section any increase in survivors insurance benefits under social security that occurs after the date of death shall not be considered, and any such offset shall be equally applicable to the survivors insurance benefits under the social security act which are received retroactively but such offset shall not apply to increases of such benefits received retroactively.

§ 24-a. Representation before the workers' compensation board

1. No person, firm or corporation, other than an attorney and counsellor-at-law, shall appear on behalf of any claimant or person entitled to the benefits of this chapter, before the board or any officer, agent or employee of the board assigned to conduct any hearing, investigation or inquiry relative to a claim for compensation or benefits under this chapter, unless he or she shall be a citizen of the United States or an alien lawfully admitted for permanent residence in the United States, and shall have obtained from the board a license authorizing him or her to appear in matters or proceedings before the board. Such license shall be issued by the board in accordance with the rules established by it. Any person, firm or corporation violating the aforesaid provisions shall be guilty of a misdemeanor. The board, in its rules, shall provide for the issuance of licenses to representatives of charitable and welfare organizations, and to associations who employ a representative to appear for members of such association, upon certification of the proper officer of such association or organization, which licenses shall issue without charge; and may provide for a license without fee in the case of all other persons, firms or corporations in an amount to be fixed by said rules. The board shall have such tests of character and fitness with respect to applicants for licenses, and such rules governing the conduct of those licensed, as aforesaid, as it may deem necessary.

2. There shall be maintained in each office of the board a registry or list of persons to whom licenses have been issued as provided herein, which list shall be corrected as often as licenses are issued or revoked. Absence of a record of a license issued as herein provided shall be prima facie evidence that a person, firm or corporation is not licensed to represent claimants. Any such license may be revoked by the board, for cause, after a hearing before the board. No license hereunder shall be issued for a period longer than three years from the date of its issuance.

3. Refusal by any person to whom a license has been issued authorizing him to appear on behalf of any claimant to answer, upon request of the board, or other duly authorized officer, board or committee of the state, any legal question or to produce any relevant book or paper concerning his conduct under such license, shall constitute adequate cause for revocation thereof.

4. Only an attorney, or a representative licensed in accordance with rules established by the board pursuant to subdivisions three-b and three-d of section fifty of this chapter, shall appear on behalf of an employer or an insurance carrier regarding a claim for compensation or any benefits under this chapter before the board or any officer, agent or employee of the board assigned to conduct any hearing relative to a claim for compensation or benefits under this chapter. The provisions of this subdivision shall not apply to a designated regular employee of a self-insured employer, or of an insurance carrier appearing on behalf of his or her employer, but the board may prohibit the appearance of any such employee for cause.

§ 32. Waiver agreements

No agreement or release except as otherwise provided in this chapter by an employee to waive his right to compensation under this chapter shall be valid.

(a) Whenever a claim has been filed, the claimant or the deceased claimant's dependents and the employer, its carrier, the special disability fund as set forth in subdivision (e) of this section, or the aggregate trust fund, if the board has directed that the present value of any unpaid compensation be paid into such fund pursuant to section twenty-seven of this article, may enter into an agreement settling upon and determining the compensation and other benefits due to the claimant or his or her dependents. The agreement shall not bind the parties to it, unless it is approved by the board. Such agreements, when so approved, notwithstanding any other provisions, shall be final and conclusive upon the claimant, the claimant's dependents, the employer, its insurance carrier, the aggregate trust fund and the special disability fund. Every insurance carrier as defined in subdivision twelve of section two of this chapter shall offer each claimant the opportunity to enter into an agreement settling upon and determining the compensation and other benefits due, in the case of disability, within two years after the date the claim was indexed by the board or six months after the claimant is classified with a permanent disability, whichever is later, and in the case of death, within six months after entitlement to benefits is established for all beneficiaries. The offer made by the insurance carrier shall clearly state what portion of the offer is (i) for compensation as defined in subdivision six of section two of this chapter, if any; (ii) for medical benefits, including prescription medicine, if any; and (iii) for the fee of the attorney or licensed representative, if any. If a claimant is represented by an attorney or licensed representative, the insurance carrier shall present such offer to such legal representative. If a claimant is not represented by an attorney or a licensed representative, the insurance carrier shall, in addition to the offer to enter into a settlement agreement, provide the claimant with a statement of his or her rights, obligations and potential liability if the offer is accepted.

(b) The agreement shall be approved by the board in a decision duly filed and served unless:

(1) the board finds the proposed agreement unfair, unconscionable, or improper as a matter of law;

(2) the board finds that the proposed agreement is the result of an intentional misrepresentation of material fact; or,

(3) within ten days of submitting the agreement one of the interested parties requests that the board disapprove the agreement.

(c) A decision duly filed and served approving an agreement submitted to the board shall not be subject to review pursuant to section twenty-three of this article. However, a decision duly filed and served disapproving an agreement submitted to the board is subject to review pursuant to section twenty-three of this article. If the board disapproves of an agreement it shall duly file and serve a notice of decision setting aside the proposed agreement.

(d) An agreement for compensation and other benefits covered by this chapter may be modified at any time by agreement of all interested parties provided it is approved by the board.

(e) The chair shall establish an office under his or her supervision to be known as the "waiver agreement management office," to negotiate and seek board approval for waiver agreements on behalf of the special disability fund. The office shall operate in accordance with guidelines or directives that the chair may issue, as approved by the special disability fund advisory committee, or in the absence of such guidelines or directives, using such discounting factors as the office determines are in the financial interest of the special disability fund. The waiver agreement management office on behalf of the special disability fund may enter into a waiver agreement with a claimant only when the special disability fund has been found liable by the board to reimburse the claimant's employer, insurance carrier or the state insurance fund. Notwithstanding any other provisions of law, no consultation or approval of any employer, insurance carrier, self-insurer or the state insurance fund shall be required before such office may enter into any waiver agreement, or before the board may approve such waiver agreement. The chair may, in his or her discretion, and as approved by the special disability fund advisory committee, terminate the operation of the waiver agreement management office, if he or she believes it no longer serves the interest of the special disability fund.

(f) A claimant's executed waiver agreement with the waiver agreement management office shall be final and conclusive upon the claimant, the claimant's dependents, and any employer, self-insurer, insurance carrier, the state insurance fund and the special disability fund as to all claims by the claimant, and as to any claim or request for reimbursement from the special disability fund for payments not yet made. The waiver agreement management office shall give written notice to any employer, insurance carrier or the state insurance fund entitled to receive reimbursement from the special disability fund in regard to any claimant, of any waiver agreement signed by the office with such claimant within fourteen days of submitting the waiver agreement to the board for approval.

(g) Nothing in this section shall prohibit any insurance carrier, employer, the state insurance fund, or the waiver agreement management office on behalf of the special disability fund from jointly entering into a waiver agreement with a claimant, by which the joint signatories may apportion responsibility for making any payments required under the agreement. The agreement shall set forth the obligations of the signatories to make such payments, and shall identify, as to each obligation thereunder: (1) the signatory that has the legal obligation to carry out that provision, or (2) that all signatories are jointly and severally liable under the provision.

(h) Neither the establishment of the waiver agreement management office, nor any action taken by that office, shall serve as grounds for the board's disapproval of any waiver agreement to which the office is not a party, or otherwise permit any party to withdraw from such a waiver agreement.

(i) (1) The waiver agreement management office may contract with any third party to manage, administer, or settle claims on its behalf, so long as (A) such contract is approved by the special disability fund advisory committee and (B) such third party shall agree to be subject to any guidelines or directives as the chair may issue.

(2) The chair, with approval of the special disability fund advisory committee and on such terms as the committee deems appropriate, shall have discretion to procure one or more private entities to assume

the liability for and management, administration or settlement of all or a portion of the claims in the special disability fund. Any such procurement shall be conducted in accordance with state finance law, except as otherwise set forth below. The chair shall not award any contract that has not been approved by the special disability fund advisory committee. Notwithstanding the foregoing, the chair of the workers' compensation board may, if approved by the special disability fund advisory committee, and on such terms as the committee deems appropriate:

(A) waive any informality in a bid, and either reject all bids and again advertise for bids, or interview at least two responsible qualified bidders and negotiate and enter into a contract with one or more of such bidders; or

(B) group claims to be assigned, in whole or in part, based on the insurance carrier, self-insured employer or state insurance fund that is receiving or will receive reimbursement on those claims from the second disability fund. Such grouping shall be permissible notwithstanding that any insurance carrier may have greater access to information, or may be able to provide better terms, in regard to claims so grouped.

(3) Any such contract shall expressly provide that the special disability fund is no longer liable for the claims covered by the contract, and require security of either cash, an indemnity policy, or such security as is otherwise sufficient to cover any losses incurred as a result of the failure or default of the entity or entities awarded any such contract, including as a result of the insolvency of any such entity. The chair may waive all or part of such security, and may impose other reasonable methods of insuring payment, upon approval of the special disability fund advisory committee.

(4) Notwithstanding any other provision of this article, the waiver agreement management office may request in writing any information relevant to its entry into or management of waiver agreements from (A) any insurance carrier, employer, or the state insurance fund, if that entity has submitted a claim for reimbursement from the special disability fund as to the claimant to whom the information relates; or (B) the special funds conservation committee. The party to whom the request is made shall provide the requested information within fourteen days of the request, unless before that date it files an objection with the board to any information which is subject to a recognized privilege or whose production is otherwise barred by law. The objecting party shall provide the requested information within five business days of the board's rejection of its objection.

(5) No carrier, self-insured employer or the state insurance fund shall assume the liability for, or management, administration or settlement of any claims under this section on which it holds reserves, beyond such reserves as are permitted by regulation of the superintendent of financial services for purposes of this provision. No carrier may assume liability for any claims in the special disability fund under this paragraph unless the carrier maintains, on a stand alone basis, separate from its parent or any affiliated entities, an interactive financial strength rating from a nationally recognized statistical rating organization that is considered secure or deemed acceptable by the special disability fund advisory committee.

(6) The director of the budget shall notify in writing the chairs of the senate finance committee and the assembly ways and means committee of any plans to transfer all or a portion of the portfolio of claims determined to be eligible for reimbursement from the special disability fund or to contract with any party to take responsibility in whole or in part for the administration of a material portion of the claims, including the procurement process to be used to select parties involved in such transfer or contract, not less than forty-five days prior to the commencement of such process. At any time borrowing is anticipated to settle claims, the chief executive officer of the dormitory authority of the state of New York and the director of the budget shall provide a report to the chairs of the senate finance committee and the assembly ways and means committee on a planned bond sale of the authority and such report shall include, but not be limited to: (A) the maximum amount of bonds expected to be sold by the authority in connection with a sale agreement; (B) the expected maximum interest rate and maturity

date of such bonds; (C) the expected amount of the bonds that will be fixed and/or variable interest rate; (D) the estimated costs of issuance; (E) the estimated level or levels of reserve fund or funds, if any; (F) the estimated cost of bond issuance, if any; (G) the anticipated use or uses of the proceeds; (H) the maximum expected net proceeds that will be paid to the state as a result of the issuance of such bonds; and (I) the process to be used to select parties to the transaction. Any such expectations and estimates in the report shall not be deemed a substantive limitation on the authority of the dormitory authority of the state of New York.

§ 45. Notice to employers

The employer to whom notice of death or disability is to be given, or against whom claim is to be made by the employee, shall be the employer who last employed the employee in the employment to the nature of which the disease was due and such notice and claim shall be deemed seasonable as against prior employers. The requirements as to notice as to occupational disease and death resulting therefrom shall be the same as required in section eighteen of this chapter, except that the notice shall be given to the employer within two years after the disablement or after the claimant knew or should have known that the disease is due to the nature of the employment, whichever is the later date.

§ 50. Security for payment of compensation

An employer shall secure compensation to his employees in one or more of the following ways:

1. By insuring and keeping insured the payment of such compensation in the state fund, or

2. By insuring and keeping insured the payment of such compensation with any stock corporation, mutual corporation or reciprocal insurer authorized to transact the business of workers' compensation insurance in this state through a policy issued under the law of this state.

3. By furnishing satisfactory proof to the chair of his financial ability to pay such compensation for himself, or to pay such compensation on behalf of a group of employers in accordance with subdivision ten of this section, in which case the chair shall require the deposit with the chair of such securities as the chair may deem necessary of the kind prescribed in subdivisions one, two, three, four and five, and subparagraph (a) of paragraph three of subdivision seven of section two hundred thirty-five of the banking law, or the deposit of cash, or the filing of irrevocable letters of credit issued by a qualified banking institution as defined by rules promulgated by the chair or the filing of a bond of a surety company authorized to transact business in this state, in an amount to be determined by the chair, or the posting and filing as aforesaid of a combination of such securities, cash, irrevocable letters of credit and surety bond in an amount to be determined by the chair, to secure his liability to pay the compensation provided in this chapter. Any such surety bond must be approved as to form by the chair. If an employer or group of employers posts and files a combination of securities, cash, irrevocable letters of credit and surety bond as aforesaid, and if it becomes necessary to use the same to pay the compensation provided in this chapter, the chair shall first use such securities or cash or irrevocable letters of credit and, when the full amount thereof has been exhausted, he shall then require the surety to pay forthwith to the chair all or any part of the penal sum of the bond for that purpose. The chair may also require an agreement on the part of the employer or group of employers to pay any awards commuted under section twenty-seven of this chapter, into the special fund of the state fund, as a condition of his being allowed to remain uninsured pursuant to this section. The chair shall have the authority to deny the application of an employer or group of employers to pay such compensation for himself or to revoke his consent furnished, under this section at any time, for good cause shown. The employer or group of employers qualifying under this subdivision shall be known as a self-insurer.

If for any reason the status of an employer or group of employers under this subdivision is terminated, the securities or the surety bond, or the securities, cash, or irrevocable letters of credit and surety bond, on deposit referred to herein shall remain in the custody of the chair for such time as the chair may deem proper and warranted under the circumstances. In lieu thereof, and at the discretion of the chair, the employer, his or her heirs or assigns or others carrying on or liquidating such business, may execute an assumption of workers' compensation liability insurance policy securing such further and future contingent liability as may arise from prior injuries to workers and be incurred by reason of any change in condition of such workers warranting the board making subsequent awards for payment of additional compensation. Such policy shall be in a form approved by the superintendent of financial services and issued by the state fund or any insurance company licensed to issue this class of insurance in this state. In the event that such policy is issued by an insurance company other than the state fund, then said policy shall be deemed of the kind specified in paragraph fifteen of subsection (a) of section one thousand one hundred thirteen of the insurance law and covered by the workers' compensation security fund as created and governed by article six-A of this chapter. It shall only be issued for a single complete premium payment in advance by the employer or group of employers and in an amount deemed acceptable by the chair and the superintendent of financial services. In lieu of the applicable premium charge ordinarily required to be imposed by a carrier, said premium shall include a surcharge in an amount to be determined by the chair to: (i) satisfy all assessment liability due and owing to the board and/or the chair under this chapter; and (ii) satisfy all future assessment liability under this section, and which surcharge shall be adjusted from time to time to reflect any changes to the assessment of group self-insured employers, including any changes enacted by the chapter of the laws of two thousand eleven amending sections fifteen and one hundred fifty-one of this chapter. Said surcharge shall be payable to the board simultaneous to the execution of the assumption of workers' compensation liability insurance policy. However, the payment of said surcharge does not relieve the carrier from any other liability, including liability owed to the superintendent of financial services pursuant to article six-A of this chapter. When issued such policy shall be non-cancellable without recourse for any cause during the continuance of the liability secured and so covered.

3-a. Group self-insurance.

(1) Definitions. As used in this chapter the term "employers" shall include: (a) employers with related activity in a given industry which shall include municipal corporations as that term is defined in sections two and six-n of the general municipal law, employing persons who perform work in connection with the given industry, (b) an incorporated or unincorporated association or associations consisting exclusively of such employers provided they employ persons who perform such related work in the given industry, and (c) a combination of employers as described in subparagraph (a) hereof and an association or associations of employers as described in subparagraph (b) hereof.

(2) (a) Any group consisting exclusively of such employers may adopt a plan for self-insurance, as a group, for the payment of compensation under this chapter to their employees, except that no new groups may adopt such a plan, and no group not composed solely of public entities set forth in paragraph a of subdivision four of this section may insure any liabilities for any employers on and after January first, two thousand twelve, except as provided for in paragraph ten of this subdivision. Under such plan the group shall assume the liability of all the employers within the group and pay all compensation for which the said employers are liable under this chapter, except that in the case of municipal corporations as herein defined no proof of financial ability or deposit of securities or cash need be made in compliance with this subdivision. The group qualifying under this subdivision shall be known as a group self-insurer and the employers participating therein and covered thereby shall be known as members.

(b) Where such plan is adopted the group self-insurer shall furnish satisfactory proof to the chair of its financial ability to pay such compensation for the members in the industry covered by it, its revenues, their source and assurance of continuance. The chair shall require the deposit with the chair of such securities as may be deemed necessary of the kind prescribed in subdivisions one, two, three, four and five, and subparagraph (a) of paragraph three of subdivision seven of section two hundred thirty-five of the banking law or the deposit of cash or the filing of irrevocable letters of credit issued by a qualified banking institution as defined by rules promulgated by the chair or the filing of a bond of a surety company authorized to transact business in this state, in an amount to be determined to secure its liability to pay the compensation of each employer as above provided. Such surety bond must be approved as to form by the chair. The chair shall require each group self-insurer to provide regular reports no less than annually, which shall include but not be limited to audited financial statements, actuarial opinions and payroll information containing proof that it is fully funded. Such reports shall also include a contribution year analysis detailing contributions and expenses associated with each specific contribution year. For purposes of this paragraph, proof that a group self-insurer is fully funded shall at a minimum include proof of unrestricted cash and investments permitted by regulation of the chair of at least one hundred percent of the total liabilities, including the estimate presented in the actuarial opinion submitted by the group self-insurer in accordance with this chapter. The chair by regulation, may set further financial standards for group self-insurers. Any group self-insurer that fails to show that it is fully funded shall be deemed underfunded, and must submit a plan for achieving fully funded status which may include a deficit assessment on members of such group self-insurer which shall be subject to approval or modification by the chair.

(c) The chair shall evaluate, no less than once every three years, a group self-insurer's compliance with the financial and regulatory requirements for self-insurance. The chair may engage any qualified person or organization to assist with such evaluation and any costs incurred by the chair shall be borne by the group self-insurer under examination. Failure to submit to such independent review or to pay such costs, upon demand of the chair, shall be sufficient grounds to terminate coverage of the group self-insurer.

(d) The chair may require reports to be prepared by an auditor, actuary or other consultant, selected by the board or, at the chair's discretion, by the group self-insurer from a list which shall be pre-approved by the chair to determine whether the group self-insurer meets the financial criteria for self-insurance. All actuaries so selected shall be fellows or associates of the casualty actuarial society.

(e) The chair may also require that any and all agreements, contracts and other pertinent documents relating to the organization of the members in the group self-insurer shall be filed with the chair.

(f) The chair shall have the authority to revoke consent furnished under this section at any time for good cause shown.

(g) Prior to the requested effective date of the participating agreement, a group self-insurer shall notify the chair on a prescribed form of a new group self-insurer member and file (1) a member application and (2) a copy of the properly executed prescribed participation agreement wherein the member acknowledges their joint and several obligation for their period of membership. The board shall, on a form promulgated by the chair, provide notice of the member's rights and responsibilities as a group self-insurer member, including the member's assumption of joint and several liability, and require the member to return a signed copy to the chair as a condition of membership.

(h) Any member terminating membership in a group self-insurer after less than four years in such group self-insurer, and any member in a group self-insurer that has defaulted, shall be precluded from obtaining prospective coverage from any group self-insurer for a period of at least three years from the effective date of termination.

(3) A member's participation in a group self-insurer shall not relieve it of its liability for compensation prescribed by this chapter except by the payment thereof by the group self-insurer or by itself. Each member shall be responsible, jointly and severally, for all liabilities of the group self-insurer provided for by this chapter occurring during its respective period of membership, and such liability shall attach to any recipient of a conveyance of assets made in violation of section two hundred seventy-three of the debtor and creditor law. As between the employee and the group self-insurer, notice to or knowledge of the occurrence of the injury on the part of the member shall be deemed notice or knowledge, as the case may be, on the part of the group self-insurer; jurisdiction of the member shall, for the purpose of this chapter, be jurisdiction of the group self-insurer and such group self-insurer shall in all things be bound by and subject to the orders, findings, decisions or awards rendered against the participating

member for the payment of compensation under the provisions of this chapter. The insolvency or bankruptcy of a participating member shall not relieve the group self-insurer from the payment of compensation for injuries or death sustained by an employee during the time the member was a participant in such group self-insurer. Notice of termination of a participating member shall not be effective until at least ten days after notice of such termination, on a prescribed form, has been either filed in the office of the chair or sent by certified or registered letter, return receipt requested, and also served in like manner upon the member. In the event such termination is due to a member's failure to pay required contributions, such member's termination shall not be rescinded more than three times.

(4) Each group self-insurer, in its application for self-insurance, shall set forth the names and addresses of each of its officers, directors, trustees, third party administrator and group administrator. Notice of any change in the officers, directors, trustees, third party administrator or group administrator shall be given to the chair within ten days thereof. No officer, director, trustee, employee, third party administrator or group administrator of the group self-insurer may represent or participate directly or indirectly on behalf of an injured worker or his dependents in any workers' compensation proceeding. All employees of members participating in group self-insurance shall be and are deemed to be included under the group self-insurance plan.

(5) (a) Each group self-insurer shall secure the services of a group administrator to be responsible for assisting the group self-insurer in complying with the provisions of this section and the rules and regulations promulgated hereunder, and for coordinating services including but not limited to claims processing, loss control, legal, accounting and actuarial services. No person, firm or corporation shall coordinate such services or otherwise carry out the tasks of a group administrator as provided in this subdivision or in the regulations issued pursuant thereto on behalf of a group self-insurer unless such person shall have obtained from the chair a license authorizing it to act as a group self-insurer administrator, which license may be revoked for good cause. The chair shall promulgate regulations setting forth any additional qualifications for such license, governing the conduct and compensation of group self-insurer administrators, and setting a license fee in an amount not less than five thousand dollars per year for such license for each group self-insurer the administrator administers. Each administrator shall post a bond in the amount of five hundred thousand dollars for each group self-insurer administered or such other amount as may be set by the chair based on the cost and availability of such bond, from which the chair may recover any recoveries or penalties against the administrator under this section. Nothing in this section shall relieve the trustees of a group self-insurer of any fiduciary obligation they hold to the other members of such group self-insurer.

(b) A group administrator that knowingly and with intent to mislead makes a material misrepresentation of a material fact in soliciting members in a group self-insurer shall be guilty of a class E felony. Additionally, the chair may impose a civil penalty of up to ten thousand dollars for each such violation.

(c) A group administrator, actuary or accountant that knowingly makes a material misrepresentation of a material fact concerning the financial status of any group self-insurer to the chair or board, or in its annual report to members of the group self-insurer, shall be guilty of a class E felony. The chair may impose a civil penalty of up to twenty thousand dollars for each such violation. A second and subsequent violation of this paragraph shall be a class D felony. The chair may recover in a civil action any damages resulting from such misrepresentations, including the value of any amount assessed against any entities that are not members of the defaulted self-insurer that resulted from any such misrepresentation.

(d) (1) A group administrator shall provide an annual written report to all members of the group self-insurer and to the board which shall include:

a. the members of the group self-insurer;

b. the group administrator and trustees;

c. the results of the most recent financial audit;

d. the percentage of total liabilities held by the self-insurer in unrestricted cash and investments permitted by regulation as determined in accordance with subparagraph (b) of paragraph two of this subdivision;

e. the number and amount of rate deviations provided to members during the prior year and whether the recipient of any such deviation was a trustee; and

f. such other information as the chair may direct.

The group administrator shall provide a copy of the most recent financial audit to any group self-insurer member upon written request.

(2) The chair shall make available to the public, on its website and in writing upon request:

a. the identity of all group self-insurers that have provided workers' compensation under this subdivision in the prior three years;

b. the group administrator of each such group self-insurer;

c. the financial condition of all group self-insurers as determined by the board in the last financial audit and the board's regulatory definition of assets; and

d. such other information as the chair may direct, but which shall not include any confidential or proprietary information.

The board may direct the disclosure of any non-proprietary information regarding any group self-insurer, including whether a member is a member thereof, to any claimant upon a showing of need.

(e) (1) The chair may condition the issuance or continuation of a license under this subdivision upon the presentation by a group administrator of such information as the board requests, at any time chosen by the chair or at regular intervals, including but not limited to the annual financial statements of the group administrator detailing the compensation the administrator and its substantially owned affiliated entities, as defined in section two of this chapter, have received or shall receive from the group self-insurer or its members, and the method by which such compensation has been or will be calculated. The chair may issue regulations governing the method of calculating compensation which a group administrator may receive, including restrictions on the process by which such compensation may be set.

(2) The chair may revoke the license of any group administrator that receives compensation in violation of such regulations, and may impose a penalty of up to two times any compensation so received.

(f) (1) No officer or director of, or person holding five percent or more ownership interest in, a group administrator shall within two years of serving in such capacity or holding such ownership interest, serve in any capacity or hold any ownership interest in a workers' compensation carrier that provides or solicits the provision of compensation under this title for any employer that is or was a member of such group self-insurer. No officer or director of, or person holding five percent or more ownership interest in a group administrator shall serve in such capacity or hold such ownership interest in a carrier that provides or solicits excess coverage for any group self-insurer administered by such administrator.

(2) The chair may impose a civil penalty of up to ten thousand dollars for each violation of this paragraph.

(g) Each group self-insurer shall submit to the chair copies of any agreement or contract with an entity that serves or will serve as its group administrator, accountant, actuary or third party administrator at least thirty days prior to becoming effective, and the effectiveness of such contract shall be conditioned on the absence of an objection by the board during the thirty day period. Contracts that shall be subject to such objection shall include any contract in violation of regulation; and any contract that does not provide reasonable cancellation or renewal terms, including any contract that requires an affirmative act by the trustees of the group self-insurer to prevent automatic renewal, or that does not permit cancellation for negligence, violation of law, or other good cause.

(6) (a) Group self-insurers must file with the board, as soon as practicable but no later than sixty days prior to the start of the fund year a rating plan which is supported by an actuarial rate study prepared by an independent, qualified actuary that is a fellow or associate of the casualty actuarial society, that clearly identifies the actuary's indicated rate assumptions therein. The rating plan must apply consistently to all members, and must provide for a common renewal date for all group self-insurer members. The rates filed can be adjusted based on an experience modification calculated for every member in accordance with the experience rating plan promulgated by the workers' compensation rating board. Experience modification formulas must be applied identically to all members. Other rate deviations may be permissible provided a plan has been approved by the board. Such deviations shall not be in excess of ten percent of the actuary's indicated rate unless otherwise approved by the board for a fully funded group self-insurer, and shall in no event result in amounts less than the actuary's overall indicated rate. The chair by regulation may set further rate plan and actuarial reporting standards.

(b) If the chair has cause to believe that a group self-insurer's contribution rates including experience modifications do not conform to the requirements of this part then he or she may require the submission of a report identifying the contributions paid by each of the members for the preceding year, the projected contributions for each group self-insurer member for the current fiscal year, and the manner in which such contributions were calculated. If, after review by the chair, the group self-insurer's contribution rates are deemed to be detrimental to its solvency, the chair may mandate that the group self-insurer modify such rates as the chair directs. The chair may impose a penalty of up to five thousand dollars for each violation of this subparagraph. A group self-insurer's failure to adhere to the rating structure determined by the board shall constitute good cause for termination.

(7) (a) If for any reason, the status of a group self-insurer under this subdivision is terminated, including by operation of law on and after January first, two thousand twelve, the securities or cash or the surety bond on deposit referred to herein shall remain in the custody of the chair for such time as the chair may deem proper and warranted. In lieu thereof, and at the discretion of the chair, the group self-insurer, its heirs or assigns or others carrying on or liquidating such group self-insurer, including the chair on the group self-insurer's behalf, may execute an assumption of workers' compensation liability insurance policy securing such further and future contingent liability as may arise from prior injuries to workers and be incurred by reason of any change in the condition of such workers warranting the board making subsequent awards for payment of additional compensation. Such policy shall be in a form approved by the superintendent of financial services and issued by the state fund or any insurance company licensed to issue this class of insurance in this state. In the event that such policy is issued by an insurance company other than the state fund, then said policy shall be deemed of the kind specified in paragraph fifteen of subsection (a) of section one thousand one hundred thirteen of the insurance law and covered by the workers' compensation security fund as created and governed by article six-A of this chapter. It shall only be issued for a single complete premium payment in advance by the group self-insurer and in an amount deemed acceptable by the chair and the superintendent of financial services. In lieu of the applicable premium charge ordinarily required to be imposed by a carrier, said premium shall include a surcharge in an amount to be determined by the chair to: (i) satisfy all assessment liability due and owing to the board and/or the chair under this chapter; and (ii) satisfy all future assessment liability under this section, and which surcharge shall be adjusted from time to time to reflect any changes to the assessment of group self-insured employers, including any changes enacted by the chapter of the laws of two thousand eleven amending sections fifteen and one hundred fifty-one of this chapter. Said surcharge shall be payable to the board simultaneous to the execution of the assumption of workers' compensation liability insurance policy. However, the payment of said surcharge does not relieve the carrier from any other liability, including liability owed to the

superintendent of financial services pursuant to article six-A of this chapter. When issued such policy shall be noncancellable without recourse for any cause during the continuance of the liability secured and so covered.

(b) The chair shall levy an interim assessment on the members of a defaulted group self-insurer within one hundred twenty days of such default or of the effective date of the chapter of the laws of two thousand eight which amended this subdivision, whichever is later, and against the members of any other terminated group self-insurer when necessary, for such an amount as he or she determines to be necessary to discharge all liabilities of the group self-insurer, including the reasonable cost of liquidation such as claims administration costs, actuarial and accounting services, and the value of future assessments on members of such group self-insurer as they are known at the time of the assessment. The chair may impose subsequent and further deficit assessments, or return funds to members, to adjust the moneys collected to reflect the time of participation, and percent of group self-insurer liabilities for such time. The time limitations included in the first sentence of this subparagraph do not apply to the imposition of any subsequent and further deficit assessments that exceed the interim assessment made by the chair against members of a defaulted group insurer or members of any other terminated group self-insurer. Notwithstanding any such action by the chair, each member of the group self-insurer shall remain jointly and severally responsible for all liabilities provided by this chapter including but not limited to outstanding and estimated future liabilities and assessments. Further, separate and apart from, and in addition to a member's joint and several liability and notwithstanding any payments made by any other members of the group self-insurer pursuant to this subparagraph, in the event that a member neglects or fails to pay an assessment levied pursuant to this subparagraph, the member shall be deemed in default in the payment of compensation. Such defaulting member is subject to the enforcement provisions of section twenty-six of this chapter for the payment of all compensation relative to awards due and owing on claims filed by the employees of such member that have neither been paid by the member or the group self-insurer. Nothing in this paragraph shall prevent the chair from offering payment plans or settling claims against members of any group self-insurer as necessary to facilitate collection.

(c) Upon the assumption of the assets and liabilities of a group self-insurer by the chair or his or her designee pursuant to regulation of the chair, all records, documents and files of whatever nature, pertaining to the group self-insurer, be they in the possession of the group self-insurer or a third party, and all remaining assets of the group self-insurer, shall become the property of the chair. All custodians of such records and/or funds shall turn over to the chair or his designee all such original records upon demand.

(8) All the provisions of this chapter relating to self-insurance and the rules and regulations promulgated thereunder shall be deemed applicable to group self-insurance. The chair shall implement the provisions of this subdivision by promulgating rules and regulations but no such rules or regulations shall be necessary for any provision of this subdivision to be effective. The chair may impose a civil penalty of up to ten thousand dollars for each violation against any group self-insurer that violates any provision of this subdivision or of any regulation issued pursuant thereto for which a civil penalty is not specified.

(10) (a) A non-municipal group of employers may make application to the chair to qualify jointly as a self-insurer, provided:

(1) The members of the group secure the services of an administrator, who shall carry out the responsibilities of such an administrator as set forth in subdivision five of this section, and who shall be subject to the restrictions and penalties applicable to an administrator under this section;

(2) The members of the group, through the administrator, (a) jointly deposit sufficient securities in accordance with subdivision three of this section or in a trust governed in accordance with Part 126 of title 11 of the New York code of rules and regulations to secure the liability of the members of the group to pay for all existing claims obligations, provided such deposit shall be made by November first,

two thousand eleven, (b) jointly deposit sufficient securities in accordance with subdivision three of this section or in a trust governed in accordance with Part 126 of title 11 of the New York code of rules and regulations to secure all anticipated present and future claims of the members of the group, by November first, two thousand fourteen, provided annual deposits are made in accordance with a schedule set by the chair on or before November first of each year, and provided that the deposit shall be deemed an asset of the group for the purpose of determining its funding status, and (c) by November first, two thousand eleven and thereafter, shall maintain funds sufficient for all other liabilities besides claims in a trust governed in accordance with Part 126 of title 11 of the New York code of rules and regulations, of which the board shall be the sole beneficiary, and the terms of the trust agreement, and the trustee, shall be approved by the chair in his or her sole discretion, and provided that any group self-insurer that does not hold such funds in a trust that meets the terms of this paragraph shall post them with the board;

(3) The group has been authorized by the chair to self-insure in accordance with this subdivision prior to the effective date of this paragraph;

(4) The group's members or participant employers either (a) are parties to collective bargaining agreements with the same unions; or (b) fall within a limited number of payroll classifications, as set by the chair, after giving due consideration to the risks associated with any group of employers self-insuring. However, employers that were active prior to the effective date of this section and whose classification codes do not meet the limitations on payroll classification codes or are not parties to collective bargaining agreements with the same unions will be permitted to remain in the trust provided (a) they continue to meet the other terms and conditions of the trust; and (b) any new members shall be subject to the limitations on the number of payroll classifications; and provided further, the chair shall revoke such permission in the event the trust violates paragraph six of this subdivision relating to filing of a rating plan;

(5) The group was fully funded for three out of the previous five years and at least ninety percent funded for one other year out of the previous five years, as determined by the chair following a financial review, and the group self-insurer has sufficient funds to meet its liabilities;

(6) The group has a safety program acceptable to the chair; and

(7) The group is subject to such other limitations and requirements of this subdivision unless waived by the chair and to regulations of the chair.

(b) The members of any such group shall enter into an agreement among themselves and with the group's administrator which shall, at a minimum:

(1) Indicate that each of the members of the group is jointly and severally liable for any liabilities of the group; and

(2) Provide for the collection of additional funds from group members in the event the deposit with the board is insufficient to meet the liabilities of the group.

(11) Former group self-insurer. Any group self-insurer that has ceased to self-insure, or has ceased to self-insure any new liabilities after January first, two thousand twelve in accordance with paragraph two of this subdivision, shall remain subject to all the provisions of this subdivision and the regulations issued pursuant thereto and any assessments provided for by this section until such time as the group self-insurer no longer possesses any liabilities.

(12) Any non-municipal group of employers authorized to self-insure under paragraph ten of this section on or after January first, two thousand twelve shall be deemed a "private self-insurer" for purposes of the assessments set forth in sections fifteen and one hundred fifty-one of this chapter.

3-b. (a) Except as provided in subdivision three-d of this section, no person, firm or corporation, other than an attorney and counsellor-at-law, shall solicit the business of representing, or engage in representing self-insurers or group self-insurers, as defined in subdivisions three and three-a of this section, before the board or any officer, agent or employee of the board assigned to conduct any hearing, investigation or inquiry relative to a claim for compensation or benefits under this chapter, unless he shall be a citizen of the United States or an alien lawfully admitted for permanent residence in the United States, or a corporation organized under the laws of the state of New York, and shall have obtained from the board a license authorizing him to appear in matters or proceedings before the board. Such license shall be issued by the board in accordance with the rules established by it. Any person, firm or corporation violating the aforesaid provisions shall be guilty of a misdemeanor. The chair may impose a civil penalty of up to one thousand dollars for each violation against any representative licensed in accordance with this section that violates any provision of this section or of any regulation issued pursuant thereto, in addition to any other sanctions provided for under this chapter.

(b) The board, in its rules, may provide for the issuance of licenses to persons, firms or corporations, upon such proof of character and fitness as it may deem necessary, without annual license fee, and for the giving of a bond running to the people of the state of New York, conditioned upon the faithful performance of all duties required of such person, firm or corporation, and in an amount to be fixed by the board in its rules. Such bond shall be approved by the board as to form and sufficiency and shall be filed with it.

(c) There shall be maintained in each office of the board a registry or list of all persons to whom licenses have been issued, as provided herein, which list shall be corrected as often as licenses are issued or revoked. Absence of record of the license issued, as herein provided, shall be prima facie evidence that a person, firm or corporation is not licensed to represent self-insurers.

(d) Any such license may be revoked by the board for cause after a hearing before it.

(e) No license shall be issued hereunder for a period longer than three years from the date of its issuance. The provisions of this section shall not apply to a regular employee of a self-insured employer or to the state insurance fund acting in accordance with an insuring agreement with the state as authorized pursuant to the provisions of section eighty-eight-c of this chapter.

3-c. Notwithstanding any provision in this chapter or in any general, special or local law contained, all cash and securities deposited with the chairman by an employer who is a party or a wholly owned subsidiary of a party to a plan heretofore or hereafter adopted under article seven of the public service law by the transit commission-metropolitan division of the department of public service, and who is, or at the time of the consummation of such plan was, a self-insurer under this chapter, may be withdrawn upon, or at any time after, the consummation of such plan as hereinafter provided. All cash and securities deposited by any such employer with and held by the chairman may be withdrawn upon, or at any time after, the consummation of such plan where any city which is a party thereto and which is a self-insurer under this chapter assumes all liabilities of or claims against such employer under this chapter, as follows: (a), where such plan provides that such city shall acquire, or that such employer or his assigns shall retain, all the right and interest of such employer in the deposited cash and securities, the chairman shall surrender and deliver such cash and securities to such city or to such employer or his assigns, as the case may be, upon its demand, and (b), where such plan provides that such city and such employer, or his assigns, shall each retain some right and interest in such cash and securities, the chairman shall surrender and deliver such cash and securities to such city and to such employer or his assigns upon their joint demand as shall be specified therein.

3-d. The state insurance fund, an insurance company duly authorized or licensed to write workers' compensation insurance in this state, a subsidiary or an affiliate of such an insurance company, or a licensed or authorized adjusting company or association may apply for a license from the board to solicit the business of representing and engage in representing self-insurers, as defined in subdivision three of this section, before the board or any officer, agent or employee of the board assigned to conduct any hearing, investigation or inquiry relative to a claim for compensation or benefits under this chapter. Any corporation formed solely for the purpose of engaging in the activities described by this subdivision shall be formed under the laws of the state of New York.

The state insurance fund, an insurance company, its subsidiary or affiliate, or such adjusting company or association shall designate those employees who are to appear in matters or proceedings before the board on behalf of self-insurers. Such employees shall obtain an authorization from the board. Upon application to the board for such authorization all such employees who, on the effective date of this subdivision, have been appearing in matters or proceedings before the board on behalf of insurers for a period of at least two years shall automatically receive a temporary authorization from the board. Such temporary authorization shall remain in effect until the applicant employee has been granted or denied final authorization by the board. The board in its rules shall provide for the issuance of authorizations to such employees and other designated employees. If the board, in its rules, provides for the issuance of authorization to persons, firms or corporations under subdivision three-b of this section upon such proof of character and fitness as it may deem necessary, the same proof of character and fitness shall be required for an authorization issued under this subdivision.

The state insurance fund, an insurance company duly authorized or licensed to write workers' compensation insurance in this state, a subsidiary or an affiliate of such an insurance company, or a licensed or authorized adjusting company or association shall apply to the board for the issuance of a license upon such proof of character and fitness as the board may deem necessary. Such proof of character and fitness shall be the same as that required by the board of persons, firms or corporations under subdivision three-b of this section. If the board charges a fee for a license issued under subdivision three-b of this section, the same amount shall be charged for a license issued under this subdivision. If the board requires for the giving of a bond running to the people of the state of New York, conditioned upon the faithful performance of all duties required of such person, firm, or corporation licensed under subdivision three-b of this section, the same shall be required for a license under this subdivision. Such bond shall be approved by the board as to form and sufficiency and shall be filed with it. All license and authorization fees collected under the provisions of this subdivision shall be paid into the state treasury. Any person, insurance company, its subsidiary or affiliate, or adjusting company or association which violates the aforesaid provisions of this paragraph shall be guilty of a misdemeanor.

There shall be maintained in each office of the board a registry list of all persons to whom authorizations and licenses have been issued as provided herein, which list shall be corrected as often as authorizations and licenses are issued or revoked. Absence of record of the authorization or license issued, as herein provided, shall be prima facie evidence that a person, firm or corporation is not authorized or licensed to represent self-insurers. Any such authorization or license may be revoked by the board for cause after a hearing before it. No authorization or license shall be issued hereunder for a period longer than three years from the date of its issuance.

The board shall make rules pertaining to when conflicts of interest arise in individual cases which shall apply to those who are licensed or authorized to represent self-insurers under subdivision three-b of this section or under this subdivision.

The provisions of article twenty-four of the insurance law, insofar as applicable, shall apply to the state insurance fund, insurance companies, their subsidiaries and affiliates or adjusting companies or associations in their activities representing self-insurers before the board.

3-e. (a) The state insurance fund and any other insurer that issues policies of workers' compensation insurance shall offer at the option of the policyholder a deductible for benefits payable under a workers' compensation policy with an annual premium of twelve thousand dollars or more, if in the opinion of the state insurance fund or such other insurer the policyholder meets the eligibility requirements of paragraph (b) of this subdivision.

(b) A policyholder is eligible for a policy deductible for any renewal period of the policy if such policyholder has paid the entire billed premium on the policy for all policy periods within forty-five days of each billing for the past three years. A policyholder will continue to be eligible for a deductible provided that no part of any premium is more than forty-five days overdue from the date billed or reimbursement for any deductible amount is unpaid by the policyholder to such insurer. The state insurance fund or any other insurer that has issued a policy with a deductible may revoke the policyholder's entitlement to a deductible if the policyholder fails to reimburse any deductible amounts, or pay any billed premium, within forty-five days after such reimbursement or premium payment has become due. Upon such revocation of a policyholder's entitlement to a deductible, the policyholder shall be entitled to cancel such policy and such policyholder will forfeit eligibility for entitlement to a deductible as provided above.

(c) Deductibles shall be offered by the state insurance fund or any other insurer in writing to eligible policyholders at the beginning of policy periods, in the amounts of one hundred dollars, two hundred dollars, three hundred dollars, four hundred dollars and five hundred dollars, and thereafter, in increments of five hundred dollars up to a maximum of two thousand five hundred dollars per occurrence. The eligible policyholder shall select, in writing, only one deductible amount which shall be binding on such policyholder throughout the policy period.

(d) If the policyholder selects a deductible under paragraph (c) of this subdivision, workers' compensation benefits payable under the policy shall be paid by the state insurance fund or other insurer liable under the policy to the person or provider entitled to such benefits without regard to any deductible applied to such policy. Upon payment of benefits on a claim up to or exceeding the deductible amount, the state insurance fund or other insurer shall be entitled to bill the policyholder for reimbursement up to the deductible amount. A policyholder's failure to pay billed deductible reimbursement amounts to the state insurance fund or other insurer under this paragraph shall be treated in the same manner as non-payment of premium and render the policy cancelable in accordance with the provisions of subdivision five of section fifty-four of this article. The deductibles paid by the insured employer during any one year period of the policy of insurance shall not exceed the annual premium for such policy of insurance.

(e) Premium reductions, in accordance with methodology approved by the superintendent of financial services shall be applied to any policy written with a deductible. Such premium reductions shall be determined before the application of any experience modification premium surcharge or premium discount.

(f) The New York workers' compensation rating board shall file for appropriate premium discounts subject to the approval of the superintendent of financial services.

(g) The state insurance fund, any other insurer or any group self-insurer for municipal corporations as defined in subdivision three-a of this section may, at its option, offer a deductible in an amount specified in paragraph (c) of this subdivision to any policyholder who is not otherwise eligible for a deductible under this subdivision.

4. a. A county, city, village, town, school district, fire district or other political subdivision of the state may secure compensation to its employees in accordance with subdivision one, two or three-a of this section, and a public corporation as defined in subdivision one of section sixty of this chapter may also secure such compensation in accordance with article five of this chapter. If compensation is not so secured, a county, city, village, town, school district, fire district or other political subdivision shall be deemed to have elected to secure compensation pursuant to subdivision three of this section and, in such case, no proof of financial ability or deposit of securities or cash need be made in compliance with such subdivision. All other requirements prescribed by this chapter for employers so electing shall be complied with and notice of such election shall be filed with the chair. For failure to file such notice of election, prescribed in form by the chair, within ten days after the election was made, the treasurer or

other financial officer shall be liable to pay to the chair the sum of one hundred dollars as a penalty, to be transferred to the state treasury.

b. The treasurer or other fiscal officer of a self-insuring county, city, village, town, school district, fire district or other political subdivision shall, upon presentation of an award of compensation forthwith begin payment of it to the person entitled thereto in accordance with this chapter.

c. The governing board of a county, city, village, town, school district, fire district or other political subdivision may authorize the treasurer or other fiscal officer of such municipal corporation, district or political subdivision, as the case may be, to pay the compensation provided for in this chapter to the person entitled thereto without waiting for an award in any case in the manner provided in section twenty-five of this chapter. The amount of such compensation payable prior to an award pursuant to such authorization shall constitute a settled claim within the meaning of the local finance law.

d. A contract of insurance issued to a county or a town in accordance with subdivision one or two of this section and in force on or after the first day of March, nineteen hundred sixty-three, in relation to fire districts and on or after the first day of January, in the year in which this paragraph as hereby amended becomes effective in relation to ambulance districts shall contain a provision reading as follows: "This contract does not provide (1) any coverage under the Workers' Compensation Law or the Volunteer Firefighters' Benefit Law or the Volunteer Ambulance Workers' Benefit Law for which any fire district or ambulance district would be liable under such laws, (2) any workers' compensation benefits for fire or ambulance district officers and employees for which any fire district or ambulance district would be liable under the Workers' Compensation Law, or (3) any volunteer firefighters' or ambulance workers' benefits for any volunteer firefighters or volunteer ambulance workers under the Volunteer Firefighters' Benefit Law or the Volunteer Ambulance Workers' Benefit Law."

e. If for any reason the status of a county, city, village, town, school district, fire district or other political subdivision of state is terminated, at the discretion of the chair, the county, city, village, town, school district, fire district or other political subdivision of state, may execute an assumption of workers' compensation liability insurance policy securing such further and future contingent liability as may arise from prior injuries to workers and be incurred by reason of any change in the condition of such workers warranting the board making subsequent awards for payment of additional compensation. Such policy shall be in a form approved by the superintendent of financial services and shall be issued by the state fund or any insurance company licensed to issue this class of policy in this state. In the event that such policy is issued by an insurance company other than the state fund, then said policy shall be deemed to be insurance of the kind specified in paragraph fifteen of subsection (a) of section one thousand one hundred thirteen of the insurance law and covered by the workers' compensation security fund as created and governed by article six-A of this chapter. It shall only be issued for a single complete premium payment in advance by the county, city, village, town, school district, fire district or other political subdivision of state and in an amount deemed acceptable by the chair and the superintendent of financial services. In lieu of the applicable premium charge ordinarily required to be imposed by a carrier, said premium shall include a surcharge in an amount to be determined by the chair to satisfy all assessment liability due and owing to the board and/or the chair under this chapter. Said surcharge shall be payable to the board simultaneous to the execution of the assumption of workers' compensation liability insurance policy. However, the payment of said surcharge does not relieve the carrier from any other liability, including liability owed to the superintendent of financial services pursuant to article six-A of this chapter. When issued such policy shall be non-cancellable without recourse for any cause during the continuance of the liability secured and so covered.

5. Self-insurance. "Self-insurance," as used herein, shall be deemed to be the system of securing compensation as provided in subdivisions three, three-a and four of this section, and article five of this chapter.

a. The chair shall administer all matters relating to self-insurance under this chapter. All penalties set forth in subdivisions three and three-a of this section shall be paid into the fund for uninsured employers provided for in section twenty-six-a of this chapter.

b. Advisory committee for individual self-insurance.

(1) To advise the chair, there shall be an advisory committee for individual self-insurance, which shall be called the advisory committee for self-insurance and consist of the chair and ten additional members appointed by the chair. Three of such members shall be named from the manufacturing and trade group of self-insurance, three from the transportation, public utilities and construction group, and one member shall be a self-insurer selected at large by the chairman, who shall be vice-chairman of the advisory committee. The chair shall be chair of the advisory committee; the secretary of the board shall act as secretary of the advisory committee. Any member appointed to such advisory committee shall be a self-insurer or an officer of a self-insurer or a person who on account of his or her employment or affiliation can be classed as a management representative of a self-insurer. The members of the advisory committee for self-insurance in office at the time this subdivision takes effect, shall be and they are hereby continued in office as such for the remainder of the terms for which they were appointed respectively.

The members of the advisory committee for self-insurance next appointed, except to fill a vacancy created otherwise than by expiration of term, shall be appointed for terms of three years, except that of the three additional members to be appointed after May first, two thousand eight, one such member shall be appointed for an initial term of one year, one such member shall be appointed for an initial term of two years, and one such member shall be appointed for an initial term of three years. No member shall be appointed to the advisory committee for individual self-insurance if he or she has been convicted of a crime under this chapter or has been subject to criminal or civil penalties under this subdivision. Vacancies shall be filled for the unexpired term by appointment by the chair. Members shall continue in office until their successors are appointed; in the event that no appointment is made within three months after a vacancy exists or after the expiration of the term of a member, the remaining members may fill the vacancy by a majority vote. If a member shall be absent from two consecutive regular meetings without adequate excuse his or her place may be declared vacant by the chair. Members of such advisory committee shall serve without pay, but shall be entitled to their reasonable and necessary traveling and other expenses incurred in connection with their duties. Regular meetings of the advisory committee shall be held twice a year, on dates to be fixed by the chair. In addition, special meetings shall be held if called by the chair or any five members of the committee. Such advisory committee shall have access to all self-insurance records except those restricted by the chair or those whose disclosure is restricted under section one hundred ten-a of this chapter, and shall have the power to require the presence before it of any employee of the board or any self-insurer as reasonable and related to matters within the purview of the committee. Information obtained by members of the advisory committee shall be deemed confidential unless disclosed by order of the committee. It shall be the duty of the advisory committee to advise the chair on all matters relating to self-insurance, particularly in respect to rules governing self-insurance, the deposit or withdrawal of securities, the standards for permitting employers to self-insure under this section, the appropriate amount of security or payments that self-insured employers must provide, and on such other matters as the chair shall request. The chair shall detail to such advisory committee such stenographic or other assistance as may be necessary. Minutes shall be kept of the meetings of the advisory committee and shall be provided within forty-five days of such meeting to the governor and legislature, including the chairs of the assembly and senate committees on insurance and labor.

c. (1) The chair and the department of audit and control as soon as practicable after May first, nineteen hundred sixty, and annually thereafter, as soon as practicable after April first in each succeeding year, shall ascertain the total amount of net expenses, including (a) administrative expenses, which shall include the direct costs of personal services, the cost of maintenance and operation, the cost of retirement contributions made and workers' compensation premiums paid by the State for or on account of personnel, rentals for space occupied in state owned or state leased buildings, and (b) all direct or indirect costs incurred by the board during the preceding fiscal year in carrying out the provisions of subdivision three and three-a of this section. Such expenses shall be adjusted quarterly to reflect any change in circumstances, and shall be assessed against all private self-insured employers, including for this purpose active and terminated group self-insurers, active individual self-insured employers, and individual self-insured employers who have ceased to exercise the privilege of self-insurance.

(2) Such expenses shall be assessed against all self-insurers including for this purpose employers who have ceased to exercise the privilege of self-insurance. The basis of apportionment of the assessment against each self-insurer shall be a sum equal to that proportion of the amount which the indemnity payment for each self-insurer bore to the total indemnity payments for all self-insurers for the calendar year which ended within the preceding state fiscal year. All such assessments when collected shall be deposited into a fund which shall be used to reimburse the appropriations theretofore made by the state for the payment of the expenses of administering this chapter.

(3) Pure premium for assessments made prior to January first, two thousand nine against individual and group self-insurers who ceased to self-insure shall be based on payroll at the time the individual or group self-insurer has ceased to self-insure, reduced by a factor reflecting the reduction in the group or individual self-insurer's self-insurance liabilities since ceasing to self-insure.

d. The chair may from time to time request the superintendent of financial services for assistance, and the superintendent of financial services is hereby authorized to render such assistance upon request of the chair, as may be necessary to insure the financial ability of such group self-insurers to pay all liabilities provided by this chapter.

e. Notwithstanding the provisions of paragraph c of this subdivision, the chair shall require that partial payments for expenses of the fiscal year beginning April first, nineteen hundred eighty-three, and for each fiscal year thereafter shall be made on March tenth of the preceding fiscal year and on June tenth, September tenth, and December tenth of each year, or on such other dates as the director of the budget may prescribe, by each self-insurer. Provided, however, that the payment due March tenth, nineteen hundred eighty-three for the fiscal year beginning April first, nineteen hundred eighty-three shall not be required to be paid until June tenth, nineteen hundred eighty-three. Each such payment shall be a sum equal to twenty-five per centum of the annual expenses assessed upon each self-insurer, as estimated by the chair. The balance of assessments for the fiscal year beginning April first, nineteen hundred seventy-three and each fiscal year thereafter, shall be paid upon determination of the actual amount due in accordance with the provisions of paragraph c of this subdivision. Any overpayment of annual assessments resulting from the requirements of this paragraph shall be refunded or at the option of the chair shall be applied as a credit against the assessment of the succeeding fiscal year. The requirements of this subdivision shall not apply to those self-insurers whose estimated annual assessment for the fiscal year is less than one hundred dollars and such self-insurers shall make a single payment of the estimated annual assessment on or before September thirtieth of the fiscal year.

f. Whenever the chair shall determine that the compensation and benefits provided by this chapter may be unpaid by reason of the default of an insolvent private self-insured employer, including a private group self-insurer, the chair shall pay such compensation and benefits from administration expenses as provided in section one hundred fifty-one of this chapter upon audit and warrant of the comptroller upon vouchers approved by the chair. Such payments shall be considered expenses of administration. The chair shall be reimbursed therefor from the surety bond, cash or securities held or, if such surety bond, securities or cash is insufficient, by the employer, its receiver, liquidator, rehabilitator or trustee in bankruptcy. All moneys reimbursed to the chair or recovered by the chair in an action or proceeding to secure such reimbursement shall forthwith be applied as a credit against the expenses on which the assessment levied upon all private self-insured employers, in accordance with paragraphs c and e of this subdivision, is calculated.

g. Whenever the chair shall determine that the compensation and benefits provided by this chapter may be unpaid by reason of the default of an insolvent private self-insured employer, including a private group self-insurer, the chair shall levy an assessment against all private self-insured employers, including private group self-insurers, in accordance with paragraphs c and e of this subdivision to assure prompt payment of such compensation and benefits. Whenever compensation and benefits are unpaid by reason of such default, the chair shall promptly pay such compensation and benefits from administration expenses as provided in section one hundred fifty-one of this chapter upon audit and warrant of the comptroller upon vouchers approved by the chair. Nothing in this paragraph shall preclude the chair from recovering the moneys it expends from its administrative expenses against the defaulted individual self-insurer, or the members of the defaulted group self-insurer, as otherwise permitted by this chapter.

6. Any policy of insurance purchased pursuant to the provisions of this subdivision six as in effect prior to the first day of March, nineteen hundred fifty-seven, shall be cancelled prior to, or as of, the twenty-eighth day of February, nineteen hundred fifty-seven.

The cost of such insurance shall be apportioned by the clerk of the board of supervisors of the county to each such city, village, fire district, fire protection district, fire alarm district, and territory outside such municipal corporations and districts, in the proportion that the agreed population bears to the entire population of the group. Refunds, dividends and discounts in relation to such insurance shall be distributed or credited according to the same apportionment. Upon notification by the clerk of the board of supervisors, the chief fiscal officer of each such city, village or fire district shall pay to the county treasurer, from moneys available or made available, the amount apportioned to such city, village or district. Upon like notification, the supervisor of each town in which a fire protection district or fire alarm district is located in whole or in part, or in which outside territory is located, shall pay to the county treasurer the amount apportioned for such district, in whole or in part, or territory, as the case may be, using moneys raised or made available for the purposes of fire protection in such district or outside territory, or if there be no such moneys or insufficient moneys, using funds of the town available or made available, which funds shall be a charge upon such district or territory for which the town shall be reimbursed. The county treasurer shall pay the cost of such insurance with such moneys, or if any apportioned share has not been paid, the county treasurer shall advance the amount necessary from moneys of the general fund upon resolution of the board of supervisors. Any such advance shall be repaid as soon as moneys are available therefor. If any apportioned share remains unpaid, the county may recover the same by action at law. If any member of the group shall fail to pay its apportioned share within thirty days after notice that such amount has become due and payable, the chairman of the board of supervisors may terminate the participation of such member in the group by notice by mail to such member on a date specified in the notice, and a copy of such notice shall be filed by the chairman of the board of supervisors with the insurance carrier, who shall notify the chairman of the workmen's compensation board of the termination of coverage in the same manner as provided for cancellation of policy under subdivision five of section fifty-four of this chapter.

If any participating fire protection district or fire alarm district includes territory in more than one town, whether or not in more than one county, the amount of cost of insurance, refund, dividend or discount apportioned to such district shall be apportioned in the proportion that the population of the district within each such town bears to the population of the entire district. The figure used for population in such case shall be the one stated in the agreement.

7. Any policy of insurance purchased pursuant to the provisions of this subdivision seven as in effect prior to the first day of March, nineteen hundred fifty-seven, shall be cancelled prior to, or as of, the close of the twenty-eighth day of February, nineteen hundred fifty-seven. The cost of such insurance

shall be a town charge and shall be levied and collected in the same manner as other town charges only in the territory of such town outside of any villages and fire districts not covered by such a policy.

8. The requirements of section ten of this chapter regarding the provision of workers' compensation insurance as to owners and trainers governed by the racing, pari-mutuel wagering and breeding law who are employers under section two of this chapter are satisfied in full by compliance with the requirements imposed upon owners and trainers by section two hundred thirteen-a of the racing, pari-mutuel wagering and breeding law, provided that in the event double compensation, death benefits, or awards are payable with respect to an injured employee under section fourteen-a of this chapter, the owner or trainer for whom the injured jockey, apprentice jockey or exercise person licensed under article two or four of the racing, pari-mutuel wagering and breeding law is performing services as a jockey, apprentice jockey or exercise person so licensed at the time of the accident shall bear the sole responsibility for the amount payable pursuant to such section fourteen-a in excess of the amount otherwise payable under this chapter, unless there shall be a failure of the responsible owner or trainer to pay such award within the time provided under this chapter. In the event of such failure to pay and the board requires the fund to pay the award on behalf of such owner or trainer who has been found to have violated section fourteen-a, the fund shall be entitled to an award against such owner or trainer for the amount so paid which shall be collected in the same manner as an award of compensation. Coverage directly procured by any owner or trainer for the purpose of satisfying the requirements of this chapter with respect to employees of the owner or trainer shall not include coverage on any jockey, apprentice jockey or exercise person licensed under article two or four of the racing, pari-mutuel wagering and breeding law to the extent that such jockey, apprentice jockey or exercise person is also covered under coverage procured by The New York Jockey Injury Compensation Fund, Inc. pursuant to the requirements of section two hundred thirteen-a of the racing, pari-mutuel wagering and breeding law, and to that extent, coverage procured by the fund pursuant to the requirements of the racing, pari-mutuel wagering and breeding law shall be considered primary.

9. The requirements of sections ten and eleven of this chapter regarding the securing and provision of workers' compensation benefits as to a central dispatch facility, as defined in article six-F of the executive law, are satisfied in full by compliance with the requirements imposed upon such central dispatch facility by such article. Insurance coverage directly procured by any central dispatch facility for the purpose of satisfying the requirements of this chapter with respect to employees of the central dispatch facility shall not include coverage of any black car operator to the extent that the black car operator is also covered under coverage secured by the New York black car operators' injury compensation fund, inc. pursuant to the requirements of article six-F of the executive law, and to that extent, coverage secured by the fund pursuant to the requirements of article six-F of the executive law shall be considered primary.

10. An individual self-insured employer or group self-insurer who fails to file or maintain the security deposit required by the chair will be deemed to have failed to secure compensation for the amount not deposited, and shall be liable for all penalties for such failure provided for under this title.

11. If at any time an individual self-insured employer or member of a group self-insurer intentionally and materially understates or conceals payroll, or intentionally and materially misrepresents or conceals employee duties or if the employer intentionally or materially misstates payroll or claims information for the purposes of determining employer contributions as provided for under subdivisions three and three-a of this section, such employer shall be deemed to have failed to secure compensation and shall be subject to sanctions applicable under section fifty-two of this article in addition to any other sanctions available under law.

12. The chair, with the approval of the director of the budget, may request the issuance of bonds by the dormitory authority for one or more of the purposes authorized by section sixteen hundred eighty-q of the public authorities law and by a self-insured bond financing agreement authorized by section fifty-c of this article. The net proceeds of such bonds shall be deposited into the self-insurer offset fund or as otherwise provided by the applicable self-insured bond financing agreement.

§ 51. Posting of notice regarding compensation

Every employer who has complied with section fifty of this article shall post and maintain in a conspicuous place or places in and about his place or places of business typewritten or printed notices in form prescribed by the chairman, stating the fact that he has complied with all the rules and regulations of the chairman and the board and that he has secured the payment of compensation to his employees and their dependents in accordance with the provisions of this chapter, but failure to post such notice as herein provided shall not in any way affect the exclusiveness of the remedy provided for by section eleven of this chapter. Every employer who owns or operates automotive or horse-drawn vehicles and has no minimum staff of regular employees required to report for work at an established place of business maintained by such employer and every employer who is engaged in the business of moving household goods or furniture shall post such notices in each and every vehicle owned or operated by him. Failure to post or maintain such notice in any of said vehicles shall constitute presumptive evidence that such employer has failed to secure the payment of compensation. The chairman may require any employer to furnish a written statement at any time showing the stock corporation, mutual corporation or reciprocal insurer in which such employer is insured or the manner in which such employer has complied with any provision of this chapter. Failure for a period of ten days to furnish such written statement shall constitute presumptive evidence that such employer has neglected or failed in respect of any of the matters so required. Any employer who fails to comply with the provisions of this section shall be required to pay to the board a fine of up to two hundred fifty dollars for each violation, in addition to any other penalties imposed by law to be deposited into the uninsured employers' fund.

§ 52. Effect of failure to secure compensation

1. (a) Failure to secure the payment of compensation for five or less employees within a twelve month period shall constitute a misdemeanor, and is punishable by a fine of not less than one thousand nor more than five thousand dollars. Failure to secure the payment of compensation for more than five employees within a twelve month period shall constitute a class E felony, and is punishable by a fine of not less than five thousand dollars nor more than fifty thousand dollars in addition to any other penalties otherwise provided by law. It shall be an affirmative defense to any criminal prosecution under this section that the employer took reasonable steps to secure compensation.

(b) Where any person has previously been convicted of a failure to secure the payment of compensation within the preceding five years, upon conviction for a subsequent violation such person shall be guilty of a class D felony, and fined not less than ten thousand nor more than fifty thousand dollars in addition to any other penalties including fines otherwise provided by law.

(c) Where the employer is a corporation, the president, secretary and treasurer thereof shall be liable for failure to secure the payment of compensation under this section. It shall be an affirmative defense to any action against any officer of a corporation under this section that the officer took reasonable steps to ensure that the corporation secured compensation, that proper internal procedures were in effect to do so, and that proper internal controls existed to monitor compliance with said procedures.

(d) If at any time an employer intentionally and materially understates or conceals payroll, or intentionally and materially misrepresents or conceals employee duties so as to avoid proper classification for calculation of premium paid to secure compensation, or intentionally and materially misrepresents or conceals information pertinent to the calculation of premium paid to secure compensation, such employer shall be deemed to have failed to secure compensation and shall be subject to the sanctions applicable to this section.

(e) A stop-work order issued because an employer is deemed to have failed to secure compensation under section one hundred forty-one-a of this chapter shall have no effect upon an employer's or carrier's duty to provide benefits under this chapter or upon any of the employer's or carrier's rights and defenses.

2. All fines imposed under this chapter, except as herein otherwise provided, shall be paid directly and immediately by the officer collecting the same to the chairman, and shall be paid by him into the uninsured employers' fund created under section twenty-six-a of this chapter, provided, however, that all such fines collected by justices of towns and villages shall be paid to the state comptroller in accordance with the provisions of section twenty-seven of the town law and section 4-410 of the village law respectively.

3. In any prosecution hereunder the failure of the employer to file with the chairman, within ten days after demand, a statement subscribed by the employer and affirmed by him as true under the penalties of perjury showing specifically (a) the name of the stock company, mutual corporation or reciprocal insurer in which such employer is insured and the number and the date of issuance and term of such policy of insurance, or (b) that the said employer is insured with the state fund in which case he shall give the number of such policy of insurance, the date of issuance and term thereof, or (c) that the said employer has been authorized to do business as a self-insurer pursuant to section fifty of this article, giving the date of said authorization, or (d) a legal reason, if any, why said employer is not required to secure compensation, shall constitute prima facie evidence that the employer has failed to secure compensation as herein required. The statement to be filed herein shall be subscribed by the employer or if the employer is a corporation by one of the officers herein named in which he shall state that he has read such statement subscribed by him and knows the contents thereof and that same is true of his own knowledge.

4. If, however, there has been an accident and the board shall have made an award against the employer as a non-insured employer, the making of such award, except in a case where the employer had secured compensation insurance which was in effect at the time of the accident but the carrier later became insolvent, shall constitute prima facie evidence of an employment by the employer of an employee in an occupation in which the said employer was required to carry compensation and of the failure of the employer to secure the payment of workers' compensation on the date of the accident involved in said award. A certified copy of such award shall be received as competent evidence of the making thereof in any criminal prosecution hereunder.

5. The chair, upon finding that an employer has failed for a period of not less than ten consecutive days to make the provision for payment of compensation required by section fifty of this article, may impose upon such employer, in addition to all other penalties, fines or assessments provided for in this chapter, a penalty of up to two thousand dollars for each ten day period of non-compliance or a sum not in excess of two times the cost of compensation for its payroll for the period of such failure, which sum shall be paid into the uninsured employers' fund created under section twenty-six-a of this chapter. When an employer fails to provide business records sufficient to enable the chair to determine the employer's payroll for the period requested for the calculation of the penalty provided in this section, the imputed weekly payroll for each employee, corporate officer, sole proprietor, or partner shall be the New York state average weekly wage, multiplied by 1.5. Where the employer is a corporation, the president, secretary and treasurer thereof shall be liable for the penalty. If the employer shall within thirty days after notice of the imposition of a penalty by the chair pursuant to this subdivision make an application in affidavit form for a redetermination review of such penalty the chair shall make a decision in writing on the issues raised on such application.

§ 54. The insurance contract

1. Right of recourse to the insurance carrier. Every policy of insurance covering the liability of the employer for compensation shall be issued by one or more stock companies, mutual corporations or reciprocal insurers authorized to transact workers' compensation insurance in this state. In the case of a policy with multiple insurers, such insurers shall share one hundred percent of the liabilities by

subscription, and one of the insurers shall serve as the lead insurer for notice and cancellation purposes. Such a policy shall contain a provision setting forth the right of the chair to enforce in the name of the people of the state of New York for the benefit of the person entitled to the compensation insured by the policy either by filing a separate application or by making the insurance carrier a party to the original application, the liability of the insurance carrier in whole or in part for the payment of such compensation; provided, however, that payment in whole or in part of such compensation by either the employer or the insurance carrier shall to the extent thereof be a bar to the recovery against the other of the amount so paid.

2. Knowledge and jurisdiction of the employer extended to cover the insurance carrier. Every such policy shall contain a provision that, as between the employee and the insurance carrier, the notice to or knowledge of the occurrence of the injury on the part of the employer shall be deemed notice or knowledge, as the case may be, on the part of the insurance carrier, or if more than one insurer, the lead carrier; that jurisdiction of the employer shall, for the purpose of this chapter, be jurisdiction of the lead insurance carrier and that such insurance carrier shall in all things be bound by and subject to the orders, findings, decisions or awards rendered against the employer for the payment of compensation under the provisions of this chapter.

3. Insolvency of employer does not release the insurance carrier. Every such policy shall contain a provision to the effect that the insolvency or bankruptcy of the employer shall not relieve the insurance carrier from the payment of compensation for injuries or death sustained by an employee during the life of such policy.

4. Limitation of indemnity agreements. Every contract or agreement of an employer the purpose of which is to indemnify him from loss or damage on account of the injury of an employee by accidental means, or on account of the negligence of such employer or his officer, agent or servant, shall be absolutely void unless it shall also cover liability for the payment of the compensation and for the payment into the special funds provided for by this chapter. Every such contract or agreement of insurance issued by an insurance carrier covering the liability of an employer for the payment of the compensation and for the payment into the special funds provided by this chapter shall be deemed to include all employees of the employer employed at or in connection with the business of the employer carried on, maintained, or operated at the location or locations set forth in such contract or agreement and employees for whose injuries a contractor may become liable under the provisions of section fifty-six of this chapter. Any employee or employees or class of employees not enumerated in section three, subdivision one, group one to seventeen inclusive, of this chapter, employed by a municipal corporation or political subdivision of the state, may by the terms of the contract or agreement be expressly excluded therefrom.

5. Cancellation and termination of insurance contracts. No contract of insurance issued by an insurance carrier against liability arising under this chapter shall be cancelled within the time limited in such contract for its expiration unless notice is given as required by this section. When cancellation is due to non-payment of premiums and assessments, such cancellation shall not be effective until at least ten days after a notice of cancellation of such contract, on a date specified in such notice, shall be filed in the office of the chair and also served on the employer. When cancellation is due to any reason other than non-payment of premiums and assessments, such cancellation shall not be effective until at least thirty days after a notice of cancellation of such contract, on a date specified in such notice, shall be filed in the office of the chair and also served on the employer; provided, however, in either case, that if the employer has secured insurance with another insurance carrier which becomes effective prior to the expiration of the time stated in such notice, the cancellation shall be effective as of the date of such other coverage. No insurer shall refuse to renew any policy insuring against liability arising under this chapter unless at least thirty days prior to its expiration notice of intention not to renew has been filed in the office of the chair and also served on the employer.

Such notice shall be served on the employer by delivering it to him, her or it or by sending it by mail, by certified or registered letter, return receipt requested, addressed to the employer at his, her or its last known place of business; provided that, if the employer be a partnership, then such notice may be so given to any of one of the partners, and if the employer be a corporation then the notice may be given to any agent or officer of the corporation upon whom legal process may be served; and further provided that an employer may designate any person or entity at any address to receive such notice including the designation of one person or entity to receive notice on behalf of multiple entities insured under one insurance policy and that service of notice at the address so designated upon the person or entity so designated by delivery or by mail, by certified or registered letter, return receipt requested, shall satisfy the notice requirement of this section. Provided, however, the right to cancellation of a policy of insurance in the state fund shall be exercised only for non-payment of premiums and assessments or as provided in section ninety-four of this chapter.

The provisions of this subdivision shall not apply with respect to policies containing coverage pursuant to subsection (j) of section three thousand four hundred twenty of the insurance law relating to every policy providing comprehensive personal liability insurance on a one, two, three or four family owner-occupied dwelling.

In the event such cancellation or termination notice is not filed with the chair within the required time period, the chair shall impose a penalty in the amount of up to five hundred dollars for each ten-day period the insurance carrier or state insurance fund failed to file the notification. All penalties collected pursuant to this subdivision shall be deposited in the uninsured employers' fund.

5-a. Issuance, amendment, endorsement or reinstatement of insurance contracts

a. Any insurance carrier or the state insurance fund who issues, reinstates, amends or endorses any contract of insurance or rider thereto covering the liability of an employer for compensation under this chapter shall file notification in the office of the chair within thirty days after such issuance, reinstatement, amendment, or endorsement of the contract. Such notice shall be filed in the manner and form prescribed by the chair.

b. In the event notice required under this subdivision is not filed with the chair within the thirty-day time period, or notice is not provided by a group self-insured trust pursuant to regulation promulgated by the board regarding notification of the trust's commencement or termination of coverage for any employer, the chair may impose a penalty of up to five hundred dollars for each ten-day period the insurance carrier or state insurance fund or group self-insurance trust failed to file the notification. All penalties collected pursuant to this subdivision shall be deposited in the uninsured employers' fund.

c. The provisions of this subdivision shall not apply with respect to insurance policies containing coverage pursuant to subsection (j) of section three thousand four hundred twenty of the insurance law relating to every policy providing comprehensive personal liability insurance on a one, two, three or four family owner-occupied dwelling.

6. a. Insurance of officers of corporations. Every executive officer of a corporation shall be deemed to be included in the compensation insurance contract or covered under a certificate of self-insurance unless that person is an unsalaried executive officer of a not-for-profit corporation or unincorporated association and such corporation or association elects to exclude that person from the coverage of this chapter. Such election to exclude such person shall be made in writing on a form prescribed by the chair and filed with the insurance carrier. Such election shall be effective with respect to all of the policies issued to the corporation or association by such insurance carrier as long as it shall continuously insure the corporation or association, provided that written notice of the continuation of the election to exclude any or all executive officers is given to the corporation or association with each renewal notice of the policy. If such election is revoked, it shall be in writing on a form prescribed by the chair, and shall be filed with the chair and the insurance carrier. Such revocation shall not be effective until thirty days after such filing. Any executive officer whose corporation or association files an election

not to be included under this chapter shall be deemed not to be an employee within the intent of this chapter; however, if not excluded, such officers and their dependents shall be entitled to compensation as provided by this chapter.

b. An executive officer of any corporation who at all times during the period involved owns all of the issued and outstanding stock of the corporation and holds all of the offices pursuant to paragraph (e) of section seven hundred fifteen of the business corporation law and who is the executive officer of a corporation having other persons who are employees required to be covered under this chapter shall be deemed to be included in the compensation insurance contract or covered under a certificate of self-insurance unless the officer elects to be excluded from the coverage of this chapter. Such election shall be made by the corporation filing a notice that the corporation elects to exclude the executive officer of such corporation named in the notice from coverage of this chapter. Such election shall be filed with the insurance carrier or the chair in the case of self-insurance upon a form prescribed by the chair of the workers' compensation board. Such election shall be effective with respect to all policies issued to such corporation by such insurance carrier as long as it shall continuously insure the corporation and shall be final and binding upon the executive officer named in the notice until revoked by the corporation in accordance with paragraph a of this subdivision.

c. An executive officer of any corporation who at all times during the period involved owns all of the issued and outstanding stock of the corporation and holds all of the offices pursuant to paragraph (e) of section seven hundred fifteen of the business corporation law and who is the executive officer of a corporation that has no other persons who are employees required to be covered under this chapter shall be deemed to be excluded from coverage under this chapter unless such officer elects to be covered. Such coverage may be effected by obtaining an insurance policy or in the case of self-insurance by the corporation submitting a form prescribed by the chair of the workers' compensation board, giving notice that the corporation elects to bring the executive officer of such corporation named in the notice within the coverage of this chapter.

d. Any two executive officers of a corporation who at all times during the period involved between them own all of the issued and outstanding stock of the corporation and hold all such offices, provided, however that each officer must own at least one share of stock, who are the executive officers of such corporation having other persons who are employees required to be covered under this chapter shall be deemed to be included in the compensation insurance contract or covered under a certificate of self-insurance unless one or both the officers elect to be excluded from the coverage of this chapter. Such election shall be made by any such corporation filing a form prescribed by the chair of the workers' compensation board with the insurance carrier or the chair in the case of self-insurance giving notice that the corporation elects to exclude one or both of the executive officers of such corporation named in the notice from the coverage of this chapter. Such election shall be effective with respect to all policies issued to such corporation by such insurance carrier as long as it shall continuously insure the corporation and shall be final and binding upon the executive officers as named in the notice until revoked by the corporation. If such election is revoked, it shall be in writing on a form prescribed by the chair and shall be filed with the chair and the insurance carrier. Such revocation shall not be effective until thirty days after such filing.

e. Any two executive officers of a corporation who at all times during the period involved between them own all of the issued and outstanding stock of such corporation and hold all such offices, provided, however that each officer must own at least one share of stock, who are the executive officers of such corporation that has no other persons who are employees required to be covered under this chapter shall be deemed to be excluded from coverage under this chapter unless one or both officers elect to be covered. Such coverage may be effected by obtaining an insurance policy or, in the case of self-insurance, by the corporation submitting a form prescribed by the chair of the workers' compensation board, giving notice that the corporation elects to bring one or both executive officers of such corporation named in the notice within coverage of this chapter.

f. Notwithstanding the provisions of paragraph a of this subdivision or any other provision of this chapter, any executive officer of a religious, charitable or educational corporation and the officers of a municipal corporation, and officers of any post or chapter of organizations of veterans of any war of the United States may be brought within the coverage of the insurance contract as if they were employees by any such corporation filing with the insurance carrier, upon a form prescribed by the chair of the workers' compensation board, a notice that the corporation elects to bring one or more executive officers of such corporation named in the notice within the coverage of this chapter. Such election shall be effective with respect to all policies issued to such corporation by such insurance carrier as long as it shall continuously insure the corporation. If such election is revoked, it shall be in writing on a form prescribed by the chair and filed with the chair and with the insurance carrier and a copy thereof furnished to each officer as to whom such revocation is applicable, upon a form prescribed by the chair. Such revocation shall not be effective until thirty days after such filing. The estimation of the wage values of executive officers within the coverage of the insurance contract shall be reasonable and separately stated and added to the valuation of the payrolls upon which the premium is computed.

g. The executive officers brought within the coverage of the insurance contract, and the dependents of any such executive officers, including executive officers of religious, charitable or educational corporations and officers of municipal corporations, and officers of any post or chapter of organizations of veterans of any war of the United States that have elected to bring their officers within the coverage of the policy, shall have the same rights and remedies as any employee and shall be entitled to compensation and medical care as provided by this chapter, and the insurance carrier shall be liable therefor and for payments into the special funds provided in this chapter as in the case of an employee. The executive officers who may be brought within the coverage of an insurance contract shall include an officer of a corporation who at all times during the period involved between them owns all of the issued and outstanding stock of the corporation and holds all of the offices pursuant to paragraph (e) of section seven hundred fifteen of the business corporation law or two executive officers of a corporation who at all times during the period involved between them own all of the issued and outstanding stock of such corporation and hold all such offices and who is the executive officer or who are the executive officers of a corporation that has no other persons who are employees required to be covered under this chapter.

h. Any officer or officers, elective or appointive, of a municipal corporation or other political subdivision of the state complying with the provisions of group nineteen of subdivision one of section three of this chapter shall be deemed executive officers subject to the provisions of this subdivision.

6-a. Insurance contracts with fire or ambulance districts. Notwithstanding any other provision of this section or of this chapter, any insurance contract to secure workers' compensation for a fire or ambulance district pursuant to subdivision one or subdivision two of section fifty of this chapter issued to take effect on or after July first, nineteen hundred sixty, in relation to a fire district and January first, in the year next succeeding the year in which this subdivision as hereby amended becomes effective, in relation to an ambulance district or any such contract renewed to continue in effect on or after such dates, shall provide workers' compensation coverage for all fire or ambulance district officers, whether elective or appointive, and all fire or ambulance district employees, whether or not they are compensated for their services, unless the board of fire or ambulance commissioners of the fire district or ambulance district by resolution elects not to provide such coverage for any one or more of such officers or employees, or class thereof. Such election not to provide such coverage shall be effective with respect to all such insurance contracts thereafter issued to such fire or ambulance district by any insurance carrier until revoked in whole or in part by resolution of the board of fire or ambulance commissioners of the fire or ambulance district. Such election not to provide such coverage shall not become effective until thirty days after a copy of such resolution has been filed with the chairman of the workers' compensation board and with the insurance carrier and a copy thereof is furnished to each officer and employee as to whom such revocation is applicable. The chairman of the workers' compensation board shall prescribe the form of such resolution. The provisions of this subdivision shall not be applicable in cases where the injury arises out of and in the course of duty as a volunteer firefighter or a volunteer ambulance worker or as a civil defense volunteer and where the computation of benefits would be made under the provisions of the volunteer firefighters' benefit law or the volunteer ambulance workers' benefit law or under article ten of this chapter.

7. Limitation of the issuance of policies by a foreign insurance company. No policy or contract of insurance issued by a foreign stock corporation or mutual association authorized to transact the business of workers' compensation insurance in this state, except a corporation organized under the laws of a state or country outside of the United States and domiciled in this state, covering or intended to cover the liability of an employer to his employees under this chapter, shall be accepted as a compliance with subdivision two of section fifty of this chapter, unless such foreign stock corporation or mutual association shall have filed with the superintendent of financial services a bond or undertaking with good and sufficient sureties to the people of the state of New York, and conditioned upon the payment in full of any and all compensation and benefits as provided in this chapter to any and all persons entitled thereto under any such policy or contract of insurance. Such bond shall be approved as to form by the attorney-general and as to sufficiency by the superintendent of financial services. The amount of such bond shall be such sum as may reasonably represent twenty-five per centum of the outstanding reserves for compensation losses on policies issued by such foreign stock corporation or mutual association upon risks located in the state of New York as determined by law or by the requirements of the superintendent of financial services, provided, however, that the amount of such bond shall in no case be less than twenty-five thousand dollars nor more than one million dollars. Such bond shall be renewed annually. Every such bond shall contain a provision authorizing the attorney-general upon the certificate of the superintendent of financial services that there has been default in the payment of compensation for thirty days or that the bonded company has become insolvent to enforce such bond in the name of the people of the state of New York for the benefit of any and all persons entitled to the compensation assured by any policy issued by such foreign stock corporation or mutual association or otherwise entitled to any benefits under such policy. In lieu of the bond required to be given hereunder any such foreign stock corporation or mutual association may deposit with the superintendent of financial services securities of the kind prescribed in section one thousand three hundred eighteen of the insurance law in an amount equal to twenty-five per centum of the outstanding reserves for compensation losses on policies issued by such foreign stock corporation or mutual association upon risks located in the state of New York, but not less than twenty-five thousand dollars nor more than one million dollars. In computing the amount of such securities they shall be valued as determined by the superintendent of financial services in valuing the assets of insurance companies. Such securities shall be held by the superintendent of financial services as a special deposit and as express security for the payment of such compensation or benefits and may be sold by the said superintendent without notice in the event that there has been default in the payment of compensation for thirty days or that the depositing company has become insolvent. The income thereon shall be collected by the superintendent of financial services and, prior to any default in the payment of such compensation or benefits, shall be paid over by him to the stock corporation or mutual association depositing the same.

However, no such bond or undertaking shall be required to be filed after July first, nineteen hundred thirty-eight, by any carrier making payment to the stock or mutual funds respectively established by sections one hundred seven and one hundred nine-d of this chapter.

8. A self-employed person, a partner of a partnership as defined in section ten of the partnership law but not including a limited partner, a partner of a registered limited liability partnership as defined in section two of the partnership law, a member of a limited liability company as defined in subdivision (m) of section one hundred two of the limited liability company law or a member of a professional service limited liability company as defined in subdivision (f) of section one thousand two hundred one of the limited liability company law, having other persons who are employees required to be covered under this chapter may be included in the compensation insurance contract or covered under a certificate of self-insurance. Such election shall be made by any such partnership, sole proprietorship, registered limited liability partnership, limited liability company or professional service limited liability company

filing with the insurance carrier or the chair in the case of self-insurance upon a form prescribed by the chair, a notice that the partnership, sole proprietorship, registered limited liability partnership, limited liability company or professional service limited liability company elects to include the partner, partners, the self-employed person or member named in the notice in the coverage of this chapter. Such election shall be effective with respect to all policies issued to such partnership, sole proprietorship, registered limited liability partnership, limited liability company or professional service limited liability company by such insurance carrier as long as it shall continuously insure the employees of the partnership, sole proprietorship, registered limited liability partnership, limited liability company or professional service limited liability company. Such election shall be final and binding upon the partner, self-employed person or member named in the notice until revoked by the partnership, sole proprietorship, registered limited liability partnership, limited liability company or professional service limited liability company. A self-employed person, a partner of a partnership, a partner of a registered limited liability partnership, a member of a limited liability company or a member of a professional service limited liability company having no other persons who are employees required to be covered under this chapter shall be deemed to be excluded from coverage under this chapter unless he or she elects to be covered. Such coverage may be effected by obtaining an insurance policy.

The self-employed persons, partners of a partnership, partners of a registered limited liability partnership, members of a limited liability company or members of a professional service limited liability company brought within the coverage of the insurance contract, and the dependents of any such self-employed persons, partners of a partnership, partners of a registered limited liability partnership, members of a limited liability company or members of a professional service limited liability company shall have the same rights and remedies as any employee or his or her dependents and shall be entitled to compensation and medical care as provided by this chapter, and the insurance carrier shall be liable therefor and for payments into the special funds provided in this chapter as in the case of an employee.

§ 60. Definitions

As used in this article, the following terms shall mean and include:

1. "Public corporation." A corporation as defined in section three of the general corporation law, except that a public benefit corporation shall not be deemed a public corporation for the purposes of this article unless it operates in a territory coterminous with the county or a tax district or districts within the county.

1-a. "Contract agency", "contract association". A not-for-profit corporation or association which provides services exclusively to a single county on a contractual basis and receives at least eighty-five percent of its funding from the local, state or federal government.

2. "Municipal corporation," "district corporation" and "public benefit corporation." A municipal corporation, district corporation and public benefit corporation, respectively, as defined in section three of the general corporation law.

3. "Plans." The plan of self-insurance provided for in this article.

4. "Committee." The committee appointed pursuant to section sixty-four of this chapter to administer the plan.

5. "Administrator." The administrator appointed pursuant to section sixty-four of this chapter to administer the plan.

6. "Participant." A public corporation participating in a plan.

7. "Liability." The liability of a participant to pay compensation, assessments and all other obligations imposed by or pursuant to this chapter, the volunteer firemen's benefit law, and the volunteer ambulance workers' benefit law except as otherwise provided in section sixty-one of this chapter.

8. "Reserve." The self-insurance reserve provided for in section sixty-nine of this chapter.

§ 62. Participants

Each plan shall have at least two municipal corporations as participants. The county shall be one of the participants in a plan. Any contract agency or contract association with the approval of the county government and any other public corporation may by resolution of its governing body elect to become a participant in a plan established in the county, or, in the case of a public corporation or contract agency or contract association located in more than one county, in a plan established in one of such counties; provided, however, that the rules and regulations adopted pursuant to section sixty-five of this chapter may exclude from participation in a plan any type of public corporation or contract agency or contract association other than the county and cities, towns and villages.

§ 114-a. Disqualification for false representation.

1. If for the purpose of obtaining compensation pursuant to section fifteen of this chapter, or for the purpose of influencing any determination regarding any such payment, a claimant knowingly makes a false statement or representation as to a material fact, such person shall be disqualified from receiving any compensation directly attributable to such false statement or representation. In addition, as determined by the board, the claimant shall be subject to a disqualification or an additional penalty up to the foregoing amount directly attributable to the false statement or representation. Any penalty monies shall be paid into the state treasury.

2. If with the knowledge of a claimant, another person knowingly makes a false statement or representation as to a material fact for the purpose of assisting a claimant in either obtaining, or influencing any determination regarding compensation pursuant to section fifteen of this chapter, such claimant may be disqualified from receiving any compensation directly attributable to such false statement or representation. In addition, as determined by the board, the claimant may be subject to a disqualification or an additional penalty up to the foregoing amount directly attributable to the false statement or representation. Any penalty monies shall be deposited to the credit of the general fund of the state.

3. If the board or any court having jurisdiction over proceedings in respect of any claim for compensation determines that the proceedings in respect of such claim, including any appeals, have been instituted or continued without reasonable ground:

(i) the cost of such proceedings shall be assessed against the party who has so instituted or continued the proceedings, which shall be payable to the board for administrative expenses pursuant to section one hundred fifty-one of this chapter;

(ii) reasonable attorneys' fees shall be assessed against an attorney or licensed representative who has instituted or continued proceedings without reasonable grounds, which assessment shall be payable to the board for administrative expenses pursuant to section one hundred fifty-one of this chapter. Fees awarded under this provision may not be recouped from the party; and

(iii) such assessments shall be in addition to any other penalty permitted under this chapter.

125. Job discrimination prohibited based on prior receipt of benefits

1. It shall be unlawful for any employer to inquire into, or to consider for the purpose of assessing fitness or capability for employment, whether a job applicant has filed for or received benefits under this chapter, or to discriminate against a job applicant with regard to employment on the basis of that claimant having filed for or received benefits under this chapter, or because the claimant is an injured veteran. An individual aggrieved under this subdivision may initiate proceedings in a court of competent jurisdiction seeking damages, including reasonable attorney fees, for violation of this subdivision.

2. An employer who violates the provisions of subdivision one of this section shall be guilty of a misdemeanor, and upon conviction shall be punished, except as in this chapter or in the penal law otherwise provided, by a fine of not more than one thousand dollars, and subject to the debarment provisions of section one hundred forty-one-b of this chapter.

§ 137. Independent medical examinations

1. (a) A copy of each report of independent medical examination shall be submitted by the practitioner on the same day and in the same manner to the board, the insurance carrier, the claimant's attending physician or other attending practitioner, the claimant's representative and the claimant.
(b) If a practitioner who has performed or will be performing an independent medical examination of a claimant receives a request for information regarding the claimant, including faxed or electronically transmitted requests, the practitioner shall submit a copy of the request for information to the board within ten days of receipt of the request. Nothing in this subdivision shall be construed to abrogate the attorney-client privilege.
(c) Copies of all responses to such requests for information as are described in paragraph (b) of this subdivision, including all materials which are provided in response to such a request, shall be submitted by the responding practitioner to the board within ten days of submission of the response to the requestor. Nothing in this subdivision shall be construed to abrogate the attorney-client privilege.

2. In any open case where an award has been directed by the board for temporary or permanent disability at an established rate of compensation and there is a direction by the board for continuation of payments, or any closed case where an award for compensation has been made for permanent total or permanent partial disability, a report of an independent medical examination shall not be the basis for suspending or reducing payments unless and until the rules and regulations of the board regarding suspending or reducing payments have been met and there is a determination by the board finding that such suspension or reduction is justified.

3. (a) Only a New York state licensed and board certified physician, surgeon, podiatrist or any other person authorized to examine or evaluate injury or illness by the board shall perform such independent medical examination. Where a claimant resides out of state a practitioner qualified to examine or evaluate injury or illness by the board shall perform such independent medical examination.
(b) Any practitioner performing the independent medical examinations shall be paid according to the fee schedule established pursuant to section thirteen of this chapter.

4. All independent medical examinations shall be performed in medical facilities suitable for such exam, with due regard and respect for the privacy and dignity of the injured worker as well as the access and safety of the claimant. Such facilities must be provided in a convenient and accessible location within a reasonable distance from the claimant's residence.

5. All independent medical examinations shall be performed by a practitioner competent to evaluate or examine the injury or disease from which the injured worker suffers. Such examination shall be performed by a practitioner who is licensed and board certified in the state of New York or any other person authorized to examine or evaluate injury or illness by the board.

6. No practitioner examining or evaluating a claimant under this chapter nor any supervising authority or proprietor nor insurance carrier or employer may cause, direct or encourage a report to be submitted as evidence in workers' compensation claim adjudication which differs substantially from the professional opinion of the examining practitioner. Such an action shall be considered within the jurisdiction of the workers' compensation fraud inspector general and may be referred as a fraudulent practice.

7. The claimant shall receive notice by mail of the scheduled independent medical examination at least seven business days prior to such examination. Such notice shall advise the claimant if the practitioner intends to record or video tape the examination, and shall advise the claimant of their right to video tape or otherwise record the examination. Claimants shall be advised of their right to be accompanied during the exam by an individual or individuals of their choosing.

8. Independent medical examinations shall be performed during regular business hours except with the consent and for the convenience of the claimant. Claimants subject to such examination shall be notified at the time of the exam in writing of the available travel reimbursement under law.

9. A practitioner is not eligible to perform an independent medical examination of a claimant if the practitioner has treated or examined the claimant for the condition for which the independent medical examination is being requested or if another member of a preferred provider organization or managed care provider to which the practitioner belongs has treated or examined the claimant for the condition for which the independent medical examination is being requested.

10. The ability of a claimant to appear for an exam or hearing shall not be dispositive in the determination of disability, extent of disability or eligibility for benefits.

11. At the time of the independent medical examination the claimant shall receive a notice from the entity performing the independent medical examination, on a form which shall be approved and promulgated by the chair, stating the rights and obligations of the claimant and the practitioner with respect to such exam, and such notice shall include but not be limited to a statement that the claimant's receipt of benefits could be denied, terminated, or reduced as a result of a determination which may be based upon the medical evaluation made after such independent medical examination, and the claimant's rights to challenge or appeal such a determination.

§ 205. Disabilities and disability periods for which benefits are not payable
No employee shall be entitled to benefits under this article:

1. For more than twenty-six weeks during a period of fifty-two consecutive calendar weeks or during any one period of disability;

2. for any period of disability during which an employee is not under the care of a duly licensed physician or with respect to disability resulting from a condition of the foot which may lawfully be treated by a duly registered and licensed podiatrist of the state of New York or with respect to a disability resulting from a condition which may lawfully be treated by a duly registered and licensed chiropractor of the state of New York or with respect to a disability resulting from a condition which may lawfully be treated by a duly licensed dentist of the state of New York or with respect to a disability resulting from a condition which may lawfully be treated by a duly registered and licensed psychologist of the state of New York or with respect to a disability resulting from a condition which may lawfully be treated by a duly certified nurse midwife, for any period of such disability during which an employee is neither under the care of a physician nor a podiatrist, nor a chiropractor, nor a dentist, nor a psychologist, nor a certified nurse midwife; and for any period of disability during which an employee who adheres to the faith or teachings of any church or denomination and who in accordance with its creed, tenets or principles depends for healing upon prayer through spiritual means alone in the practice of religion, is not under the care of a practitioner duly accredited by the church or denomination, and provided such employee shall submit to all physical examinations as required by this chapter.

3. for any disability occasioned by the willful intention of the employee to bring about injury to or the sickness of himself or another, or resulting from any injury or sickness sustained in the perpetration by the employee of an illegal act;

4. for any day of disability during which the employee performed work for remuneration or profit;

5. for any day of disability for which the employee is entitled to receive from his employer, or from a fund to which the employer has contributed, remuneration or maintenance in an amount equal to or greater than that to which he would be entitled under this article; but any voluntary contribution or aid which an employer may make to an employee or any supplementary benefit paid to an employee pursuant to the provisions of a collective bargaining agreement or from a trust fund to which contributions are made pursuant to the provisions of a collective bargaining agreement shall not be considered as continued remuneration or maintenance for this purpose;

6. for any period in respect to which such employee is subject to suspension or disqualification of the accumulation of unemployment insurance benefit rights, or would be subject if he were eligible for such benefit rights, except for ineligibility resulting from the employee's disability;

7. for any disability due to any act of war, declared or undeclared, if such act shall occur after June thirtieth, nineteen hundred fifty;

8. for any disability commencing before the employee becomes eligible to benefits hereunder or commencing prior to July first, nineteen hundred fifty, but this shall not preclude benefits for recurrence after July first, nineteen hundred fifty, of a disability commencing prior thereto.

§ 208. Payment of disability benefits

1. Benefits provided under this article shall be paid periodically and promptly and, except as to a contested period of disability, without any decision by the board. The first payment of benefits shall be due on the fourteenth day of disability and benefits for that period shall be paid directly to the employee within four business days thereafter or within four business days after the filing of required proof of claim, whichever is the later. Thereafter benefits shall be due and payable bi-weekly in like manner. The chairman may determine that benefits may be paid monthly or semi-monthly if wages were so paid, and may authorize deviation from the foregoing requirements to facilitate prompt payment of benefits. Any inquiry which requires the employee's response in order to continue benefits uninterrupted or unmodified shall provide a reasonable time period in which to respond and include a clear and prominent statement of the deadline for responding and consequences of failing to respond.

2. The chairman may, whenever such information is deemed necessary, require any carrier to file in form prescribed by the chairman a report or reports as to any claim or claims, including (but without limitation) dates of commencement and termination of benefit payments and amount of benefits paid under this article. The chairman may also require annually information in respect to the aggregate of benefits paid, the number of claims allowed and disallowed, the average benefits and duration of benefit periods, the amount of payrolls covered and such other information as the chairman may deem necessary for the purposes of administering this article. If the carrier is providing benefits in respect to more than one employer, the chairman may require that such information be shown separately as to those employers who are providing only benefits that are substantially the same as the benefits required in this article.

VOLUNTEER FIREFIGHTERS' BENEFIT LAW

§ 3. Definitions
As used in this chapter:

1. "Volunteer fireman" means an active volunteer member of a fire company.

2. "Fire company" means:

a. A fire company of a county, city, town, village or fire district fire department, whether or not any such company has been incorporated under any general or special law,

b. A fire corporation incorporated under or subject to the provisions of article ten of the membership corporations law, which is not included within paragraph a above, if such corporation is by law under the general control of, or recognized as a fire corporation by, the governing board of a city, town, village or fire district, or

c. A fire corporation incorporated under, or established pursuant to the provision of, any general or special law, which is not included within paragraphs a and b above, if such corporation is by law under the general control of, or recognized as a fire corporation by, the governing board of a city, town, village or fire district or Indian reservation.

Any district corporation which has the general powers of and operates as a fire district shall be considered as a fire district for the purposes of this chapter. A "fire department" may be composed of one or more fire companies.

3. "Line of duty" means the performance by a volunteer firefighter as a volunteer firefighter of the duties and activities described in subdivision one of section five of this chapter and the same such duties and activities performed for a specialized team established pursuant to the provisions of section two hundred nine-bb of the general municipal law for which the volunteer firefighter does not receive any remuneration or a gratuity and shall be deemed to include any date of injury as determined by the workers' compensation board pursuant to the provisions of section forty-one of this chapter. The following shall not be deemed to be remuneration or a gratuity: reimbursement of expenses for meals, lodging and actual and necessary travel; the receipt of a mileage allowance in lieu of travel expense; reimbursement of expenses for registration and tuition fees payable under section seventy-two-g of the general municipal law, and the acceptance of transportation, food, drink, shelter, clothing and similar items while on duty or engaged in such activities.

4. "Injury" includes any disablement of a volunteer fireman that results from services performed in line of duty and such disease or infection as may naturally and unavoidably result from an injury.

5. "Child" includes a posthumous child, a child legally adopted prior to the injury of the volunteer fireman; and a step-child or acknowledged child born out of wedlock dependent upon the deceased volunteer fireman.

6. "Surviving spouse" means the legal spouse of a deceased volunteer firefighter, but shall not include a spouse who has abandoned the deceased. The term "abandoned", as used in this subdivision, means such an abandonment as would be sufficient under section two hundred of the domestic relations law to sustain a judgment of separation on that ground.

7. "Dependent" includes a surviving spouse entitled to receive benefits under this chapter, whether or not actually dependent upon a volunteer fireman, unless a contrary meaning is clearly intended.

8. "Earning capacity", except as herein provided, means:

a. The ability of a volunteer fireman to perform on a five-day or six-day basis either the work usually and ordinarily performed by him in his remunerated employment or other work which for any such worker would be a reasonable substitute for the remunerated employment in which he was employed at the time of his injury, or

b. The ability of a volunteer fireman to perform on a five-day or six-day basis either the work usually and ordinarily performed by him in the practice of his profession or in the conduct of his trade or business, including farming, and from which he could derive earned income or other work which for any such person would be a reasonable substitute for the profession, trade or business in which he was engaged at the time of his injury.

Every volunteer fireman shall be considered to have earning capacity and, if the provisions of paragraphs a and b above are not applicable in any given case, the workmen's compensation board, in the interest of justice, shall determine the reasonable earning capacity of the volunteer fireman with due regard to the provisions of such paragraphs and the work he reasonably could be expected to obtain and for which he is qualified by age, education, training and experience. The ability of a volunteer fireman to perform the duties of a volunteer fireman, or to engage in activities incidental thereto, may be considered in determining loss of earning capacity, but the inability of a volunteer fireman to perform such duties or to engage in such activities shall not be a basis of determining loss of earning capacity.

9. "State" includes all territory within the boundaries of the state of New York, including territory which has been or may hereafter be ceded to the federal government or to the United Nations and territory within the boundaries of Indian reservations.

10. "Political subdivision" mean a county, city, town, village or fire district.

11. "State fund" means the state insurance fund provided for in article six of the workmen's compensation law.

12. "County plan of self-insurance" means a county plan of self-insurance under article five of the workmen's compensation law.

13. "Insurance carrier" means the state fund, the stock corporations, mutual corporations or reciprocal insurers described in subdivision nine of section thirty of this chapter, a county plan of self-insurance, or a self-insuring political subdivision. For purposes of this chapter, a nonprofit property/casualty insurance company which is licensed pursuant to subsection (b) of section six thousand seven hundred four of the insurance law shall be deemed a stock corporation and a nonprofit property/casualty insurance company which is licensed as a reciprocal insurer pursuant to subsection (c) of section six thousand seven hundred four of the insurance law shall be deemed a reciprocal insurer.

14. "Emergency" includes the search for persons and the search for, and attempts to recover or the recovery of, bodies of persons even though it is possible or is known that all hope of life is gone.

15. "Fund raising activity" means a method of raising funds to effectuate the lawful purposes of a fire company, but shall not include any method prohibited by the state constitution or the penal statutes of this state, public fireworks displays unless conducted in compliance with section 405.00 of the penal law. Such term "fund raising activity" shall not include drills, parades, inspections, reviews, competitive tournaments, contests or public exhibitions, described in paragraphs e and i of subdivision one of section five of this chapter, even though prizes are awarded at such events. Such fund raising activity must comply with all the requirements of section two hundred four-a of the general municipal law.

16. "Minor" or "infant" means a person who has not attained the age of eighteen years.

17. The "workers' compensation rating board" or the "New York workers' compensation rating board" shall have the meaning set forth in section two of the workers' compensation law.

§ 5. Coverage

1. The duties and activities in relation to which benefits shall be paid and provided pursuant to this chapter are:

a. Necessary travel to, working at, and necessary travel returning from a fire, alarm of fire, hazardous material incident or other emergency to which his fire department, fire company, or any unit thereof, either has responded or would be required or authorized to respond, including necessary travel during such work or incidental thereto.

b. While, within the state, personally assisting another fire department, fire company, or any unit thereof pursuant to the provisions of section two hundred nine-i of the general municipal law, including, after his services have been duly accepted, necessary travel to and returning from such work and necessary travel during such work or incidental thereto.

c. While, within the state and pursuant to orders or authorization, performing duties at the firehouse, or elsewhere, directly related to (1) the prevention of fires or other disasters, (2) the investigation of fires or other disasters, (3) the inspection of property for fire hazards or other dangerous conditions, including necessary travel directly connected therewith.

d. While, within this country or in Canada and pursuant to orders or authorization, instructing or being instructed in fire duties, attending a training school or course of instruction for firemen, or attending or participating in any noncompetitive training program, including necessary travel directly connected therewith, as well as necessary travel to and necessary travel returning from such activity.

e. While, within this country or in Canada and pursuant to orders or authorization, attending or participating in any drill, parade, funeral, inspection or review in which his fire department, fire company, or any unit thereof, is engaged, including necessary travel directly connected therewith, as well as necessary travel to and necessary travel from such activity.

f. While, within the state and pursuant to orders or authorization, attending or working at meetings of his fire department or fire company, or any organized unit thereof, at the firehouse or other regular or special headquarters of the department, company or unit, including necessary travel directly connected therewith other than travel to or returning from such meetings.

g. While, within the state and pursuant to orders or authorization, working in connection with the construction, testing, inspection, repair or maintenance of (1) the firehouse and the fixtures, furnishings and equipment thereof, and (2) the fire fighting vehicles, fire apparatus and equipment used by the fire department, fire company, or other unit thereof, including necessary travel directly connected therewith other than travel to or returning from such work.

h. While, within the state and pursuant to orders or authorization, working in connection with the construction, testing, inspection, repair or maintenance of the fire alarm system, water supply system, fire well, fire cistern or fire suction pool, used by the fire department or fire company, including necessary travel directly connected therewith, as well as necessary travel to and necessary travel from such activity.

i. While, within this country or in Canada and pursuant to orders or authorization, practicing for, or participating as a contestant or an official in, any competitive tournament, contest or public exhibition conducted for firefighters which is intended to promote the efficiency of the fire department, fire company or any unit thereof, including necessary travel directly connected therewith other than travel to and returning from such practice. The actual rendition of fire or other emergency service shall not be deemed "practicing" within the meaning of this paragraph.

j. While, pursuant to orders or authorization, engaged in the inspection of fire fighting vehicles and fire apparatus prior to delivery under a contract of purchase, or performing duties in relation to the delivery thereof, including necessary travel directly connected therewith, as well as necessary travel to and necessary travel returning from such activity.

k. Necessary travel to, work in connection with, and necessary travel returning from a call for general ambulance service by a member of an emergency rescue and first aid squad which has been authorized to furnish such service pursuant to section two hundred nine-b of the general municipal law, including necessary travel during such work or incidental thereto.

l. While, within this country or Canada and pursuant to orders or authorization, attending a convention or conference of firemen or fire officers or fire district officers as the authorized delegate or representative of his fire department, fire company or any unit thereof, including necessary travel directly connected therewith, as well as necessary travel to and necessary travel returning from such activity.

m. While, within the state and pursuant to orders or authorization, working in connection with a fund raising activity of his fire company, as defined in subdivision fifteen of section three of this chapter including necessary travel directly connected therewith, as well as necessary travel to and necessary travel returning from such activity, but shall not include competitive events in which volunteer firemen are competitors, such as baseball, basketball, football, bowling, tugs of war, water-ball fights, donkey baseball, boxing, wrestling, contests between bands or drum corps, or other competitive events in which volunteer firemen are competitors and which involve physical exertion on the part of the competitors.

n. While, within the state and pursuant to orders or authorization, performing work or service leading or directing a youth program established pursuant to section two hundred four-b of the general municipal law, including necessary travel directly connected therewith, as well as necessary travel to and necessary travel returning from such activity. This paragraph shall not be interpreted as providing coverage for participants in such youth programs.

o. While, within the state and pursuant to orders or authorization, performing the duty of pumping out water or any other substance from the basement or other part of a building, including necessary travel directly connected therewith.

p. While, within the state and pursuant to orders or authorization, instructing, supervising, being instructed or participating in a supervised physical fitness class, group session or program for the purpose of promoting or maintaining the performance of their duties as firefighters, as well as necessary travel to and necessary travel from such activity, but shall not include competitive sporting events in which volunteer firefighters are competitors.

2. Benefits shall not be paid and provided pursuant to this chapter in the following instances:

a. Work or service rendered by a volunteer firefighter while on a leave of absence pursuant to either section two hundred-b or section two hundred-c of the general municipal law, unless such work or service is performed pursuant to subdivision one-a of section two hundred-b or subdivision one-a of section two hundred-c of the general municipal law, or pursuant to any other general, special or local law, charter or ordinance or pursuant to the constitution, by-laws, rules or regulations applicable to the fire company or fire department of which he is a member.

b. Practice for and participation in any recreational, social, or fund raising activity other than a fund raising activity for which coverage is provided under paragraph m of subdivision one of this section.

c. Work or service rendered by a volunteer fireman while suspended from duty pursuant to section two hundred nine-l of the general municipal law, article eight of the village law or pursuant to any other general, special or local law, charter or ordinance or pursuant to the constitution, by-laws, rules or regulations applicable to the fire company or fire department of which he is a member.

d. Work or service not rendered as a volunteer fireman, but rendered as an officer, official or employee of a public corporation or any special district thereof, whether with or without remuneration, even though by law a requirement for such office, position or employment shall be that such officer, official or employee shall have been or must be a volunteer fireman.

e. Work or service not rendered as a volunteer fireman, but rendered in the course of his employment for a private employer.

f. Work or service not rendered as a volunteer fireman, but rendered as a civil defense volunteer.

g. Work, service or activities in which the volunteer fireman has been ordered not to participate. This subdivision shall not be deemed to enumerate all of the activities engaged in by volunteer firemen for which mandatory coverage is not provided by this chapter, or to prohibit any of the activities described in this subdivision, or to prevent the securing of insurance pursuant to section two hundred twenty-two of the insurance law to cover volunteer firemen when engaged in activities other than those for which mandatory coverage is provided by this chapter.

This subdivision shall not be deemed to enumerate all of the activities engaged in by volunteer firemen for which mandatory coverage is not provided by this chapter, or to prohibit any of the activities described in this subdivision, or to prevent the securing of insurance pursuant to section four thousand two hundred thirty-seven of the insurance law to cover volunteer firemen when engaged in activities other than those for which mandatory coverage is provided by this chapter.

§ 30. Liability for and payment of benefits

Except as otherwise provided in article five of the workmen's compensation law, in section two hundred nine-i of the general municipal law and in section twenty-one of this chapter:

1. If at the time of injury the volunteer fireman was a member of a fire company of a county, city, town, village or fire district fire department, any benefit under this chapter shall be a county, city, town, village or fire district charge, as the case may be, and any claim therefor shall be audited in the same manner as other claims against the county, city, town, village or fire district and the amount thereof shall be raised and paid in the same manner as other county, city, town, village or fire district charges.

2. If at the time of injury the volunteer fireman was a member of a fire company incorporated under the membership corporations law, or any other law, and located in a city, village, or fire district, protected under a contract by the fire department or fire company of which the volunteer fireman was a member, any benefit under this chapter shall be a city, village or fire district charge, as the case may be, and any claim therefor shall be audited in the same manner as other claims against the city, village or fire district and the amount thereof shall be raised and paid in the same manner as other city, village or fire district charges.

3. If at the time of injury the volunteer fireman was a member of a fire company incorporated under the membership corporations law, or any other law, and located in a fire protection district, or fire alarm district, protected under a contract by such fire company, any benefit under this chapter shall be a town charge and any claim therefor shall be audited and paid in the same manner as town charges and the amount thereof shall be raised upon the property liable to taxation in the fire protection district or fire alarm district in the same manner as town charges therein are raised.

4. If at the time of injury the volunteer fireman was a member of a fire company incorporated under the membership corporations law, or any other law, and located outside of a city, village, fire district, fire protection district or fire alarm district, any benefit under this chapter shall be a town charge and any claim therefor shall be audited and paid in the same manner as town charges and the amount thereof raised upon the property liable to taxation in such outside territory protected by such fire company in the same manner as town charges therein are raised.

5. If at the time of injury the volunteer fireman was a member of a fire company or fire department operating in, or maintained jointly by two or more villages, or two or more towns, or two or more fire districts, any benefit under this chapter shall be a charge against such villages, towns or fire districts, in the proportion that the full valuation of taxable real estate in each bears to the aggregate full valuation of the taxable real estate of all such villages, towns or fire districts and the amount thereof shall be audited, raised and paid in the same manner as other village, town or fire district charges. Full valuation shall be determined by dividing the assessed valuations of taxable real estate of each such village, town or fire district as shown by the latest completed assessment roll of the village, town or fire district by the equalization rate established by the authorized state agency or officer for such roll; provided, however, in a county having a county department of assessment the full valuation in towns and fire districts shall be determined by applying the state equalization rate established for the town, or the town in which the fire district is located, to the appropriate portion of the last completed county roll.

6. The provisions of subdivisions one to five, inclusive, of this section shall not apply if the injury results from services performed when assistance is being rendered to:

a. Another city, town which has a town fire department, village or fire district, including one protected under a contract by the fire department or fire company of which the volunteer fireman is a member,

b. A fire protection district or fire alarm district, including one protected under a contract by the fire department or fire company of which the volunteer fireman is a member,

c. The area of a town protected by a fire company incorporated under the membership corporations law, or any other law, and located outside of a city, village, fire district, fire protection district, or fire alarm district,

d. The unorganized area of a town (outside of a city, village, fire district, fire protection district, fire alarm district, and also outside the area protected by a fire company incorporated under the membership corporations law, or any other law, and located outside of a city, village, fire district, fire protection district or fire alarm district),

e. The joint area protected by a fire company or fire department operating in, or maintained jointly by two or more villages, or two or more towns, or two or more fire districts,

f. A fire department of a county which has a fire department, or

g. A county which has requested fire aid pursuant to section two hundred nine-e of the general municipal law, pursuant to a call to furnish assistance to any such municipal corporation, district or area in cases of fire or other emergencies, or for other authorized purposes, or while going to or returning from the place where the assistance is to be or was rendered, or if death shall result from the effects of any such injury, and in any such case any such benefit shall be a charge against such aided municipal corporation, district or area and after audit shall be paid and the amount thereof shall be raised upon the property liable to taxation in such municipal corporation, district or area, in the same manner as other charges against the same are raised, except that in the cases described at paragraphs b, c and d of this subdivision, the town in which the district or area is located shall be primarily liable for such payment. If there is no property liable to taxation in any area described in paragraph d, the benefit shall be a town charge and any claim therefor shall be audited and paid in the same manner as town charges and the amount thereof shall be raised upon the taxable real property in the town in the same manner as town charges therein are raised.

In the case of a false call for assistance, any such benefit shall be audited, raised and paid in the manner provided in subdivisions one to five, inclusive, of this section, as the case may be.

The term "assistance", as used in this section, includes the services of firefighting forces, fire police squads, emergency rescue and first aid squads rendered in case of a fire or other emergency, including stand-by service, to aid (1) a fire department, fire company, or any unit thereof, other than that of which the volunteer fireman is a member and (2) owners or occupants of property, and other persons, whether or not such owners, occupants or persons are receiving fire or other emergency service from a fire department, fire company, or any unit thereof, other than that of which the volunteer fireman is a member.

Except as otherwise provided by law in the case of natural disaster emergencies, a call to furnish assistance may be made by any person aware of the peril involved and the need for assistance or pursuant to any legally authorized or recognized plan for the furnishing of mutual aid in cases of fire or other emergency. The call need not originate in the municipal corporation, district or area ultimately liable for benefits under this section and may be relayed through one or more persons or mediums of communication.

The provisions of this subdivision six shall not apply if the injury results from services performed by the volunteer fireman in a natural disaster emergency and he was serving as part of the civil defense forces activated pursuant to section six hundred fifty-six-a of the county law, section two hundred nine-n of the general municipal law, section two hundred nine-o of the general municipal law as added by chapter six hundred thirty-one of the laws of nineteen hundred fifty-seven, or section ten of the executive law, and when assistance is being so rendered the benefits to be paid and provided under this chapter shall be paid and provided by the political subdivisions which would be liable under subdivisions one to five, inclusive, of this section.

If death or injury results from the performance of duty by a volunteer fireman serving as fire chief while inspecting a public or private school pursuant to paragraph c of subdivision seven of section eight hundred seven-a of the education law for fire prevention and protection purposes in a fire district, fire protection district or fire alarm district furnished fire protection pursuant to a contract by his fire department or fire company, or from necessary travel directly connected with any such duty, then the benefits to be paid and provided under this chapter shall be a charge against such fire district, fire protection district or fire alarm district so protected pursuant to contract and after audit shall be paid and the amount thereof shall be raised upon the property liable to taxation in any such district in the same manner as other charges against the same are raised, except that in the case of a fire protection district or fire alarm district, the town in which the district is located shall be primarily liable for such payment.

If death or injury results from the performance of duty under subdivision four of section three hundred three of the multiple residence law, or from necessary travel directly connected with any such assignment, and the building or property inspected or to be inspected is not located in the area regularly served and protected by the fire department or fire company of which the volunteer fireman is a member, but is located in a city, town which has a fire department, village, fire district, fire protection district or fire alarm district served and protected pursuant to a contract for fire protection by the fire department or fire company of which the volunteer fireman is a member, then the benefits to be paid and provided under this chapter shall be a charge against such political subdivision, fire protection district or fire alarm district so protected pursuant to contract and after audit shall be paid and the amount thereof shall be raised upon the property liable to taxation in such political subdivision or district in the same manner as other charges against the same are raised, except that in the case of a fire protection district or fire alarm district, the town in which the district is located shall be primarily liable for such payment.

If death or injury results from the performance of duty by a volunteer fireman while inspecting buildings for fire hazards in a city, village, fire district, fire protection district or fire alarm district furnished fire protection pursuant to a contract by his fire department or fire company, or from necessary travel directly connected with any such duty, then the benefits to be paid and provided under this chapter shall be a charge against such city, village, fire district, fire protection district or fire alarm district so protected pursuant to contract and after audit shall be paid and the amount thereof shall be raised upon the property liable to taxation in any such city, village or district in the same manner as other charges against the same are raised, except that in the case of a fire protection district or fire alarm district, the town in which the district is located shall be primarily liable for such payment. This paragraph shall not be applicable in any city, however, unless a city charter or other law under which the city operates, or a local law adopted by the city, authorizes such an inspection in areas of the city receiving fire protection pursuant to a contract. The term "building," as used in this paragraph, does not include a multiple dwelling which may be inspected by such fire department or company under and pursuant to the provisions of subdivision four of section three hundred three of the multiple residence law.

The foregoing provisions of this subdivision six shall apply only in cases where volunteer firemen are injured in line of duty prior to the first day of March, nineteen hundred sixty-four; and in death cases where death results from injuries sustained prior to such date. Where volunteer firemen are injured in line of duty on or after the first day of March, nineteen hundred sixty-four, and in death cases where death results from injuries sustained on or after such date, the liability for benefits under this chapter shall be determined pursuant to subdivisions one to five, inclusive, of this section, except as otherwise provided in article five of the workmen's compensation law, section two hundred nine-i of the general municipal law and in section twenty-one of this chapter.

6-a. The provisions of subdivisions one to six, inclusive, of this section shall not apply if the injury results from services performed when general ambulance service is furnished under a fire protection contract pursuant to section two hundred nine-b of the general municipal law for (1) another city, village or fire district, protected under a contract by the fire department or fire company of which the volunteer fireman is a member or (2) a fire protection district or fire alarm district, protected under a contract by the fire department or fire company of which the volunteer fireman is a member, pursuant to a call to furnish such service in any such municipal corporation or district, or while going to or returning from the place where the service is to be or was furnished, or if death shall result from the effects of any such injury, and in any such case any such benefit shall be a charge against such municipal corporation or district and after audit shall be paid and the amount thereof shall be raised upon the property liable to taxation in such municipal corporation or district, in the same manner as other charges against the same are raised, except that in the case of a fire protection district or fire alarm district the town in which the district is located shall be primarily liable for such payment.

The foregoing provisions of this subdivision six-a shall apply only in cases where volunteer firemen are injured in line of such general ambulance service duty prior to the first day of March, nineteen hundred sixty-four, and in death cases where death results from injuries sustained prior to such date. Where volunteer firemen are injured in line of such general ambulance service duty on or after the first day of March, nineteen hundred sixty-four, and in death cases where death results from injuries sustained on or after such date, the liability for benefits under this chapter shall be determined pursuant to subdivisions one to five, inclusive, of this section, except as otherwise provided in article five of the workmen's compensation law, section two hundred nine-i of the general municipal law and section twenty-one of this chapter.

7. Any political subdivision may finance the payment of any benefits to be paid and provided under this chapter by the issuance of serial bonds or capital notes pursuant to the local finance law unless it is required by some law, other than this chapter, to pay such benefits from current funds.

8. Any political subdivision may contract for insurance indemnifying against the liability imposed by this chapter and the cost of such insurance shall be audited, raised and paid in the same manner as benefits are required to be audited, raised and paid in this section.

9. Insurance authorized to be purchased pursuant to subdivision eight of this section may be secured from the state fund or any stock corporation, mutual corporation or reciprocal insurer authorized to transact the business of workers' compensation in this state. If such insurance is not secured, the political subdivision liable shall be deemed to have elected to be a self-insurer unless it is a participant in a county plan of self-insurance or its liability for benefits under this chapter is covered by a town's participation in a county plan of self-insurance as provided in subdivision three of section sixty-three of the workers' compensation law. Every such self-insurer shall file with the chair of the workers' compensation board a notice of such election prescribed in form by such chair. For failure to file such notice within ten days after such election is made, the treasurer or other fiscal officer of such political subdivision shall be liable to pay to the chair of the workers' compensation board the sum of one hundred dollars as a penalty, to be transferred to the state treasury. A notice of election to be a self-insurer for compensation and benefits to volunteer firefighters under the provisions of the workers' compensation law and the general municipal law in effect prior to March first, nineteen hundred fifty-seven, which was filed prior to such date pursuant to the provisions of subdivision four of section fifty of the workers' compensation law as in effect prior to such date shall be deemed to be a notice of election filed under this section unless the chair of the workers' compensation board is notified to the contrary. The provisions of subdivision five of section fifty of the workers' compensation law shall be applicable to such self-insurers.

10. The governing board of a political subdivision liable for the payment of such benefits may authorize the treasurer or other fiscal officer thereof to pay the financial benefits provided for in this chapter to the person entitled thereto without waiting for an award in any case in the manner provided in section forty-nine of this chapter. The amount payable prior to an award pursuant to such authorization shall constitute a settled claim within the meaning of the local finance law.

11. A contract for fire protection, for the purposes of this section, shall be deemed in full force and effect if negotiations are pending for the renewal thereof.

12. Where a city, village, fire district or town on behalf of a fire protection district or fire alarm district is furnished service by a fire company, fire department, or any unit thereof pursuant to a contract with another city, village, fire district, or an incorporated fire company having its headquarters outside the city, village, fire district, fire protection district or fire alarm district receiving such service and the liability for benefits under this chapter in relation to volunteer firefighters rendering such service pursuant to such contract is not covered pursuant to a county self-insurance plan pursuant to section sixty-three of the workers' compensation law, such contract shall provide for payment to the city, village, fire district or town in which such incorporated fire company has its headquarters, of a sum in addition to the amount to be paid for such service pursuant to the contract, to provide for any increase in cost, or any new or added cost for insurance coverage for the liability for benefits under this chapter by reason of the service rendered pursuant to such contract, unless such additional sum has been specifically included in the contract amount for such service. Any such additional sum so paid shall not be subject to division with a volunteer fire company as otherwise provided by law in the case of contracts for such service.

NEW YORK CODES, RULES AND REGULATIONS

PART 315. REGULATIONS

§ 315.1 Application

(a) Every employer desiring to become a self insurer shall make application in form prescribed by the chairman. This application shall contain:

(1) a payroll report filed by classification code, for the five preceding annual fiscal periods;

(2) a report in a format determined by the chairman indicating compensation and medical losses (payments plus reserves), for a period up to 10 years prior to the date of application;

(3) the most recent, certified, independently audited financial statement of the employer, and copy of form 10K, if any, filed by the employer with the Securities and Exchange Commission. A subsidiary company may submit the consolidated financial statement of the parent company in lieu of its own individual financial statement. In such event, however, the parent company must guarantee the liability of the subsidiary company under the Workers' Compensation Law, by filing with the chairman, an Agreement of Assumption and Guarantee in form approved by the chairman;

(4) a description of the safety organization maintained by the employer for the prevention of accidents; and

(5) a description of the business operations performed or to be performed by the employer.

(b) If, upon examination of the certified, independently audited financial statement and other data submitted, the chairman is satisfied as to the ability of the employer to make current compensation payments and that the employer's tangible assets and profit and loss history make the payment of all obligations that may arise under the Workers' Compensation Law, reasonably certain, the application may be granted subject to the conditions herein provided. The chairman will notify the employer of approval or nonapproval of his or her application within 120 days.

§ 315.2 Agreement

The employer shall execute and file with the chairman an agreement, in prescribed form:

(a) to pay to injured employees and to the dependents of deceased employees, from time to time, all compensation as required by the provisions of the Workers' Compensation Law;

(b) to deposit with the chair securities, and/or cash, and/or a surety bond, and/or irrevocable letters of credit, in form approved by the chair, in amounts or penal sum as hereinafter provided;

(c) to pay annually such share of the expense of administration and other expense or assessment as provided by the Workers' Compensation Law;

(d) to permit the chairman's authorized representatives access to the premises of the employer for the purpose of examining operations and records pertaining to the employer's financial condition and status as a self-insurer under the Workers' Compensation Law;

(e) that the chair may sell any part of the securities deposited, draw on the letters of credit or require the surety to pay forthwith to the chair all or any part of the penal sum of the bond, and from the proceeds of the securities, from such penal sum, from the amount drawn, or from the employer's deposit of cash pay any compensation obligations, expense, or assessments imposed by law when such employer may neglect or refuse to pay such obligations, expense, or assessments or within 30 days prior to the expiration date of any letters of credit when the employer shall have failed to renew or replace such letters or have substituted cash, securities or a surety bond; and

(f) if the chairman shall so require, to pay any awards commuted under section 27 of the Workers' Compensation Law into the aggregate trust fund.

§ 315.3 Securities, cash, surety bond and/or letters of credit

(a) The applicant shall deposit with the chairman securities of the kind specified in subdivisions 1, 2, 3, 4, 5, and paragraph (a) of subdivision 7 of section 235 of the New York State Banking Law. Such securities shall be registered in the name of "Chairman, Workers' Compensation Board, State of New York." Interest paid on securities on deposit will be regularly remitted to the self-insurer for whose account they are deposited, so long as such self-insurer complies with this Subchapter and the provisions of the Workers' Compensation Law, and is not in default in the payment of compensation or other obligation under the Workers' Compensation Law.

(b) A cash deposit may be deposited in lieu of securities, surety bond or letters of credit. Such cash deposit will be deposited in an interest-bearing account in the name of "Chair, Workers' Compensation Board, State of New York" and shall be in an account authorized by the Comptroller of the State of New York. Such cash deposit is to be by certified check. Interest paid on the cash deposit will be regularly remitted to the self-insurer for whose account it is deposited so long as such self-insurer complies with the provisions of the Workers' Compensation Law and is not in default in the payment of compensation or other obligation under the Workers' Compensation Law.

(c) Surety bonds accepted in lieu of securities, cash, or letters of credit shall be undertaken and enforced in the name of the "Chair, Workers' Compensation Board, State of New York" and shall be in form approved by the chair and issued by a company authorized by the Superintendent of Insurance to write business as a surety in the State of New York.

(d) To be acceptable, a letter of credit must comply with all requirements set forth in Regulation 133 of the New York State Insurance Department, codified as Part 79 of Title 11 of the Official Compilation of Codes, Rules and Regulations of the State of New York, except that:

(1) the beneficiary shall be the Chair, Workers' Compensation Board, State of New York;

(2) the evergreen clause shall provide for at least 60 days written notice to the Chair of the Workers' Compensation Board prior to expiry date for nonrenewal;

(3) a bank, to be a qualified bank, may in lieu of a determination by the Securities Evaluation Office of the National Association of Insurance Commissioners for purposes of 11 NYCRR, section 79.1(e)(3), have either a long-term debt rating equal to Baa/BBB or better by Moody's or Standard & Poor's or the equivalent thereto from any other securities rating service, and/or a short-term debt rating of P2/A2 from Moody's or Standard & Poor's or the equivalent thereto from any other securities rating service;

(4) the letter of credit shall additionally provide that any legal proceedings with respect thereto be subject to the jurisdiction of the courts of the State of New York; and

(5) the form and content thereof shall be acceptable to the chair.

§ 315.4 Periodic reports

(a) Reports shall be filed with the chairman, by each self-insurer as follows:

(1) the most recent certified, independently audited financial statement and copy of form 10K, if any, filed by the employer with the Securities and Exchange Commission, to be filed not later than three months after the close of the self-insurer's fiscal year. A subsidiary company may submit the consolidated financial statement of the parent company in lieu of its own individual financial statement.

In such event, however, the parent company must guarantee the liability of the subsidiary company under the Workers' Compensation Law by filing with the chairman, an Agreement of Assumption and Guarantee in form approved by the chairman;

(2) a payroll report filed by classification code, for the 12-month period ending March 31st of each year;

(3) a statement of all outstanding death and disability claims as of September 30th of each year, segregated by State fiscal year (April 1st through March 31st) of accident occurrence;

(4) a statement of compensation and medical losses incurred by the self-insurer for the 12-month period ending September 30th, analyzed by State fiscal year of accident occurrence; and

(5) additional or more frequent reports or statements as may be requested by the chairman.

(b) The reports called for in paragraphs (a)(2), (3), and (4) of this section shall be filed no later than November 1st of each year.

PART 316. RULES

§ 316.1 The minimum exposure deposit required

The self-insurer shall deposit securities, and/or cash, with the chair, Workers' Compensation Board, and/or file an acceptable surety bond and/or irrevocable letters of credit, in an aggregate amount and/or penal sum determined by the chair, but not less than the lesser of either:

(a) the product of the statutory maximum weekly compensation rate for total disability multiplied by 52, multiplied by 30; or

(b) one and one-half times the self-insurer's retention as specified on the certification of excess reinsurance contracts filed with the chair, but in no event less than $ 200,000.

§ 316.3 Increase or reduction in the amount of deposit

The chair may require the deposit of additional securities and/or cash, an increase in the penal sum of the surety bond and/or an increase in the aggregate amount of the letters of credit, or, on application of the self-insurer, return a part of the securities or cash on deposit, permit a reduction in the penal sum of the surety bond and/or a reduction in the aggregate amount of the letters of credit, in such amounts as he or she may deem necessary or determine to be advisable to secure the self-insurer's liability under the Workers' Compensation Law.

§ 316.5 Consolidation of security deposits

(a) A corporation which has qualified as, or has applied to become, a self-insurer pursuant to the provisions of subdivision 3 of section 50 of the Workers' Compensation Law may apply to the chair for permission to establish a consolidated deposit with one or more subsidiary corporations of which it is the owner, directly or indirectly, of at least a majority of the voting shares. Such application shall be accompanied by an agreement, in the form prescribed by the chair, duly approved by the board of directors of each corporation that the corporate parties and the aggregate amount of securities and/or cash, the aggregate amount of the penal sums of the surety bonds and/or the aggregate amount of the letters of credit deposited or to be deposited with the chair by them, individually and collectively, at all times shall be liable and shall be available, at the discretion of the chair, for the payment of any and all compensation, death benefits, administrative expenses, assessments, and/or other charges or obligations for which the corporation and/or each and every one of the subsidiary corporations shall be liable under the Workers' Compensation Law and under the rules and regulations of the Workers' Compensation Board and/or of its chair.

(b) A not-for-profit corporation which has qualified as, or has applied to become, a self-insurer pursuant to the provisions of subdivision 3 of section 50 of the Workers' Compensation Law may apply to the chair for permission to establish a consolidated deposit with one or more not-for-profit corporations of which it is the owner, directly or indirectly, of at least a majority interest. For purposes of this section, a determination of majority interest shall be based on: (1) the majority of the members of each such entity; or (2) the majority of the board of directors or comparable governing body of each such entity; or (3) the same central authority which appoints or controls the appointment of the board of trustees or similar body and exercises direct, complete and active control over the finances, properties, operations and activities of separate legal entities. Such application shall be accompanied by an agreement, in the form prescribed by the chair, duly approved by the board of directors of each not-for-profit corporation that the corporate parties and the aggregate amount of securities and/or cash, the aggregate amount of the penal sums of the surety bonds and/or the aggregate amount of the letters of credit deposited or to be deposited with the chair by them, individually and collectively, at all times shall be liable and shall be available, at the discretion of the chair, for the payment of any and all compensation, death benefits, administrative expenses, assessment, and/or other charges or obligations for which the corporation and/or each and every one of the entities in which the not-for-profit corporation has a majority ownership interest shall be liable under the Workers' Compensation Law and under the rules and regulations of the Workers' Compensation Board and/or of its chair.

(c) The chair, in his or her discretion, may permit the establishment of a consolidated deposit of securities and/or cash in an amount and/or the filing of surety bonds in an aggregate penal sum and/or of letters of credit in an aggregate amount which shall be determined in accordance with the provisions of the Workers' Compensation Law and with the rules and regulations promulgated thereunder.

PART 317. GROUP SELF-INSURANCE

317.2 Definitions.

For purposes of these rules:

(a) *American institution,* shall mean an institution created or existing under the laws of the United States of America or of any State, district or territory thereof.

(b) *Board of trustees,* shall mean that body, identified in the trust agreement, which is responsible for all operations of the group self-insurer and which shall take all necessary action to protect the assets of the group self-insurer.

(c) *Claims* shall mean, for purposes of financial reporting and determining trust liabilities, the present value of all workers' compensation claims, including those incurred but not reported, and the expenses associated therewith which the group is obliged to settle and adjust. Such claims must be determined on an actuarial basis and may be discounted at a reasonable rate. The board may reject discount rates considered to be unreasonable. *Claims* may be variously referred to as claim reserves, loss reserves or reserves for loss and loss adjustment expenses in group self-insurers' financial statements and actuarial reports.

(d) *Claims administrator* or *third party administrator* shall mean an individual or entity licensed by the Workers' Compensation Board pursuant to subdivision (3-b) or (3-d) of section 50 of the Workers' Compensation Law which is responsible for the administration and defense of workers' compensation claims of members of an authorized group self-insurer.

(e) *Contribution* shall mean the annual charge to individual members of a group self-insurer to cover its workers' compensation liabilities and assessments.

(f) *Excess insurance* shall mean insurance, purchased from an insurance company authorized by the superintendent of insurance, which reduces the exposure of the group self-insurer:

(1) for workers' compensation claims; and

(2) for employers' liability.

Such excess insurance may be specific, aggregate or other insurance, singly or in combination, in amounts and form acceptable to the chair.

(g) *Group administrator* shall mean an individual or entity that is responsible for ensuring compliance with the provisions of these rules and the coordination of outside services including but not limited to claims processing, loss control and legal, accounting, and actuarial services.

(h) *Group member* or *employer* shall mean an individual employer that is participating in a group self insurance arrangement in accordance with subdivision (3-a) of section 50 of the Workers' Compensation Law.

(i) *Group self-insurer, employer group, group,* or *self-insurance trust,* shall mean an association of employers performing related activities in a given industry that contractually agree, in accordance with section 50(3-a) of the Workers' Compensation Law, to assume the workers' compensation liabilities of each associated member.

(j) *Marketing materials* shall mean any financial statement, pamphlet, circular, graphic, form letter, sales literature, advertising or other communication, whether written, recorded, electronic or verbal, intended for or directed to current or prospective members of the group self insurer.

(k) *Municipal corporation,* shall mean a county, town, city, village, school district (except a school district in a city with a population of 125,000 or more), board of cooperative educational services, fire district, a district corporation or a special improvement district governed by a separate board of commissioners.

(l) *Related activities in a given industry,* as described in section 317.3(a) of this Part, shall mean that there exists a homogeneity in the nature of the group members' business activities.

(m) *Trust account* or *trust fund* shall mean a trust account or fund, financed by the contributions of and assessments on members of a group self-insurer, for the exclusive purpose of paying for and otherwise administering workers' compensation liabilities incurred by members of the group self-insurer.

(n) *Trust assets* shall mean cash and deposits in a bank or trust company insured under the provisions of the Federal Deposit Insurance Act or investments permitted pursuant to section 317.8(c) of this Part. For purposes of these rules, *assets* shall not include fixed assets nor shall they include the security posted by the group self-insurer under section 317.5 of this Part.

(o) *Trust liabilities* shall mean all claims, accrued Workers' Compensation Board assessments, accrued expenses including administrative costs, costs of excess insurance policies, and other fixed costs, accounts payable, loans, bonds and notes payable, unearned contributions and all other trust obligations.

(p) *Qualified actuary* shall mean an individual who:

(1) is a member in good standing of the Casualty Actuarial Society;

(2) is a member in good standing of the American Academy of Actuaries who has been approved as qualified for signing casualty loss reserve opinions by the Casualty Practice Council of the American Academy of Actuaries; or

(3) satisfies the requirements of 11 NYCRR 95.5(d).

(q) *Termination* shall mean:

(1) such action taken by a group self-insurer to remove a group member from participation in the group; or

(2) the cessation of a group's status as a self-insurance trust.

(r) *Withdrawal* shall mean such action taken by a group member to remove itself from a group self-insurer.

317.3 Qualification to operate as a group self-insurer.

To qualify as a group self-insurer and to maintain authorization to operate as a group self-insurer, the following requirements must be satisfied.

(a) The group must include two or more employers that perform related activities in a given industry and that have been in business for a period of time which is acceptable to the chair. With the exception of groups consisting of municipal corporations, a group self-insurer must demonstrate the related nature of the group members' business activities, to the satisfaction of the chair, by one or more of the following methods:

(1) all group members must be classified within the same or a related standard industrial classification code (SIC code) division structure as published in the United States Department of Commerce's *Standard Industrial Classification Code Manual,* or must share a predominant payroll classification;

(2) all group members must be members in good standing in an industry-specific trade association, which shall not have been established for the primary purpose of obtaining group self-insurance status and shall have been in existence for at least five years prior to applying for such status; or

(3) through the furnishing of such other information as may be required by the chair in order to demonstrate the related nature of the participating employers' business activities.

(b) With the exception of groups consisting of municipal corporations, the group must have and maintain an aggregate net worth of members which is at least $1,000,000, unless otherwise authorized by the chair. The net worth of any related or subsidiary companies which are not signatories to the trust agreement shall not be included in the calculation of aggregate net worth.

(c) With the exception of groups consisting of municipal corporations, the group must have and maintain a combined annual payroll of group members which, when multiplied by the current manual rates promulgated by the New York compensation insurance rating board, is at least $500,000, unless otherwise authorized by the chair. Such payroll shall only include amounts paid to workers in New York State who are covered by the self-insured group.

(d) With the exception of groups consisting of municipal corporations, the group must demonstrate:

(1) sufficient aggregate financial strength and liquidity as described in the capitalization requirements set forth in section 317.6 of this Part;

(2) adequate security, as described in section 317.5 of this Part; and

(3) adequate excess insurance, as described in section 317.10 of this Part, to guarantee the payment and administration of all obligations arising under the Workers' Compensation Law.

(e) A group self-insurer that fails to satisfy the requirements set forth in this Subpart to maintain authorization to operate as a group may be subject to dissolution at the direction of the chair.

317.15 Changes in legal status of group members.

Any group member which undergoes any changes in its legal status which results in the issuance of a new taxpayer identification number or unemployment insurance number shall be required to complete a new participation application and shall execute a new participation agreement. A group self-insurer shall, within 10 days, notify the chair in writing of any such change and shall, at that time, file the new application and agreement.

PART 361. SELF-INSURANCE

§ 361.1 Application

(a) Every employer and every association of employers or employees, or trustee or trustees paying benefits under a plan or agreement authorized under subdivision 4 or 5 of section 211 of the Workers' Compensation Law desiring to provide for the payment of benefits through approved self-insurance under subdivision 3 of section 211 of the Workers' Compensation Law shall apply to the chair for the privilege of becoming a self-insurer. Such application shall be in form prescribed by the chair.

(b) If the applicant is an association of employers or of employees, or a trustee or trustees, each employer of employees for whom benefits under a plan pursuant to subdivision 4 or 5 of section 211 of the Workers' Compensation Law are to be provided by the applicant shall apply, in form prescribed by the chair, for acceptance of the plan of the association of employers or employees, trustee or trustees as the plan of the employer.

(c) If the chair shall be satisfied as to the financial and administrative ability of the applicant to make payment of the benefits provided and that the applicant's tangible assets make reasonably certain the payment of all obligations that may arise under article 9 of the Workers' Compensation Law, the application may be granted on the conditions herein provided and such other conditions as, in the discretion of the chair, may be necessary or desirable in any case.

(d) Each applicant for self-insurance shall file the most recent certified, independently audited financial statement and copy of form 10K, if any, filed by the applicant with the Securities and Exchange Commission. A subsidiary corporation may submit the consolidated financial statement of the parent corporation in lieu of its own individual financial statement. In such event, however, the parent corporation must guarantee the liability of the subsidiary corporation under article 9 of the Workers' Compensation Law by filing with the chair an agreement of assumption and guarantee, in form approved by the chair.

§ 361.2 Agreement

Each applicant for self-insurance shall execute and file with the chair an agreement, in form prescribed by the chair:

(a) to pay benefits to employees eligible under section 203 of the Workers' Compensation Law:

(1) as provided under section 204 of the Workers' Compensation Law, if there is no plan applicable to such employees;

(2) as provided by a plan accepted under subdivision 4 or 5 of section 211 of the Workers' Compensation Law for employees covered by the plan;

(b) to deposit securities, and/or cash, and/or file a surety bond and/or irrevocable letters of credit with the chair as required by section 361.3 of this Part;

(c) to pay all obligations, including benefits, fines, expenses and assessments imposed pursuant to article 9 of the Workers' Compensation Law;

(d) to permit the chair's authorized representatives access to the premises of applicant and of each employer, for the purpose of examining operations and records pertaining to financial conditions and all obligations under article 9 of the Workers' Compensation Law;

(e) that the chair may sell any part of the securities deposited, draw upon the letters of credit or require the surety to pay forthwith to the chair all or any part of the penal sum of the bond, and from the proceeds of the securities, from such penal sum, from the amount drawn, or from the applicant's deposit of cash pay any benefit, obligations, expense, or assessments imposed by law:

(1) when such applicant neglects or refuses to pay such benefit, obligations, expense, or assessments; or

(2) within 30 days prior to the expiration date of any letters of credit when the applicant shall have failed to renew or replace such letters or have substituted cash, securities or a surety bond.

§ 361.3 Required deposit or surety

(a) An applicant which has been approved to become a self-insurer shall either:

(1) deposit with the chair, and keep on deposit, securities of the kind specified in subdivisions 1, 2, 3, 4, and 5 and paragraph (a) of subdivision 7 of section 235 of the New York State Banking Law, in amount required by the chair. Securities deposited shall be registered in the name of "Chair, Workers' Compensation Board, State of New York." Interest paid on securities deposited with the chair shall be remitted to the self-insurer for whose account they are deposited, as long as the self-insurer complies with article 9 of the Workers' Compensation Law and with these regulations and rules; or

(2) deposit with the chair and keep on deposit cash in an amount required by the chair. Cash deposits shall be deposited in an interest bearing account in the name of "Chair, Workers' Compensation Board, State of New York" and shall be in an account authorized by the Comptroller of the State of New York. Such cash deposit is to be by certified check. Interest paid on the cash deposit shall be remitted to the self-insurer for whose account the cash is deposited, so long as such self-insurer complies with article 9 of the Workers' Compensation Law and with these regulations and rules; or

(3) file irrevocable letters of credit issued by a qualified bank; or

(4) in lieu of securities, cash or letters of credit and at the discretion of the chair, file with the chair the bond of a surety company authorized to do business in this State, in form and penal sum acceptable to the chair and conditioned on the payment by the self-insurer of all its obligations and the obligations of each and every employer for whose employees the self-insurer provides benefits under article 9 of the

Workers' Compensation Law. Each surety bond shall be undertaken and may be enforced in the name of "Chair, Workers' Compensation Board, State of New York"; or

(5) deposit or file with the chair a combination of such securities, cash, irrevocable letters of credit and surety bonds.

(b) To be acceptable, a letter of credit filed pursuant to paragraph (a)(3) of this section must comply with all requirements set forth in Regulation 133 of the New York State Insurance Department, codified as 11 NYCRR Part 79, except that:

(1) the beneficiary shall be the "Chair, Workers' Compensation Board, State of New York";

(2) the evergreen clause shall provide for at least 60 days' written notice to the chair of the Workers' Compensation Board prior to expiry date for nonrenewal;

(3) a bank, to be a qualified bank, may in lieu of a determination by the Securities Evaluation Office of the National Association of Insurance Commissioners for purposes of 11 NYCRR 79.1(e)(3), have either a long-term debt rating equal to Baa/BBB or better by Moody's or Standard & Poor's or the equivalent thereto from any other securities rating service, and/or a short-term debt rating of P2/A2 from Moody's or Standard & Poor's or the equivalent thereto from any other securities rating service;

(4) the letter of credit shall additionally provide that any legal proceedings with respect thereto be subject to the jurisdiction of the courts of the State of New York; and

(5) the form, amount and content thereof shall be acceptable to the chair.

(c) The self-insurer shall deposit securities and/or cash with the chair, and/or file an acceptable surety bond and/or irrevocable letters of credit, in an aggregate amount and/or penal sum determined by the chair, but not less than the lesser of:

(1) one-half the estimated contributions of the employees of the employer for the ensuing year or one-half of the contributions of the employees which would have been paid by the employees during the preceding year, whichever is the greater; or

(2) if such amount calculated under paragraph (1) of this subdivision is more than $ 50,000, an amount not less than $ 50,000.

(d) Notwithstanding the provisions of subdivision (c) of this section, the initial deposit of securities and/or cash, and/or the initial filing of a surety bond and/or irrevocable letters of credit, shall be in an amount and/or penal sum of at least $ 10,000.

§ 361.4 Periodic reports

(a) Each self-insurer, and each employer, shall file annually verified reports in form prescribed by the chair, which (without limitations) shall report the following information:

(1) number of eligible employees;

(2) amount of covered payrolls;

(3) number of employees who received benefits;

(4) amount of benefits paid;

(5) amount of employee contributions; and

(6) estimate of amount of employee contributions in the ensuing year.

(b) The information under paragraphs (1) to (6) inclusive of subdivision (a) of this section shall be reported for the calendar year, and such report shall be filed not later than January 31st of the following year.

(c) Other reports required from time to time shall be filed not later than 15 days after notice of such requirement.

GLOSSARY OF TERMS
UNDER THE WORKERS' COMPENSATION DISABILITY BENEFITS VOLUNTEER FIREFIGHTERS' BENEFIT LAWS

CONTENTS

Page

GLOSSARY OF TERMS
UNDER THE WORKERS' COMPENSATION DISABILITY BENEFITS VOLUNTEER FIREFIGHTERS' BENEFIT LAWS

A

ACCIDENT, NOTICE AND CAUSAL RELATIONSHIP - (W). The finding made by presiding Referee or the Board that the claimant "sustained an accidental injury arising out of and in the course of employment; that he gave timely notice thereof to his employer; and that the disability is causally related to the accidental injury. (Sec. 2, Subd., 7; Sec. 18)

ACCIDENTAL INJURY - (W). A personal injury which is accidental and which arose out of and in the course of employment, and such disease or infection as may naturally and unavoidably result there from. The term implies an unlocked for mishap or untoward event, and should be construed in line with the common sense view of the average man. (Sec. 2, Subd. 7)

ACTUAL REDUCED EARNINGS (ARE) - (W). The difference between the claimant's post-accident earnings and his pre-accident earnings. (Sec. 14)

ADJOURNMENT ASSESSMENT - (A). A $25.00 assessment which the Board may impose in its discretion for each adjourned hearing held at the request of the carrier.

AFFIDAVIT - (A). A written statement under oath or affirmation made or taken before an officer having authority to administer such oath.

AGGREGATE TRUST FUND - (W). An indivisible trust fund established under Section 27 to assure the payment of worker's compensation in claims involving permanent total disability, the loss of major members and fatal injuries. A private carrier is required and a self-insured employer under certain circumstances is permitted to pay the actuarial value of a claimant's future compensation payments in the above type case into the fund, and upon such payment, the carrier and the self-insured employer are discharged from further liability to such claimant for compensation or death benefits. (Section 27).

ANCR - (W). The abbreviation for ACCIDENT, NOTICE AND CAUSAL RELATIONSHIP. See explanation of the Findings under "Accident, Notice and Causal Relationship," above.

APPEAL - (A). The legal action taken by one of the parties in the Appellate Division, Third Department, to reverse or amend a decision or direction made by a Board Panel or the imposition of an assessment made by the Chairman, Worker's Compensation Board, pursuant to Section 52 (5) of the Law. (Sections 23, 224, W.C.L. and Section 46, V.F.B.L.)

APPLICATION FOR REVIEW - (A). A written request to the Worker's Compensation Board for modification or rescission or review of an award or decision of a Referee, specifying the grounds on which it is made. It must be filed within 30 days after notice of the filing of the decision sought to be reviewed, and should be directed to the Worker's Compensation Board. (Sections 23,224, Board Rule 13 W.C.L. and Section 46, V.F.B.L.)

ARISING OUT OF AN IN THE COURSE OF EMPLOYMENT - (W). The injury that "arises out of" the employment is one that was caused by a hazard of the employment. The injury that is "in the course of employment" is one that arose at a time, place and under circumstances related to the employment. Both conditions must be satisfied in order to establish a work-connected accidental injury. (Section 2, Subd. 7)

AUTHORIZED PHYSICIAN - (A). A physician licensed to practice medicine in the State of New York who has been authorized by the Chairman of the Workers' Compensation Board to render medical care or treatment under the Workers' Compensation Law. The authorization specifies the character of the medical care which the physician is authorized to render. (Section 13-b, Subd. 2; Reg. 110)

AUTHORIZED PODIATRIST - (A). A podiatrist licensed to practice podiatry in the State of New York who has been authorized by the Chairman of the Workers' Compensation Board to render podiatric care or-treatment under the Workers' Compensation Law. When care is required for injury to the foot, the injured worker may select to treat him any authorized physician or podiatrist. (Section 13-k; Reg. 110)

AUTHORIZED CHIROPRACTOR - (A). A chiropractor licensed to practice chiropractic in the State of New York who has been authorized by the Chairman of the Workers' Compensation Board to render chiropractic care under the Workers' Compensation Law within the limits prescribed by the Education Law.

AVERAGE WEEKLY WAGE - (W). The average weekly wage is one-fifty second part of the average annual earnings of the injured worker. Such average annual earnings are computed in one of the following ways: If the claimant worked in the employment in which he was injured, substantially the whole year preceding the injury, whether for the same employer or not, his average annual earnings will consist of three hundred times his average daily wage if he was a six-day worker, and two-hundred and sixty times his average daily wage if he was a five-day worker. A claimant who has worked ninety percent of the year preceding the injury, is deemed to have worked substantially the whole of the year. In the event the claimant has not worked a substantial part of the year, the average daily wage of another employee of the same class, who has worked substantially the whole of such immediately preceding year in the same or similar employment, in the same or a neighboring area will be used to fix the claimant's average annual earnings. Where the employment itself as distinguished from the claimant's relationship to it, is intermittent or discontinuous, and the multiplication of claimant's average daily wage by either the three-hundred multiple or the two-hundred and sixty multiple will not accurately reflect his annual earning capacity, the claimant's average annual earnings will be fixed at two-hundred times his average daily wage in the employment in which he was injured. (Section 14)

AVERAGE WEEKLY WAGE - (D). The amount determined by dividing the total wages of an employee in the employment of his last covered employer for the eight weeks or portion thereof that the employee was in such employment immediately preceding and including his last day worked prior to the commencement of such disability, by the number of weeks or portion thereof of such employment. (Section 201, Subd. 12)

B

BINDER - (A). A temporary insurance contract which, except for specified differences, contains the terms of the contract which will replace it. The binder obligates the carrier to fulfill the terms of the contract just as if the final contract were in effect.

BOARD OF CONSULTANTS - (W). Two compensation examining physicians appointed by the Board Medical Director to examine a claimant when objection is taken to the report of another compensation examining physician in schedule type cases exclusive of eye and ear cases.

BOARD DENIAL - (A). A Board decision denying the relief sought in an application for review of a Referee decision because the record developed at the Referee hearing(s) supports the Referee decision. (Sections 23, 224)

BOARD PANEL - (A). A panel of three Board Members who render decisions on applications for review of Referee decisions. The decision of a Board Panel is deemed the decision of the Board. (Section 142)

BOARD REVIEW - (A). Where a Referee decision is disputed, the aggrieved party may file an application for a review thereof with the Board. The Board's decision on the application will contain a statement of the facts which formed the basis of its action on the issue raised. Appeals from Board decisions may be taken to the Appellate Division of the Supreme Court, Third Department, and thereafter to the Court of Appeals. (Sections 23, 224, Board Rule 13)

C

CALENDAR - (A). A list of cases scheduled to be heard on a given date at a specific part or hearing point. (Section 141; Board Rules 4, 7, 8, and 9)

CARRIER - (W.V). The term applies to the State Fund, stock corporations, mutual corporations or reciprocal insurers with which employers cover their liability under the Workers' Compensation Law, the Disability Benefits Law and the Volunteer Firefighters' Benefit Law. The term also applies to self-insured employers. The carrier is liable for the payment of benefits and where indicated, medical care. (Section 2, Subd. 12; Section 50, Subd. 3)

CARRIER - (D). The term applies to the State Fund, stock or mutual corporations, and reciprocal insurers which insure the payment of disability benefits; and employers and associations of employers or of employees and trustees authorized or permitted to pay benefits. (Section 201, Subd. 11)

CAUSAL RELATIONSHIP - (W,V). The connection between the claimant's physical condition and his accidental injury or occupational disease. (Section 2, Subd. 7)

CHIROPRACTIC FEE SCHEDULE - (W.V.). The schedule established by the Chairman of the Workers' Compensation Board of changes and fees for chiropractic treatment and care furnished to workers' compensation claimants. (Section 13-1).

CLAIM - (W). A request on a prescribed form C-3 for workers' compensation for work-connected injury, occupational disease disablement, or death (form C-62) resulting from either cause. A claimant must file a claim within a two-year period from the occurrence of the accidental injury, occupational disablement or death. Failure may bar an award for compensation unless the employer has made advance benefit payments in which event the claim filing requirement is deemed waived. (Sections 20, 28)

CLAIM - (D). A request for disability benefits on a prescribed form DB-450, used if the employee becomes sick or disabled (a) while employed, (b) while on a paid leave of absence or paid vacation, or (c) within four weeks after termination of employment. Completed Claim form DB-450 should be mailed to the employer or his disability benefits insurance carrier. Also, a request for disability benefits on a prescribed form DB-300, used by the employee if he becomes sick or disabled after four weeks of unemployment. Completed claim form DB-300 should be mailed to the Chairman, Workers' Compensation Board, Disability Benefits Bureau, 1949 North Broadway, Albany, New York 12204

COMMITTEE - (A). A responsible person or persons appointed by a court to protect the interests of a mental incompetent. If a committee has not been appointed, the time limitations under the Workers' Compensation Law do not run. (Section 115)

COMMUTED AWARD - (W,V). The actuarially determined value of an award, payable biweekly for a period of future disability, which is changed into a single fixed or gross sum payable into the Aggregate Trust Fund or which forms the basis for a payment to a nonresident alien. (Section 15, Subd. 5-b; Sections 17, 25, 25-b, 27, W.C.L. and Sections 17, 54, V.F.B.L.)

COMPENSATION EXAMINING PHYSICIAN - (A). A physician appointed under Civil Service Regulations to examine claimants for the Workers' Compensation Board. (Section 19)

CONSEQUENTIAL ACCIDENT - (W,V). A second accident resulting from a prior accidental injury which arose out of and in the course of employment. For example, a claimant falling down a flight of stairs at home while using crutches because of a leg injury incurred at work. (Section 2, Subd. 7)

CONTINUING JURISDICTION - (A). The jurisdiction of the Workers' Compensation Board over a workers' compensation claim is continuing, and the Board may from time to time within its discretion, reconsider a claim, change its findings, and either make new awards or modify outstanding awards as in its opinion may appear just. (Section 123)

CONTROVERTED CLAIM - (A). A claim rejected by the carrier on stated grounds. A hearing for the determination of these grounds is set by the Board, and the parties are directed to appear and present their case. (Section 25)

COVERED EMPLOYER - (D). An employer of one or more employees on each of at least 30 days in any calendar year becomes a covered-employer from and after the expiration of four weeks following such 30th day. An employer of personal or domestic employees in a private home becomes a covered employer from and after the expiration of four weeks following employment of four such employees on each of at least 30 days in any calendar year. (Section 202)

D

DATE CERTAIN - (A). An action taken by a Referee at ahearing in which he arranges for the next hearing of the case on a particular day and time when required witnesses may appear.

DAY OF DISABILITY - (D). Any day on which the employee was prevented from performing work because of disability and for which he has not received his regular remuneration. (Section 201, Subd. 14)

DEFICIENCY COMPENSATION-(W.V.)The difference between the net recovery in a third party action instituted by a claimant on account of a work-connected accidental injury and the amount of workers' compensation payable for such injury, if such amount is larger. Deficiency compensation is payable by the workers' compensation carrier. (Section 29, W.C.L. and Section 20 V.F.B.L.)

DEPENDENCY - (W,V). Death benefits in a fatal injury case may be payable, under certain circumstances, to surviving blind or crippled dependent children over the age of 18, dependent grandchildren, brothers and sisters under the age of 18, and dependent parents and grandparents. These claimants must prove their dependency upon the deceased employee. The regular receipt of contributions by the alleged dependent upon which he relies and which he needs, even if only partially, to sustain him in his customary mode of living, constitutes dependency. The surviving widow, or children under 18 years of age are not required to prove dependency. (Section 15, Subd. 4; Section 16)

DEPOSITION - (A). Evidence of testimony of a witness based upon a series of questions drawn up for the purpose of ascertaining the facts. Depositions are taken where witnesses cannot appear at a hearing before the Board. The questions and answers are part of a proceeding before an official person. (Section 121; Board Rule 19)

DISABILITY (TOTAL)* - (W,V). Disability, medically established, which precludes a claimant from earning any wages. (Section 15, Subds. 1,2)

DISABILITY (PARTIAL) - (W,V). Disability which allows a claimant to engage in some kind of gainful employment. The difference between the claimant's pre-accident earnings and his post-accident earnings is determinative of his reduced earnings rate. In the absence of actual post-accident earnings, the Board may in the interest of justice fix such wage earning capacity as is reasonable. (Section 15, Subds. 5, 5-a)

DISABILITY COMMENCING DURING EMPLOYMENT - (D). The inability of an employee, as the result of injury or sickness not. arising out of and in the course of employment, to perform the regular duties of his employment or the duties of any other employment which his employer may offer him at his regular wages. (Section 201, Subd. 9)

DISABILITY COMMENCING DURING UNEMPLOYMENT - (D). The inability of an employee, as the result of injury or sickness not arising out of and in the course of employment, to perform the duties of any employment for which he is reasonably qualified by training and experience. (Section 201, Subd. 9)

DISABILITY BENEFITS LAW (DEL) - (D). The non-occupational Disability Benefits Law which provides for the payment of benefits to workers out of work because of illness or disabling accidents not connected with their employment.

DOUBLE COMPENSATION - (W). A duplicate award of either compensation or death benefits made on the ground that the injured employee, at the time of the accident, was under the age of 18 years and was permitted or suffered to work in violation of the New York Labor Law or of a rule of the Board of Standards and Appeals. The employer alone and not his carrier is liable for the additional compensation. (Section 14-a)

DOUBLE INDEMNITY - (W). The same as Double Compensation. See explanation appearing immediately above.

E

EARNING CAPACITY - (W). The ability of a claimant, who has suffered a work-connected disabling injury, to earn wages in the labor market. A claimant's earning capacity is determined by his actual post-accident earnings. In the event he has no actual earnings, the Board may establish a theoretic wage earning capacity which is reasonable on the basis of the record but not in excess of 75% of the claimant's former full time actual earnings. (Section 15, Subd. 5-a)

ELECTION OF REMEDIES - (W). The right of a claimant whose employer was uninsured at time of the accident, to bring a court action against such employer in lieu of claiming workers' compensation (Section 11)

EMPLOYEE CONTRIBUTIONS - (D). An employee may be required to contribute 1/2 of 1% of the first $60.00 of his weekly wage, but not more than 30 cents per week. Where benefits are being provided under a plan approved by the Chairman, contributions of employees may be reduced or eliminated; or may be at a higher rate if the employer and employees have agreed thereto and the employee contribution is reasonably related, in the judgment of the Chairman, to the value of the benefits payable. (Section 209, Subd. 3)

EXCLUSIVENESS OF WORKERS' COMPENSATION REMEDY - (W). The legislature has established the Workers' Compensation Law as the exclusive remedy of an employee and his personal representatives against his employer who has secured workers' compensation. It is the sole recourse that the injured employee, his dependents or representatives have against the employer for injuries or death resulting from a work-connected accident or occupational disease. If an employer who is required to secure workers' compensation insurance fails to do so, his employee if disabled due to a work-connected injury, has the right to elect to either claim workers' compensation or to maintain an action against the uninsured employer for damages. (Section 11)

---

*For definition of "disability" under the off-the-job Disability Benefits Law see DAY OF DISABILITY, DISABILITY COMMENCING DURING EMPLOYMENT AND DISABILITY COMMENCING DURING UNEMPLOYMENT.

F

FACIAL DISFIGUREMENT AWARD - (W). An award of compensation for serious permanent facial or head disfigurement.

FINAL ADJUSTMENT (FA) - (W.V). A hearing held in cases involving the loss or loss of use of a member or organ of the body in which the principal issue is the extent of loss or loss of use. (Section 15, Subd. 3)

FUND FOR REOPENED CASES - (W,V). A fund created under the Workers' Compensation Law to assume liability for claims of compensation in certain "stale" cases where specified time limits have elapsed. (Section 25-a, W.C.L. and Section 51, V.F.B.L.)

G

GENERAL EMPLOYER - (W). The general employer is the regular or parent employer who makes his employee available to a special employer. The general employer usually exercises indirect control and the special employer exercises direct control. If the employee is injured, either employer or both may be liable for the compensation due to the injured employee. (Section 2, Subds. 3,4)

H

HEARING - (W.V). The Law provides that "No case shall be closed without notice to all parties interested and without giving to all such parties an opportunity to be heard." These "hearings" are held before Referees who hear and determine claims for compensation for the purpose of ascertaining the substantial rights of the parties. (Sections 20, 150)

HEARING - (D). When an employee files with the Chairman a notice that his claim for disability benefits has not been paid, ahearingis held only if requested by the claimant, carrier or employer, or if the issue cannot be resolved administratively.

HEARSAY EVIDENCE - (A). Testimony based upon second-hand information not known directly by the witness but related to him by someone else, constitutes hearsay evidence. It is admissible in a workmen's compensation proceedings. Declarations of a deceased employee concerning the accident are receivable in evidence, and if corroborated by circumstances or other evidence are sufficient to establish the accident and the injury. (Section 118)

I

IN LINE OF DUTY - (V). Injuries to volunteer firefighters are deemed to be in line of duty if incurred in the course of necessary travel to and from, and work at a fire, alarm of fire or other emergency to which the fire company or any unit thereof has responded, or would be required or authorized to respond and necessary travel during such work. It also covers (1) the performance, pursuant to orders of authorization, including necessary travel directly connected therewith, of duties in the firehouse or elsewhere and the investigation thereof as well as the inspection of property for fire hazards or other dangerous conditions; (2) instruction in fire duties and authorized attendance at a fire school; (3) attendance or work at meetings of the fire department or fire company or any unit thereof; (4) work in connection with the construction, testing, inspection, repair or maintenance of the firehouse and the fixtures, furnishings and equipment thereof, the fire fighting vehicles, fire apparatus and equipment, the fire alarm system, water supply system, fire well, fire cistern or fire suction pool used by the fire department or fire company or other unit thereof; (5) engaging in the inspection of fire fighting vehicles and fire apparatus prior to delivery under a contract of purchase, or performing duties in relation to the delivery thereof; (6) authorized participation in any drill, parade, inspection or review or any competitive tournament, contest or public exhibition in which the fire company or department or any unit thereof is engaged, and attendance at a convention or conference as an authorized delegate of the fire department, company or unit thereof; (7) authorized work in connection with a fund-raising activity of the fire company within the limits of Section 204-a of the General Municipal Law. It also extends to necessary travel to, work in connection with, and necessary travel returning from a call for general ambulance service by a member of an emergency relief squad which has been authorized to furnish such service pursuant to Section 209-b of the General Municipal Law. (Section 3, Subd. 3; Section 5, Volunteer Firefighters' Benefit Law)

INDEXED CLAIM - (W,V). A claim case folder when assembled is referred to as an indexed claim. (Section 141)

INJURY - (D). Injury and sickness mean accidental injury, disease, infection or illness which do not arise out of and in the course of employment. (Section 201, Subd. 8)

J

JURISDICTION - (W). The Workers' Compensation Board has the right to hear and determine a workmen's compensation case if the employment was located in New York. Proof of the latter would be some of the following contacts with New York State: (1) hiring in New York, (2) work in New York, (3) control of out-of-state employment from New York, (4) residency of claimant in New York, (5) understanding that claimant is to return to New York, following completion of the out-of-state assignment, and (6) occurrence of injury in New York.

JURISDICTION - (D). The Workers' Compensation Board has the right to hear and determine a disability benefits case if the employment is localized in New York; i.e., if it is performed entirely within the State or is performed both within and without the State but that performed without the State is incidental to the employment within the State or is temporary or transitory in nature or consists of isolated transactions; or where the employment is not localized in any state, if the employee's base of operations is in New York; or where there is no base of operations in any state, if the place from which the employment is directed or controlled is in New York; or where the base of operations or place from which the employment is controlled or directed is not in any state in which some part of the service is performed, if the employee's residence is in New York. (Section 201, Subd. 6-c)

L

LACHES - (A). The failure by a party to assert a right or request the enforcement of a right for a period of time which is unreasonable and unexplained.

LICENSED REPRESENTATIVE - (A). A person other than an attorney who is authorized by the Workers' Compensation Board to represent claimants before the Board, and in some instances, to receive a fee, fixed by the Board, for such services. Also, a person other than an attorney who is authorized by the Workers' Compensation Board to represent self-insurers before the Board. (Sections 24-a, 50(3-b); 225); Board Rule re Licences)

LOST TIME (LT) - (A). The phrase indicates that the claimant's disability has caused lost time and loss of earnings beyond the waiting period (the first seven days of disability). In workmen's compensation cases only, if the disability exceeds 14 days, compensation will be payable from the first day of disability. There is no waiting period in V.F.B.L. cases. (Sections 12, 204-1)

LUMP-SUM NON-SCHEDULE ADJUSTMENT - (W.V). A lump sum paid to a claimant in a non-schedule disability case in which the continuance of disability and of future earning capacity cannot be ascertained with reasonable certainty. Such lump sums must be submitted to the Board for approval after they have been agreed to by the claimant and the carrier. (Section 15, Subd. 5-b)

M

MEDICAL FEE SCHEDULE - (W,V). The schedule established by the Chairman of the Workers' Compensation Board of charges and fees for medical treatment and care furnished to workmen's compensation claimants. (Section 13, Subd. (a))

MODIFY PREVIOUS AWARD (MPA) - (A). A direction by a presiding Referee or a Board Panel ending, reducing or increasing the workers' compensation previously awarded to the claimant. (Sections 22, 223)

MOTION CALENDAR HEARING - (W,V). A regularly scheduled hearing on a case in which no controversy exists. The notice of hearing contains the proposed decision, and the interested parties are advised that they need not be present at the hearing.

MR-30 - (W,V). Request by Board's Medical Registration Office for decision relative to com-pensability of claim or other issue triable by a Referee, as a prerequisite to taking action on a disputed medical bill. It is instituted following receipt of Form A-1.

N

NO CLAIM PAPER - (W). A form, paper or correspondence receivedby the Board which does not warrant the indexing of a claim case folder. These papers are filed in the No-Claim File.

NO-DEPENDENCY DEATH CASE - (W,V). A death case in which there are no persons eligible to receive workmen's compensation benefits. In such case, the employer or his insurance carrier pays the funeral expenses, not exceeding $750.00 and $1,000 into the Vocational Rehabilitation Fund, and $1,500 into the Special Fund for Reopened Cases. Under certain circumstances, the $1,500 payment is paid to the Uninsured Employers' Fund instead. (Sections 15(9), 16(1) and 25-a(3), W.C.L. and Sections 15, 51, V.F.B.L.)

NO LOST TIME (NLT) - (W). Claimant has not lost time beyond the waiting period (the first seven days of disability) as a result of his work-connected injuries. (Section 12)

NON-INSURER - (W,D). A subject employer who has failed to provide for the payment of benefits to his employees either under the Workers' Compensation Law or under the Disability Benefits Law. (Sections 50, 220)

NOTICE - (W). Employees who are injured on-the-job must give their employers notice in writing of the occurrence as soon as possible but not later than 30 days thereafter. The Board may excuse the failure to give notice on the ground that notice for some sufficient reason could not have been given or on the ground that the employer had knowledge of the accident or on the ground that the employer had not been prejudiced thereby. In addition, a claim must be filed with the Board within two years. Failure to file a claim may bar an award of compensation unless the employer has made advance payments to the injured worker or has failed to raise the issue at the first hearing at which all parties were present. (Sections 18, 28, 40 and 45)

NOTICE AND PROOF OF CLAIM - (D). Employees who are disabled due to an off-the-job injury or illness must furnish written notice of disability to the employer within fifteen days and must furnish proof of disability (completed by the employee's physician or podiatrist or chiropractor) within twenty days. The prescribed notice and proof are the Claim Forms DB-300 and DB-450. Failure to furnish proof of disability within the 20-day period does not invalidate the claim, but no benefits are required to be paid for any period of disability more than two weeks prior to the date on which the proof was furnished, unless it be shown to the satisfaction of the Chairman that it had not been reasonably possible to furnish it within the prescribed time and that it was done as soon as possible. However, no benefits shall be paid unless the proof of disability was furnished within twenty-six weeks after the commencement of disability.

NOTICE - (V). Under the Volunteer Firemen's Benefit Law, notice of injury or death must be given by the injured volunteer fireman or his dependents within 90 days after the injury or death. (See Q. and A. 14 under the Volunteer Firefighters' Benefit Law)

O

OCCUPATIONAL DISEASE - (W,V). A disease arising from the conditions to which all employees of a class are subject and which produces the disease as a natural incident of a particular occupation as distinguished from and exceeding the hazard and risk of ordinary employment. A disease does not become an occupational disease merely because it is contracted on the employer's premises'in the course of the employment; it must be one which is commonly regarded as natural to, inhering in, or an incident of the work in question. There must be a recognizable link between the disease and some distinctive feature of the claimant's job. (Sections 3(2), 37, 49-a)

P

PLAN BENEFIT - (D). Disability Benefits provided under a plan or agreement accepted by the Chairman. An employer, unilaterally or as a result of collective bargaining may provide plan benefits, i.e. benefits that differ from statutory benefits in amounts of benefits paid, duration of benefits and waiting period. Plan benefits may also include hospital, surgical and/or medical care benefits. (Section 211)

PODIATRY FEE SCHEDULE - (W.V). The schedule established by the Chairman of the Workers' Compensation Board of charges and fees for podiatric treatment and care furnished to workers' compensation claimants. (Section 13-K)

PRESUMPTIONS - (W). In a claim for workers' compensation, it is presumed in the absence of substantial evidence to the contrary, that the claim falls within the Law; that sufficient notice was given; that the injury was not occasioned by the willful intention of the injured employee to bring about the injury or death of himself or another; and that death did not result solely from the intoxication of the injured employee. (Sections 21, 47)

PROTRACTED HEALING PERIOD - (W,V). In case of temporary total disability and permanent partial disability both resulting from the same schedule injury, if the period of temporary total disability continues for a longer period than the normal healing period as set forth in Section 15, Subd. 4-a, the period of temporary total disability in excess of such normal healing period is added to the schedule award. (Section 15, Subd. 4-a, W.C.L. and Section 9, V.F.B.L.)

PROOF OF CLAIM - (D). See "Notice and Proof of Claim".

R

RED SEAL SUMMONS - (W,D). A summons issued by the Board requiring an employer to appear at the Board or to furnish information by mail regarding his compliance with either the Workmen's Compensation Law or the Disability Benefits Law.

REDUCED EARNINGS (RE) - (W). A compensation rate based on the claimant's reduced earnings or his reduced earning capacity due to a condition related to his compensable work-connected injury. (Section 15)

REFEREE - (A). A quasi-judicial officer appointed by the Workers' Compensation Board to hear and determine claims and to conduct such hearings and investigations and make such orders, decisions, and determinations as may be required in the adjudication of the claims. His decision is deemed the decision of the Board unless the Board modifies or rescinds such decision. (Section 150)

REFORMATION OF INSURANCE POLICY - (A). The Workers' Compensation Board has the power to reform or rectify an insurance policy whenever the policy fails through fraud or mutual mistake to reflect the real agreement or actual intention of the parties.

REHABILITATION - (W,V). The process of restoring injured workers to productive employment through physical means, medical procedures, vocational retraining, selective placement, and social readjustment. Rehabilitation is an integral part of the medical care and other services furnished a claimant under the Law. (Section 13, Subd. a)

REMARRIAGE AWARD - (W,V). An award of two years' compensation paid in a lump sum, to the surviving widow or surviving dependent widower of a fatally injured worker upon her or his remarriage. (Section 16, Subd. 2)

REOPENED CASE - (A). A case which has been closed by a Referee or the Board, and is subsequently made active again to determine the claimant's eligibility for benefits. (Sections 22, 23 and 224)

REOPENED CASES FUND - (W,V). When an application to reopen a closed case is made more than seven years from the date of injury and more than three years from the date of the last payment of compensation, liability for any additional workers' compensation awarded in the case is imposed against the Reopened Cases Fund. The latter is financed through payments in non-dependency death cases and through assessments made periodically against all carriers. (Section 25-a, W.C.L. and Section 51, V.F.B.L.)

REQUEST FOR REIMBURSEMENT - (A). A request by an employer for reimbursement of wages paid to an employee for a period during which he was eligible to receive workers' compensation or disability benefits. Also, a request by a Compensation carrier for reimbursement out of the Special Disability Fund (Second Injury Fund); and a request by a Disability Benefits carrier for reimbursement of benefits paid to a claimant while his workmen's compensation case was being litigated. (Section 15(8), 25, 206(2))

REVIEW ASSESSMENT - (A). An assessment made by the Board where the decision of a Referee is affirmed by the Board upon review. A carrier or employer seeking such a review is assessed $25; all other parties may be assessed $5. (Section 151)

S

SCHEDULE LOSS - (W,V). The number of weeks of compensation payable for permanent partial disability due to the loss or loss of use of certain members of the body or organs as listed in Section 15, Subd. 3 of the Law. (Section 10, V.F.B.L.)

SECOND INJURY FUND - (W). A Fund, technically known as the Special Disability Fund, created to encourage employers to hire physically handicapped persons by protecting them against a disproportionate liability in the event of subsequent employment injury. At the same time, the Second Injury Law assures the injured handicapped worker full workers' compensation benefits. (Section 15, Subd. 8)

SECOND INJURY LAW - (W). This Law is designed to encourage the employment of handicapped workers by limiting the liability of an employer in the event they sustain further permanent disability due to work-connected injury. (Section 15, Subd. 8) See also Second Injury Fund, above.

SELF-INSURANCE - (W,D,V). A method by which an employer or group of employers may secure the payment of workers' compensation or disability benefits to his or its employees by depositing securities or a surety bond in an amount required by the Chairman of the Workers' Compensation Board. This method is in lieu of purchasing insurance from an insurance company. (Sections 50, 211, W.C.L. and Section 3, Subd. 13, V.F.B.L.)

SICKNESS - (D). See "Injury".

SLOW-STARTING OCCUPATIONAL DISEASE - (W). The Law identifies the diseases in this category as those caused by compressed air illness or its sequelae, or by latent or delayed pathological bone, blood or lung changes or malignancies due to occupational exposure or contact with arsenic, benzol, beryllium, zirconium, cadmium, chrome, lead or fluorine or to exposure to X-rays, radium, ionizing radiation or radioactive substances. (Sections 28, 40)

SPECIAL FUNDS - (A). These are Funds specifically created in the Workers' Compensation and Disability Benefits Laws. There are ten such Funds. They are designed mainly to assure payment of benefits to claimants. In certain instances, (Section 15, Subd. 8, and Section 25-a) the liability of the employer for compensation to his injured worker is transferred to the Fund, and the employer is relieved in part or in whole of such liability. (Sections 15, Subd. 9, 25-b, 26-a, 107, 109-d, 214, 319)

SPECIAL FUNDS CONSERVATION COMMITTEE - (W). A committee created in accordance with Se'ction 15, Subd. 8 and Section 25-a of the Law to defend claims made against the Special Funds created under those sections.

SPECIAL FUND FOR DISABILITY BENEFITS - (D). Administered by the Chairman and used to pay benefits to (1) unemployed claimants whose disability commences more than four weeks following termination of employment; (2) employees of covered employers who have failed to comply with the requirement to have disability benefits insurance; and (3) employees of a covered employer whose insurance carrier fails to'pay the benefits. (Section 214)

STATE INSURANCE FUND - (A). A Fund created by the State pursuant to Section 76 of the Law for the purpose of insuring employers in the field of workmen's compensation, disability benefits and volunteer firemen's benefit insurance.

STATUTE OF LIMITATIONS - (A). Statutory enactments that prescribe the periods within which actions may be brought upon certain claims or within which certain rights may be enforced. Some of the statutes of limitations in the Workers' Compensation Law are:

Section 15, Subd. 8. In a Second Injury Law case, the employer or carrier must file notice of claim for reimbursement from the Special Disability Fund within 104 weeks after the date of disability or death, or in a reopened case, no later than the determination of permanency upon such reopening.

Section 18. Written notice of injury or death must be given to the employer within 30 days after the accident causing such injury. (Note: The Board may excuse the failure to do so on specified grounds.)

Section 23. An application for Board review must be made within 30 days after notice of the filing of the award or decision of the Referee. An appeal to the Appellate Division, Third Department, must be taken within 30 days after notice of the Board decision.

Section 25-a. An application for compensation may be made against the Reopened Cases Fund after a lapse of seven years from the date of injury or death and also a lapse of three years from the date of the last payment of compensation. Awards made against the Reopened Cases Fund are not retroactive for a period of more than two years immediately preceding the date of filing of the application for reopening.

Section 28. The right to claim compensation is barred unless a claim for compensation is filed with the Chairman of the Board within two years after the accident. An employer is deemed to have waived the bar of this statute unless the objection to the failure to file the claim within two years is raised at the first hearing on such claim at which all parties in interest are present. Also, no case in which an advance payment is made is barred by the failure to file a claim. (IMPORTANT: The Board may not excuse the failure to file a claim within the two-year period.)

Section 40. The time limitation between contraction of an occupational disease and disablement therefrom is 12 months, but such time limitation is inapplicable in the slow-starting diseases enumerated in the Law. It is also inapplicable in the case of an employee who has continued in the same employment with the same employer from the time of contracting the disease up to the time of his disablement thereby.

Section 54, Subd. 5. No contract of workers' compensation insurance may be cancelled within the time limits in such contract, prior to its expiration, until at least 10 days after notice of cancellation is filed in the office of the Chairman and also served on the employer.

Section 110. Every employer shall report within 10 days the occurrence of an accident resulting in personal injury which causes a loss of time beyond the day of the occurrence or which requires medical treatment beyond ordinary first aid or more than two medical treatments by a person rendering first aid.

Section 115. No limitation of time shall run as against any person who is mentally incompetent or a minor so long as he has no committee or guardian.

Section 123. No awards of compensation or death benefits may be made after a lapse of 18 years from the date of injury or death and a lapse of 8 years from the date of the last payment of compensation.

All sectional references are to the Workmen's Compensation Law unless otherwise indicated

Section 217. In a Disability Benefits Law case, notice of disability must be furnished to the employer within fifteen days; and proof of claim, within twenty days. Late filing of proof of claim does not invalidate claim - (See "Notice and Proof of Claim"). No benefits are payable unless proof of disability is furnished within twenty-six weeks after start of disability. In the case of an unemployed claimant, the disability must commence within 26 weeks following termination of employment. (Section 207)

STATUTORY BENEFITS - (D). Under the Disability Benefits Law, the statutory weekly benefit rate is 50% of the employee's average weekly wage; maximum $95.00 per week, minimum $20.00 per week or average weekly wage if latter is less than $20.00. Statutory disability benefits are payable, after a 7-day waiting period, for a maximum period of twenty-six weeks in any fifty-two consecutive weeks or during any one period of disability. (Section 204, Subd. 2, Section 205, Subd. 1)

STATUTORY COVERAGE - (D). The benefits specified in the Disability Benefits Law which an employer must provide for his employees unless the Board has approved an employer's plan which provides benefits which are different but at least as favorable as the statutory benefits. In the case of an existing obligated plan which was in existence prior to April 13, 1949, the benefits provided may be less than statutory. (Article 9)

STATUS QUO ANTE - (W,V). The term signifies that a claimant's health has returned to what it was before the occurrence of the accient.

SUBPOENA - (A). A legal writ commanding a designated person to appear and give testimony at a workmen's compensation hearing under penalty for failure to do so. The Chairman, Board Members, Referees, officers of the Board designated by the Chairman and any attorney may sign and issue a subpoena, or a subpoena duces tecum, the latter requiring the production of records. (Sections 119, 142(3), 231)

SUBROGATION - (A). The assignment of a cause of action against a third party by the claimant to the carrier. Failure of a claimant to commence a third party action, if cause therefor exists, within the period of time specified in Section 29 (in a Workmen's Compensation case) and 227 (in a Disability Benefits case) operates as an assignment of the cause of action to the carrier liable for the payment of compensation or disability benefits provided that proper notice of such subrogation is given to the claimant. (Sections 29, 227, W.C.L.; Section 20, V.F.B.L.)

T

TEMPORARY REDUCED EARNINGS RATE (TRE) - (W). A temporary reduced earnings rate of compensation pending adjudication of the actual amount of reduced earnings or the determination of the claimant's reduced wage earning capacity. (Section 15, Subds. 5, 5-a)

TENTATIVE RATE (TR) - (W). The tentative rate of compensation pending final adjudication of the issues relating to rate. (Sections 14, 15)

THIRD PARTY SETTLEMENT - (A). When an employee is injured by the negligence or wrong of a party he may sue such party other than the employer or a fellow employee, if injured in the course of employment. The carrier which has paid compensation or disability benefits to the employee has a lien against any recovery in the third party action. A settlement of such action is called a third party settlement. (Sections 29, 227, W.C.L.; Section 20, V.F.B.L.)

U

UNINSURED EMPLOYERS' FUND - (W). A special fund which provides for the payment of workmen's compensation in cases where the employer was not insured nor self-insured, and he has defaulted in the payment of workmen's compensation. (Section 26-a)

W

WAGE EXPECTANCY - (W). The wages of a claimant, who is a minor at the time of the occurrence of the accident, are presumed to increase under normal conditions, and the Board may consider that fact in establishing the claimant's compensation rate if his injuries are permanent. (Section 14, Subd. 5)

WAGES - (W,D). The money rate at which employment with an employer is recompensed under the contract of hiring with the employer and shall include the reasonable value of board, rent, housing, lodging or similar advantage received under the contract of hiring. (Section 2, Subd. 9, Section 201, Subd. 12)

WAITING PERIOD - (W,D). Neither workmen's compensation nor disability benefits are allowable for the first seven days of disability, except that (1) in the case of an on-the-job accident, if disability exceeds 14 days, cash compensation is allowable from the date of the disability; and (2) in the case of disability benefits, (a) the sick unemployed, receiving unemployment insurance at the time they become sick, are not subjected to a waiting period, and (b) under a plan or agreement accepted by the Chairman, the waiting period may be less than 7 days or eliminated entirely. There is no "waiting period" in V.F.B.L. cases. (Sections 12, 204, 2D7, 211)

CPSIA information can be obtained
at www.ICGtesting.com
Printed in the USA
BVHW011025060120
568691BV00014B/359/P

9 781731 808806